MODERNIZING AMERICAN GOVERNMENT

The Demands of Social Change

MURRAY S. STEDMAN, JR.,
is Professor of Government
and Chairman of the Department,
Trinity College, Connecticut.
He is the author of
Religion and Politics in America
and *Exporting Arms,*
and is the co-author of several other books.
He has written numerous articles
on political science and government.

MODERNIZING AMERICAN GOVERNMENT

The Demands of Social Change

MURRAY S. STEDMAN, JR.
Editor

PRENTICE-HALL, Inc. Englewood Cliffs, N. J.

A SPECTRUM BOOK

CONTENTS

vii

MODERNIZING AMERICAN GOVERNMENT

The Demands of Social Change

1

INTRODUCTION: THE IMPACT OF SOCIAL CHANGE

Murray S. Stedman, Jr.

Rapid social change is the hallmark of the twentieth century. Americans accept this observation quite placidly when it serves to make possible a distinction, sometimes invidious, between the material conditions of the highly developed and the lesser developed nations. But precisely because we tend to think of social change in such international terms, we often overlook the fact that the United States itself has been and continues to be in a phase of very rapid social development. Yet the evidence is incontestable that this is so.

What has obscured our perception in this matter is plain enough. In the first place, social change is more or less taken for granted by most Americans, especially by the generation that has grown up during the period since the end of World War II. In the midst of continuing and extensive development, it has also been difficult to appreciate the sheer extent of the changes that have taken place. Secondly, unanticipated difficulties in ending poverty in America and the various delays in achieving the Great Society have conspired to create a popular mood of considerable frustration. Partly as a consequence of this, the temptation has been strong to concentrate attention on the static elements of American society while downgrading or ignoring the more dynamic elements. A by-product of this emphasis has been a widespread feeling of skepticism as to the possibilities of the rational management of social change through our existing political institutions.

Yet however imperfect has been the popular perception of social change, social scientists have charted with considerable precision the

MURRAY S. STEDMAN, JR., is Professor of Government and Chairman of the Department at Trinity College, Hartford, Conn. He has previously taught political science at Columbia and Brown Universities and at Swarthmore College. His experience in government includes service with UNESCO in Paris and with the United States Department of State. He is the author of several books on politics, including *Religion and Politics in America* (1964).

very powerful social trends that have been in operation in the United States during the last two decades. Economists have pointed to the generally unbroken period of prosperity and to the tremendous growth in the demand for consumer goods. At the same time, sociologists have stressed the substantial population growth and also the very high degree of population mobility.

With an assurance that would have delighted Nostradamus, social analysts have identified five basic trends that will be of outstanding importance in the remaining decades of the twentieth century. The propositions, not necessarily in order of significance, are these:

1. Nuclear power will increasingly challenge coal, gas, and oil as sources of energy and power.
2. Computer development will affect American life in numerous and substantial ways.
3. Space exploration will uncover new scientific as well as spatial horizons.
4. Mass communications, including the recent devices of space satellites, radar, and TV, will have profound implications on international as well as on national politics.
5. Transportation changes will in effect shrink international distances and will also bring about the redistribution of communities inside nations.

Awesome as future developments may be, those that have occurred during the last twenty or twenty-five years are impressive enough. The following survey of key indices illustrates the extent and nature of recent social change in the United States.

Population

There has been a tremendous increase from 131,700,000 persons in 1940 to 200,000,000 in 1967—a growth of 50 per cent.

AGE FACTOR. The main increase from 1940 to 1957 was due to an increase in the birth rate, which is now showing a tendency to drop. There are more young people—almost half of the population is now 26 or under. There are also more older people because of greater longevity. Life expectancy is now 70 years.

SHIFTING POPULATION. The migration from rural to urban areas has resulted in a vast decrease in the farm population. In 1920, some 30 per cent of the population lived on farms. In 1940, the figure was 23 per cent. In 1966, it had dropped to 6 per cent. The number of farms declined 50 per cent between 1940 and 1960.

URBAN SHIFT. In 1966, about 70 per cent of the population lived in urban, metropolitan areas, about half of them in suburbs.

NEGRO MIGRATION. Migration of Negroes has exceeded that of whites. The pattern of flow is from rural South to urban areas, especially to Western and North Central cities. In absolute numbers, the greatest receiving cities have been New York City, Chicago, Philadelphia, Detroit, and Washington. In 1960 the population of New York City was 14 per cent Negro; Chicago stood at 23 per cent; Washington, at 54 per cent.

URBAN SPRAWL. On the basis of present trends, three out of five Americans by the year 2000 will be crowded into five strip cities: Boston–Washington, Buffalo–Chicago, San Francisco–Los Angeles, San Antonio–Dallas–Houston, and Jacksonville–Miami.

Economic Indices

GROSS NATIONAL PRODUCT. From a market value of $212 billion in 1945 gross national product rose to $785.1 billion in 1967.

PRICES. From 1945 to 1966 consumer prices doubled, wholesale prices rose 154 per cent, and wages quadrupled. There was extensive inflation. The 1945 dollar in 1964 could buy only $0.58 worth of goods.

INCOME REDISTRIBUTION. The whole level has been rising: per cent distribution of families by income level (in constant 1964 dollars)

	1947	1950	1960	1964
Under $3,000	31%	30%	20%	18%
Over $10,000	7%	7%	17%	22%

OUTPUT PER MAN-HOUR. For the private economy (1957-58 = 100), the output rose from 70.9 in 1947 to 80.9 in 1950 to 120.5 in 1964.

EMPLOYMENT. (All noninstitutional persons 14 years and older, in 1,000's.)

	Employed	Unemployed	Per cent unemployed
1940	100,400	8,120	14
1950	110,900	3,351	5.3
1965	136,200	3,456	4.6

NUCLEAR REACTORS. Electric generation.

Gross output
(*in 1,000 megawatt hours*)

1960	*1961*	*1962*	*1963*	*1964*	*1965*
590.6	1,884.2	2,471.0	3,807.6	3,810.6	4,350.3

DEFENSE EXPENDITURES.

	Total (*in millions of dollars*)	Per cent of gross national product
1940	1,498	1.5
1945	81,277	38.3
1955	40,695	10.2
1965	50,163	7.4
1967	60,541 (estimated)	—

PUBLIC DEBT, STATE AND FEDERAL. The total rose from $215.8 billion in 1940 to $566.4 billion in 1950, $1,037.2 billion in 1960, and $1,450.7 billion in 1965.

SOCIAL WELFARE SERVICES. (Expenditures include social insurance, health, veterans, education, and public housing categories.)

	Total (*in millions of dollars*)	Per cent of gross national product
1940	8,766	9.2
1945	8,860	4.2
1960	52,380	10.6
1965	77,726	12.0

Communications

TELEVISION. Television broadcasting for public audiences began in the United States in 1946. By 1955 some 67 per cent of all households had TV receiving sets. By 1965 the figure had climbed to 92 per cent.

TELEPHONES. The number of telephones per 1,000 population soared from 164.9 in 1940 to 479.1 in 1965. In the latter year some 80.6 per cent of all households had telephones.

DAILY NEWSPAPERS. In 1945 net paid daily newspaper circulation was calculated at 48,400,000 copies. In 1965 the figure stood at 60,358,000.

Education

SCHOOL ENROLLMENT. (Including both public and nonpublic, kindergarten through higher education.)

	Total (in thousands)	Higher education only
1940	29,600	1,101
1950	31,319	2,659
1960	45,228	3,216
1963	51,194	4,234

Transportation

TOTAL HORSEPOWER OF ALL PRIME MOVERS. The increase has been tremendous—from 2.7 million in 1940 to 11 million in 1960 to 15 million in 1965. The largest factors in this increase have been the greater numbers of automobiles, mechanization of farms, and the increased production of electrical energy.

MOTOR VEHICLE TRAVEL. Measured in terms of vehicle miles, the total rose from 302,200 million in 1940 to 841,900 million in 1964. Motor vehicle registration was put at 32,525,000 in 1940 and at 90,357,000 in 1965. In 1965 some 79 per cent of all families owned cars.

SCHEDULED AIR CARRIERS. Revenue miles flown increased from 119 million in 1940 to 464 million in 1950; to 983 million in 1960; to 1,172 million in 1964.

Some of the forces highlighted by the preceding survey of key indicators, such as nuclear energy and television, have been novel in the sense that they did not exist prior to World War I. Other forces—for example, population growth and expansion of the telephonic network—have been extensions of previous trends. But whether the forces constituted an aggravation of earlier trends or were novel, the cumulative effect of them has been to place great strain upon the social, economic, and political institutions of the country.

The Triple Revolution

Public awareness of basic social trends was heightened by the appearance in the spring of 1964 of a remarkable mimeographed document issued under the auspices of the Ad Hoc Committee on the Triple Revolution. Entitled "The Triple Revolution," the statement argued that three "separate and mutually reinforcing revolutions" were taking place. These were identified as the Cybernation Revolution, the Weaponry Revolution, and the Human Rights Revolution. Though the "manifesto" dealt at length with only cybernation, it maintained vigorously that the conjuncture of the three "revolutions" had produced a crisis that called for a "fundamental reexamination of existing values and institutions." It was the conviction of the thirty-two signers of the document that cybernation "proffers an existence qualitatively richer in democratic as well as material values." [1]

As the sponsors of the Triple Revolution manifesto pointed out, rapid social change may produce opposing effects on institutions. There is the possibility that newer currents may bring with them vitality and adaptation. But there is also the possibility that such currents may be largely debilitating and destructive. What is crucial is the relationship between stability and change. A kind of challenge and response mechanism is set in motion. Some institutions successfully adapt to new conditions; others decay.

Whether political institutions are considered individually, or as parts of an inclusive political system, there is always tension between the institutions themselves and the forces of change. In addition, it is clear that pressures on one part of the system may lead to countervailing pressures on another part of the system.[2] The system as such, at least in the United States, is not static.

Political Modernization

It is now generally agreed that the movement of a society from primitive beginnings to advanced industrialization may be viewed as a process of "modernization." Originally employed primarily to describe stages of economic development in lesser-developed nations, the term is increasingly being applied to political evolution as well. The overall proposition is that all political systems go through a developmental process. "Political development," however, is considered to be a more general

[1] The leading spirits behind the statement were Robert Theobald, a consulting economist; W. H. Ferry, vice-president of the Fund for the Republic; and Ralph Helstein, president of the Packinghouse Workers Union. The statement was the subject of front-page stories in both the *New York Times* and the *Washington Post* on March 23, 1964, the day after its release. It generated hundreds of newspaper and magazine editorials and columns.

[2] For an illustration of this concept, *see* the discussion on legislatures in Harry Lazer, *The American Political System in Transition* (New York: Thomas Y. Crowell Company, 1967), p. 136.

term than "political modernization." The latter designation is more precise and can easily be subdivided into stages or phases for analytical purposes.[3]

Political modernization, then, is a convenient expression to describe the adaptation of political institutions so that they may cope with changed and novel conditions of society. As a working definition, the following is offered: *Political modernization is the process by which the power-allocating institutions of society improve their ability to meet the new demands resulting from social change.*

This definition rests on the assumption that the essence of politics is the distribution of power, just as, analogously, the allocation of resources is the chief concern of economics. There is the further assumption that while the social system affects and limits the role and functions of the institutions that comprise the political system, the relationship is reciprocal. In other words, political institutions can and do change social systems.

Social change is the factor that creates a discrepancy between what political institutions are doing and what they could be doing. It stimulates people to question the adequacy of such institutions to deal with new conditions and situations. But the timing of institutional development also depends on the social ideas that important segments of the public find acceptable. Unless there is popular support for changes in institutional behavior, the changes, however logical, are unlikely to be made.[4] The social forces tending to create conditions favorable for political modernization are not, therefore, sufficient in themselves to account for institutional change. There must, in addition, be a considerable measure of popular support for the change. The psychological, even ideological, factor must be taken into account.

Fortunately, studies of political development in a variety of newly emerging nations have identified some of the characteristics associated

---

[3] The March, 1965, issue of *The Annals of the American Academy of Political and Social Science* (Vol. 358) is entitled "New Nations: The Problem of Political Development." Lucian W. Pye examines ten definitions of "political development," and finds difficulties with each of them, in an article entitled "The Concept of Political Development," pp. 1-13. In the same issue of the journal, Marion J. Levy, Jr., who has also written extensively elsewhere on the subject, defines modernization by the ratio of inanimate to animate sources of power. *See* in the same issue of *The Annals* his article "Patterns of Modernization and Political Development," pp. 29-40. Organski defines political development as ". . . increasing governmental efficiency in utilizing the human and material resources of the nation for national goals." *See* A. F. K. Organski, *The Stages of Political Development* (New York, Alfred A. Knopf, Inc., 1965), p. 7. Political modernization as nation-building is considered on a comparative basis by Samuel P. Huntington in "Political Modernization: America vs. Europe," *World Politics*, XVIII (April, 1966), 378-414.

[4] This point is well demonstrated in Richard Hofstadter, *Social Darwinism in American Thought* (Boston: Beacon Press, 1955).

with social change. Three recurrent themes have been noted: a general spirit or drive toward equality; the capacity of a political system; and the fact of differentiation and specialization.[5] It is the first characteristic that is relevant here. The studies have shown that the spirit of equality goes in the direction of popular participation and perhaps rule, universality of laws, and open recruitment to political office.[6] In short, political development in the newer nations has been associated with a favorable public attitude toward the concept of equality.

Of more immediate concern is the question of whether this same general consideration applies to political development in the very highly industrialized United States of the twentieth century. It would, of course, be premature to attempt a definitive reply to this query. But the hypothesis is well worth investigating that the broad attitudinal forces tending to favor political modernization in this country are those associated with the drive toward equality. Furthermore, there is a good deal of evidence to support such an hypothesis.

As an illustration, consider the civil rights movement of recent years. The forces working for equal protection under the law and for equal treatment in social and economic affairs have been strongly associated with those working for political modernization. Conversely, the forces seeking to deny or retard the civil rights drive have in general been highly opposed to political modernization. They have sought, in short, to maintain the institutional status quo.

Whether social or psychological, the specific factors tending either to impel or to retard political modernization vary with the particular political institution. These factors can be identified only through careful study of the institutions concerned, and the expectation is that verifiable and verified generalizations will in due time result from the individual investigations. Furthermore, it is noteworthy that some political institutions have proceeded further along the path toward political modernization than others, for example, the Presidency further than political parties.

The essays in this volume deal with the degree of political modernization achieved by the principal American political institutions. It is the objective of the individual authors to ascertain the approximate answers to these questions:

1. How well is the institution under examination equipped to cope with the new problems of the post–World-War-II era?
2. What is needed to bring about modernization?
3. What are the prospects for achieving such modernization?

[5] *See* Pye, *op. cit.*
[6] *Ibid.*, p. 12.

The first question relates to evaluation; the second, to reconstruction; the third, to perspective. These general queries constitute the overall framework for the investigations of specific institutions. Subjected to this scrutiny are the Presidency, the Congress, the Supreme Court, national administrative agencies, political parties, federalism, and state-and-local government.

Each of the eight essayists is a specialist in the subject on which he writes. That these men continue to publish the results of their ongoing research and reflection is hardly surprising. This is part of the art of being a scholar. What is different and, one trusts, of value in the present collection is that all of the essays are focused on the difficult but important and urgent problem of political modernization in the United States. If this volume contributes to public discussion and analysis of this significant issue, it will have served its purpose.

2

THE PRESIDENCY

Louis W. Koenig

The Presidency enjoys a well-established record as an adaptive office, exceptionally able to adjust to swift and drastic change. It has prevailed in the severe tests of major war and economic depression; it has been at the center of the nation's transitions from an agricultural economy to one predominantly industrial, from an era of relative isolation from international affairs to the deepest and most intensive involvements. In the interval since 1945 the Presidency has provided leadership in profound adjustments at home and abroad. In enterprises such as the Marshall Plan and the Truman Doctrine, the Presidency led in the rescue of western Europe from the heritage of destruction and despair left by World War II, resisted effectively Communist thrusts, built an elaborate structure of alliances with nations in the West and East, and compiled a tolerably good record in supporting the several goals of the United Nations. At home, the economy has grown in productivity at a dazzling rate, with marked rises in the standard of living and an ironing out of curves in the business cycle, and all of this in an interval when the President, more than anyone else, deserves to be called the principal administrator of the economy. Civil rights legislation has been enacted under his leadership, and by public appeals, administrative action, and firmness in several civil rights crises, he has done much to raise the standards of behavior that the several races of American citizens employ in dealing with one another.

Louis W. Koenig is Professor of Government at New York University. He has previously taught at Bard College and worked in Washington with the Bureau of the Budget, the State Department, and the first Hoover Commission. He has also served as a consultant to the New York State Civil Service Commission. His special field of interest is the Presidency, concerning which he has written *The Chief Executive* (Harcourt, Brace and World, 1964), *The Invisible Presidency* (Holt, Rinehart and Winston, 1960), and, with Edward S. Corwin, *The Presidency Today* (New York: New York University Press, 1956).

For all of his good progress, the President in the 1960's and beyond seems to be faced with problems that race on at a pace well outstripping his achievements. Both now and in the foreseeable future, he seems destined to struggle with at least three central revolutions, all of which are now well visible to us.[1] One is the weaponry revolution. We know all too well that weaponry has been developed, and is still being developed, that in mere minutes could destroy millions of lives and, in time, threaten civilization itself. The President of the nation that boasts the most advanced weaponry has a self-evident duty to take steps to limit the arms race and improve the prospects of world peace.

A second revolution, the human rights revolution, seeks to bring the Negro citizen into a full share of the nation's economic, political, and social life. Such goals are fostered by considerations of simple justice and, in cities across the nation, by conditions of despair and rioting that threaten to displace large sectors of the social order with guerrilla warfare. Despite the President's achievements, the problem of the Negro in American life grows in severity. Despite new laws and enterprising Presidential action, the picture continues grim. The schools are predominantly segregated. The Negro, rather than gaining in the economy, is losing ground. Nearly 45 per cent of American Negroes live in poverty, or have yearly incomes of less than two thousand dollars. Their unemployment rate continues to be staggering; they are the most vulnerable to changes of technology that eliminate jobs and banish the victims into the exile of continuing unemployment.

A third revolution, the automation revolution, promises a future of almost unlimited productive capacity, requiring progressively less human labor. So far the Negro is its chief victim, but the white middle-class worker is beginning to come within its reach. This revolution threatens to break the link between jobs and income, and in time it may even require a remaking of social attitudes toward work and leisure, and at least a transition of massive undertakings in the public sector, in education, public works, housing, and the like.

In the face of these and other possible revolutions, the tasks facing the Presidency are clear. People must be aroused, Congress moved, the bureaucracy stirred, and alliances redirected. It is wholly appropriate that the Presidency be looked to for leadership, in light of its past successes, its possession in greater degree than the other branches of government of the means of action, and its distinction, as Max Lerner has put it, as "the greatest majority-weapon our democracy has thus far shaped." [2] In considering the adequacy of the Presidency for present and future

---

[1] The Ad Hoc Committee on the Triple Revolution, *The Triple Revolution* (Santa Barbara, Calif.: Center for the Study of Democratic Institutions, 1964), p. 5.
[2] Max Lerner, *Ideas for the Ice Age* (New York: The Viking Press, Inc., 1941), p. 390.

problems, it is profitable to consider how well the Presidency serves as a majority weapon, what limitations it suffers, and how these limitations can be overcome. A majoritarian Presidency is most in accord with the democratic ideal that a national popular majority should be able to effect its will, subject to the safeguards against the abuse of minority and individual freedoms contained in the Bill of Rights. A national popular majority, this discussion will assume, is most apt to reflect the nation's most urgent social and economic needs. This discussion further assumes that an opposite kind of rule, that is, rule by minority or minorities, particularly if they already enjoy positions of political and economic advantage or privilege, will be apt to resist change in public policy designed to match change in society and the world. Minority rule will be more protective of the status quo, of established privilege, and will be less inclined to move with the tides of change.

The Founding Fathers hedged in their choice between majority and minority rule, and probably wisely so. But in light of the enormous forces of change that we are witnessing, it may also be wise to reconsider some of the arrangements in our political system that permit the minority to thwart the majority.

Presidential Elections

We can start at the beginning, which is the election of the President. Our historic reliance is the Electoral College, and while the system has worked reasonably well, with only several breakdowns, it could also be viewed as a powder keg that in some future election might blow the nation sky-high with trouble. The danger is that a Presidential candidate receiving a minority of the popular vote will defeat the candidate receiving a majority of that vote, as Hayes triumphed over Tilden in 1876 and Harrison over Cleveland in 1888. Not only is the majority of the people thwarted, but the minority President who gains the victory can do less than the foe he defeated, for his tenure is under a cloud, and he may, as Harrison and Hayes did, represent a more restrictive philosophy of public policy than that of their more popular opponents.

Under our present system of choosing the President, if a candidate fails to secure a majority of the electoral votes, the election is thrown into the House of Representatives, where each state, regardless of the size of its delegation, has one vote. A majority of House votes so cast chooses the President. Recent Presidential elections have witnessed an attempt to exploit these constitutional provisions in an effort to frustrate the popular majority. The attempt is coupled with violations of the traditional practice that an elector will cast his vote in true reflection of the popular vote of his state, and with the introduction of a new practice, at least in modern times, of putting up slates of unpledged electors. Thus, in 1960 Senator Harry F. Byrd of Virginia, who was not a candidate on any Presidential ticket, received six of the eleven electoral votes of Alabama, which went Democratic, Mississippi's eight votes, one vote in Oklahoma, or a total of 15 electoral votes. In 1964, unpledged elector slates were eventually entered in Alabama and Mississippi, but they were foiled when the popular vote in both states chose electors committed to the Republican candidate, Senator Barry Goldwater. These violations of standard Electoral College practice are based upon the belief that by withholding enough electoral votes from the two major Presidential candidates, the necessary majority might be lacking to both. The election is then thrown into the House of Representatives, where each state will have one vote and each Southern state will therefore be as powerful as the largest states, New York and California. The eleven Southern states, comprising a substantial bloc of votes, could allot them to the Presidential candidate promising the most concessions, especially on the overriding issue of civil rights. Quite conceivably a cabinet position could be part of the bargain, and a takeover of the secretaryship of the Department of Health, Education, and Welfare, which administers many programs bearing upon civil rights, also might lend zest to the maneuver. Fortunately, these several kinds of tinkering with the Electoral College system have achieved no success, but they conceivably might work real mischief in a future close Presidential election.

Our processes for choosing the President carry still other features that may deny the national popular majority a fair opportunity to get the candidate they want, or at least the type of candidate. The age of television in Presidential campaigning is also an age of rocketing campaign costs. Herbert E. Alexander, in his study *Financing the 1964 Election*, found that the two major parties spent a combined total of $29 million on the 1964 election, of which $11 million was allotted to radio and television alone.[3] Outlays on such an exorbitant scale sharply narrow the circle of men available to run for the Presidency to those who have substantial wealth or who have access to the wealthy. The arrangement violates the democratic ideal of a widely available citizenry for office-holding and is more apt to produce candidates whose experience, interest, and instinct is with the status quo and limited change rather than a course of bold innovation that the nation's problems seem to call for. Modern America is a nation of emigrés, of millions on the move, changing their residences, often leaving one state for another, annually. Outmoded residence laws result in sweeping disenfranchisement of millions of citizens in a Presidential election year. It is all too

[3] Herbert E. Alexander, *Financing the 1964 Election* (Princeton: Citizens Research Foundation, 1965), *passim.*

self-evident that Presidential election issues have little to do with local residence.

The Twenty-second Amendment is another contrived restraint for thwarting the popular will and one that also seriously affects the ability of an incumbent President whose tenure is limited by its provisions from dealing with problems of the day through policies of strength. The amendment is a kind of posthumous revenge against Franklin D. Roosevelt for breaking the two-term tradition. Dwight Eisenhower, the first victim of the amendment, demonstrated how the amendment can weaken the President's influence during much of his second, and final, term. In 1957, the first year of Eisenhower's second term, the President was handicapped by an apparent weakening of his hold on Republican legislators and a decline of his earlier support from business and the press. Yet, only a year earlier, Eisenhower had been returned to power with a fresh and overwhelming mandate. Even worse is the amendment's potential mischief in a foreign affairs crisis. The nation could conceivably be on the brink of war or engaged in limited war, or involved in important disarmament negotiations when the tenure of its President might suddenly be cut off. The nation would have no choice, thanks to the amendment, but to violate that wise old adage that warns against changing horses in midstream. Regardless of its wishes, the electorate would be forced to choose a new leadership at a juncture when national unity was imperative, and be deprived of a President whose experience and knowledge of ongoing affairs could not be matched. At bottom, the Twenty-second Amendment is antidemocratic in spirit, a frustration of the will of the people out of fear that the people might choose unwisely.

The very worst tragedy that could befall us would be for the Presidency to become vacant, with no one immediately known and available to fill the post. The Founding Fathers made no explicit provisions for Presidential illness, mental or physical, or his being lost or missing, any of which might temporarily deprive the nation of a chief executive, and perhaps at a crucial interval. The worst of this kind of experience was suffered when Woodrow Wilson suffered a paralytic stroke and was incapacitated for more than a year. Matters such as the League of Nations struggle and the question of United States membership were neglected or badly managed. President Eisenhower's several illnesses resulted in a necessary curtailment of his Presidential activity, and some observers felt that one casualty was public policy toward the economic recession of 1958, that the recession might have been dealt with earlier and more vigorously if the President had enjoyed better health and been more available for his duties. After President Kennedy's assassination, the thought stirred in many Congressional quarters that, as former Senator Kenneth Keating stated, "A matter of inches spelled the difference between the painless death of John F. Kennedy and the possibility of his permanent incapacity to exercise the duties of the highest office of the land." [4]

The awareness that swept through Congress that more careful provision had to be made to protect the nation from headless government led to the adoption of the Twenty-fifth Amendment in 1967. The amendment permits the President to determine his inability to perform the Presidential job and to designate the Vice President to serve as Acting President for the duration of the inability. When the President is unable or unwilling to make the finding of inability, the amendment provides that the Vice President and a majority of the cabinet or such "other body" as Congress might provide could make the finding. The "other body" was described in Congressional debate as a commission of private citizens, doctors, or psychiatrists, who might be summoned to pass judgment upon the President's competence. The amendment also empowers the President to find that his disability has ended and to resume his powers and duties. If the President tries to get back to work too soon, before he is sufficiently recovered from his inability, the amendment specifies that, if the Vice President and a majority of the cabinet or of the "other body" did not agree that the President had recovered, Congress would resolve the issue. It could, by two-thirds vote of each house, decide that the President was still unable to discharge his duties, whereupon the Vice President would continue as Acting President. During debate on the amendment, some legislators argued that Congress was causing more trouble than it was curing. Senator Albert Gore of Tennessee warned that "this nation could undergo the potentially disastrous spectacle of competing claims to the power of the Presidency." [5] Still other critics have imagined a wilder confusion if Congress were controlled by a party other than the President's.

Presidential-Congressional Relations

In the interval since World War II, the President has compiled a highly spotty record in securing legislation urgently needed for the nation's social problems. Except for Lyndon Johnson's extraordinary successes in 1965 in moving an avalanche of Great Society legislation through Congress, the Presidential landscape is filled with monuments of failure, of legislation asked for but denied on Capitol Hill. John Kennedy, at the time of his death, still was deprived of legislation he deemed of the highest importance—public school aid, civil rights, Medi-

[4] Hearings before the Subcommittee on Constitutional Amendments of the Senate Judiciary Committee, 88th Congress, 1st Session (1963), p. 10.
[5] New York Times, February 11, 1967.

care, a cabinet-level urban affairs department, and stand-by authority to lower income taxes. Harry Truman, despite a miraculous election victory in 1948, which raised him to heights of political prestige, and put his own party solidly in control of both houses of Congress, was unable to win the passage of any substantial part of his 24-part program of legislation. His only major victory was in the field of housing, which materialized only because of the substantial support of the Senate leader of the Republican Party, Robert A. Taft. President Eisenhower soon saw the glow of his electoral victory subside in the repeated hostility of his fellow Republicans who were solidly in control of Congress. So much did he despair from their rebuffs that for a time he considered forming a new party. The lopsided results of the 1964 elections gave Lyndon Johnson enormous, abnormal Democratic majorities in Congress, which he quickly exploited, and presided over more legislative innovations on the home front than any other President in any other single session of Congress in the twentieth century. Items such as education, Medicare, civil rights, which had been on the Democratic agenda since the end of World War II, were finally passed after a wait of twenty years. The 1966 elections reduced the President's party margins substantially in Congress, and since then Johnson too has experienced rebuff and lean results on Capitol Hill. The Great Society programs have been starved by meager appropriations and the President has suffered defeats on civil rights legislation with open-housing provisions, on "home rule" for the District of Columbia, and on the repeal of section 14(B) of the Taft-Hartley Act, permitting the states to enact laws banning the union shop.

While the President hobbled along in the postwar era in his ventures on Capitol Hill, across the Atlantic the British Prime Minister, operating under an altogether different political arrangement, could count on the enactment of 100 per cent of the measures he proposed to the legislature. Even with a slender majority of four votes in 1965, which soon fell to one vote, Harold Wilson as Prime Minister dared to undertake an ambitious and controversial foreign and domestic program, while simultaneously surviving votes of confidence.

The President has no dependable way, as the British Prime Minister has, to command the legislature's support. A complex of forces prompts Congress to resist or oppose the President much of the time. Because the method of electing the President differs from the method of electing Congress, their constituencies, and therefore their outlooks and interests, differ. The President and Vice President alone are chosen by the nation. Senators and Congressmen are essentially local officers responsible to the voters of a single state or Congressional district. Congress neither chooses the President nor is chosen by him, and is therefore not beholden to him, and cannot be pushed by him. Only once in four years are the President and members of the House of Representatives elected simultaneously, and even then only one-third of the Senate is elected. At the President's mid-term, the House and another one-third of the Senate are chosen, usually with local issues predominating. The results usually worsen the President's own party support in both Congressional houses. At no point in his four-year term does the President face a Senate wholly elected during his tenure, owing to the Senate's six-year term and system of staggered elections.

Presidents come and go, but the most powerful legislators—the chairmen of the standing committees—stay on, sometimes rolling up tenures of a third of a century and more. In most of the years since World War II, the President who has sought important social and economic legislation has faced a hard wall of opposition from the legislative leaders of his own party. These are the committee chairmen who have risen by seniority because they come from "safe" districts. These districts have been situated chiefly in Southern and in rural and small-town areas, although it must be noted that the number and proportion of noncompetitive seats held by Northern Congressmen has been on the increase for the last decade or so. Through most of the postwar years, until 1966, the chairman of the House Rules Committee was Howard K. Smith, a small-town Virginian, who over three decades of intermittent service in that post compiled an imposing record of thwarting Presidential legislation. He fought off most of Truman's Fair Deal program, and throttled education and welfare measures of both the Eisenhower and Kennedy administrations. When the 1966 elections removed him from Congress, he was replaced by William Colmer, who was in every way a replica, except for the slight variation that he came from Mississippi. In both the Senate and the House, in Democratic Congresses since World War II, committee chairmanships have been dominated by Southerners and Southwesterners.

From the President's standpoint, Congress is an elaborate obstacle course full of procedural traps that delay and boggle his program. The Senate filibuster, the intricate rules of the House, the treaty procedure, all can be sources of trouble by which a minority of the legislature can thwart not only the President but the legislative majority. In 1966, the filibuster killed two key measures of President Johnson, the civil rights bill, and the bill to repeal section 14(B) of the Taft-Hartley Act. The requirement that two-thirds of the Senate approve treaties serves to make treaties the President brings to the Senate prey to a minority— the ⅓ of the Senate plus one that can defeat a treaty—and makes the President vulnerable to concessions and reservations and puts him to the difficult test of winning support from the opposition party. Significantly, it was at the request of the Senate Republican leader, Senator Everett Dirksen, that President Kennedy sent a letter to the Senate, when the test ban treaty was in its hands, listing a series of "assurances." [6] All of this shows that in the period since World War II, the original plan of the Founding Fathers for the place of the Presidency in the political system has not been especially disturbed, or amended. Distrustful of majorities and of power, the Fathers took pains to check both the popular will and to limit the Presidency. By instilling the principles of checks and balances and separation of powers into the Constitution, the Fathers preordained that neither Congress nor the executive was to become the dominant force, but each shared the powers of the other, whether making laws, appointments, or treaties, and each therefore could check the other's assertion.

Although the Fathers did not foresee political parties, their rise has not hampered in any significant way the intended effects of checks and balances. President Eisenhower was not long in office when he perceptively observed, "Now let's remember there are no national parties in the United States. There are . . . state parties." Experience in the post–World-War-II era has not disturbed the condition that our parties function effectively as national organizations only once every four years, when control of the White House is at stake. Otherwise, the party is a confederation of state and local organizations, ridden with sectional cleavages and factional differences. The President and members of Congress, although they march under the same party banner, are nominated by different party organizations and are chosen by different electorates, a condition hardly conducive to unity. Even in the pressure of an election, which presumably would encourage party members into the closest unity, differences may push to the surface between the President and his Congressional party colleagues. Just how far the divisions may go is suggested by an episode during President Eisenhower's second term, in the Congressional elections of 1958. Richard M. Simpson of Pennsylvania, then chairman of the Republican Congressional Campaign Committee, went so far as to counsel Republican candidates for the House of Representatives to forget about Eisenhower's favor and support and "make known" to voters any "disagreement with the President's policies." [7] A conservative Republican, Simpson often opposed the President's "modern Republicanism."

The President and the Bureaucracy

The national popular majority, working through the President, relies upon the departments and agencies of the executive branch to achieve

[6] *New York Times*, September 12, 1963.
[7] See Hugh A. Bone, *Party Committees and National Politics* (Seattle: University of Washington Press, 1958), pp. 167-68.

its purposes. The bureaucracy can serve the national majority well or frustrate it, by indifference and ineptitude, and by responsiveness to special interest, including its own. The bureaucracy itself is a power center, with a high capacity for self-direction. Its own vested interests center upon program, policy, and personal power. It nurtures indigenous work habits and cherishes ties with group interests that have a stake in its operations, and Congressional committees. All these forces may be asserted against the President and the interests of the national majority that he may embody. President Kennedy testified on more than one occasion to the troubles the executive bureaucracy can give the President. Forewarned by Adlai Stevenson that he would find the State Department a "tremendous institutional inertial force," Kennedy soon spoke of the department as "a bowl of jelly" and complained bitterly, "They never have any ideas over there; never come up with anything new." [8]

The vast bureaucracy, with its layers of specialists, its enormous paper work, its addiction to routine, its distaste for the risks of innovation, its tenacity to the status quo in policy, its slowness in deciding and acting, all militate against the needs of a President faced with urgent problems in a fast-changing world. The President, fortunately, is not without means in his dealings with bureaucracy and many have either originated or have undergone rapid development in the period following World War II. The White House staff has expanded to comprise a score of assistants devoted to responsibilities concerning the press, Congressional relations, national security, and so on. The White House staff are the President's personal aides, his "lengthened shadow" and "other self." They extend his reach into the executive branch, as prodders and trouble-shooters; help prepare his messages and speeches; oversee his communications, both incoming and outgoing; analyze and refine and propose solutions to problems he confronts and the decisions he must make. Leading White House staff figures, such as the special counsel and the assistant for national security affairs, have in the postwar period sometimes achieved an importance that only several cabinet secretaries can rival.

Beyond this personal staff is an institutional staff that includes the Bureau of the Budget, the Office of the Special Assistant for Science and Technology, the Council of Economic Advisers, and the National Security Council. All except the Budget Bureau were created since World War II and reflect the President's growing involvements in science, national defense, and economic policy. The President may also use the more traditional institution, the cabinet, whose proceedings since the Eisenhower administration have become more organized because of the use of an agenda and a recording of decisions taken. The general tend-

[8] Quoted in *New York Times*, February 20, 1967.

ency of this collection of Presidential agencies is to centralize in the President's hands control of several processes that previously were handled with large autonomy by the departments. Legislative relations of the departments have become subject to stronger direction from the White House staff, which also has become the chief source of the legislative agenda. In press relations, "good news" about administration achievements, in bygone days often released by the departments, now tends to be conveyed by the White House. On the other hand, most Presidents since World War II have relied heavily upon the departments to take initiatives in dealing with policy problems. Their occasional disappointment with the departments is suggested by Kennedy's outcry against the State Department and the tendency of Presidents such as Johnson to turn over new problems to study groups of leading private citizens and to invite from the universities proposals to be included in his annual legislative program.

Modernization of the Presidency

The postwar era has also witnessed considerable discussion, the development of several strong trends, and concrete action to bring about adjustments of the Presidency to the new demands upon it. The Twenty-fifth Amendment is a concrete effort of modernization, of updating the arrangements for the contingency of Presidential inability for the rigors of the nuclear age.

PRESIDENTIAL ELECTIONS. In the processes by which the President is selected, there is a spreading conviction that the Electoral College has long outlived its usefulness and has become a dangerous anachronism. Several kinds of proposals are in circulation for dealing with it, for erasing the glaring contradiction between the Presidency as a majoritarian office and the method of his selection, which may deny the will of the popular majority. The most modest proposal advanced is that although the plan of the electoral vote might be kept, the electors themselves should be abolished. In a word, the Electoral College should be automated to reflect the popular vote of each state. The proposal rests upon the simple proposition that if the elector is faithful to the popular vote, he is useless; if he is not, he is dangerous.

Several proposals have been advanced on the altogether correct assumption that there are ways more democratic than the Electoral College for choosing the President, ways that will more assuredly reflect the popular will. Of these, one is outstandingly in accord with the ideal of a President truly chosen by the people. This is the proposal of a constitutional amendment by which the President would be chosen by the majority of the national popular vote. A national popular election of the President would best harmonize with the ideal proclaimed by the United States Supreme Court in its reapportionment decisions, of one man, one vote, or of equal voting influence for all Americans regardless of geographical location. Under the workings of the Electoral College system, this ideal is grossly violated; a popular voter in Nevada can command a far greater percentage of an electoral vote than a voter in the far more heavily populated state of California. The new reapportionment plans required by the courts for the state legislatures and the national House of Representatives have deflated the traditional argument that the Electoral College system, operated by the general ticket principle (the Presidential candidate who wins most of a state's popular votes receives all of its electoral votes) is the only sure defense of large urban areas against rural-dominated state legislatures, malapportioned Congressional districts, and a United States Senate weighted in favor of the small states. With the Senate now strongly representative of the urban factor, and with the growing reflection of the House and the state legislatures of the Supreme Court's ideal of one man, one vote, the undeniable logic of political progress requires that the Presidency too be brought into accord with that ideal.

The two plans most discussed for the national popular election of the President have been put forward by the American Bar Association and Senator Birch Bayh of Indiana. Both plans realistically foresee that there would be more candidates in the field than under the present system. Both would require the President to win a minimum of 40 per cent of the popular vote for election. If no candidate won 40 per cent, the Bar Association proposal calls for a national run-off election between the two high candidates. The run-off election would be more in accord with the ideal of popular selection than Bayh's provision, in the event the first national balloting presents no definitive result. Bayh would have all 535 members of Congress choose a President from the two high men, by majority vote. Congress conceivably might not be controlled by the party of the top Presidential vote-getter and it would be prone then to choose the second man. A narrowly divided Congress would put a premium on promises and deals and a President who emerged from such a process would probably have mortgaged much of his future incumbency.

The Bar Association's proposal for a run-off election would substantially increase the already enormous expenditure required for Presidential candidacy. The desirability and practicality of this feature can be weighed only as it is seen in conjunction with proposals to improve the financing of Presidential campaigns. In light of the enormous costs and outlays in the age of television, in light, too, of the democratic ideal to make Presidential candidacy as widely available as possible rather than the preserve of a wealthy class, improvement of campaign financing becomes of paramount importance. It has become a topic of Presidential recommendation and Congressional discussion.

CAMPAIGN FINANCING. In 1967, President Johnson sent a wide-ranging message to Congress on campaign financing.[9] He urged Congress to provide for each Presidential election a substantial fund to finance party expenses incurred in bringing "issues before the public." This would include expenditures for radio and television, for newspaper and periodical advertising, and for travel costs and preparation and distribution of literature. The fund would not cover staff salaries, telephones, and administration, and outlays for them would still depend upon private contributions. Primary and convention expenses also would not be supported by the fund. Only official party candidates could qualify for its benefits. The maximum expendable in a state could not exceed 140 per cent of the relation of that state's population to the national population. Thus in a state with 10 per cent of the national population, no more than 14 per cent of a party's share of the subsidy could be spent. The major parties would share equally, and a minor party, defined as one that polled between 5 and 25 per cent of the vote in the current election, would be reimbursed immediately after the election. The Comptroller General would audit the fund and report abuses to the Secretary of the Senate and Clerk of the House.

Several objections can be and have been raised to the plan. It lacks any provision for controlling radio and television rates for broadcasts financed by federal funds. This defect, of course, could be overcome by at least an effort to include a schedule of rates. Even better, what with television commanding such a large percentage of campaign outlays, is it not well to ask a medium that exists through free use of the air waves belonging to all the people to donate a goodly number of hours to the task of choosing a President? Reliance upon the Secretary of the Senate and Clerk of the House for enforcement of the fund's restrictions does not augur firmness and initiative. More promising, probably, would be a committee of leading private citizens who might in periodic public reports comment on the efficacy of the fund. The plan would not escape a loophole that present-day financing suffers: the expenditures of committees and individuals working independently of the political parties. Even so, a half-step gain is preferable to none at all, and governmental subsidy seems an undeniable necessity in light of rocketing campaign costs. The most serious objection raised against the plan is that it would work a drastic redistribution of power in the party structure. In effect, by enormously increasing the financial resources of the national party committees, it would grasp power away from state and local party organizations. It would centralize power in the hands of Presi-

[9] Quoted in *New York Times*, May 26, 1967.

dential candidates and national committees and give them leverage to reward or punish local candidates by withholding Presidential campaign efforts and even to intervene in local nominating processes. To reduce this objection, a division conceivably could be made of the fund between Presidential elections, Congressional elections, and local elections. The division could be according to a formula incorporated in law. Presumably, the formula, to find its way into law, would have to be acceptable by the Senatorial, Congressional, and state organizational interests.

Because of widespread opposition to a plan of direct national subsidy, it is necessary to look at other plans—plans that would avoid the hazard of national party domination of local party institutions. More simple in form and substantially effective in purpose to provide relief to Presidential and other candidates for public offices against soaring costs is the proposal advanced by various members of Congress for a tax credit, which would be subtracted from taxable income just as deductions are for charitable contributions, with the balance subject to taxation. To begin with, a credit of $5 could be given on contributions up to $10, and if general inflation in the economy or still rising campaign costs required an upward adjustment of the tax credit, such an adjustment could be simply made. A tax credit would benefit most taxpayers, especially those in lower income brackets, and encourage broader participation in campaign financing. It would avoid the objection made to a national subsidy, that it centralizes campaign funds. By its nature it would help preserve the federal character of the party structure and the autonomy enjoyed by state and local organizations. It would also contribute effectively to our immediate objective of helping Presidential candidates.

BROADENING THE FRANCHISE. For our migrating Americans who are deprived of their franchise in Presidential elections by residence requirements, we could ideally abolish all such requirements, but we would get nowhere because of its political infeasibility. More viable politically would be to lower the requirement to the point where one would be eligible to vote in a Presidential election if he had established residence in a new state prior to September 1. Such a recommendation has been made to Congress by President Johnson and deserves support.

PRESIDENTIAL TENURE. We ought to bolster the President's tenure, the strength of which is itself a source of Presidential power. The chief blow that we could strike in its behalf would be to repeal the Twenty-second (two-term) Amendment and thus spare ourselves the potential hardships of a rigid procedure. In this case, to modernize the Presidency is to return to the original arrangement of the Founding Fathers, which placed no limit on Presidential reeligibility.

Although the Twenty-fifth Amendment, in dealing with disability, carries flaws, with the possibility of deep and dark maneuver for control of the Presidency that Senator Gore warned us of, it is probably wise, for the immediate future, to leave the subject at rest. The disability problem, with all its complexities, defies any neat and wholly satisfactory solution. The subject has long been discussed and agitated about and it is doubtless wisest to rely on the expectation that in a crisis of Presidential disability the pressures of national expectations would compel all concerned, including legislators of both parties, to act constructively and responsively. We can be confident, too, that anything done in such a crisis would have to reflect a broad national consensus.

PRESIDENTIAL SUCCESSION. In our concern that the Presidency always be filled in the nuclear age, we might well extend the line of succession now provided in the Presidential Succession Act of 1947. The act brings into the succession the Speaker of the House, the President pro tempore of the Senate, and most members of the cabinet. All those now in the line are present in Washington most of the time, a fact that makes possible the extinction of the entire body of successors in a nuclear attack on the capital. Congress might desirably add to the succession public officials distributed around the country. One possibility might be to include the governors ranked according to the population of their states in the last census.

Strengthening the Presidential System

Despite the strong record of the British Prime Minister in securing legislation in comparison with the President, there is no sufficient cause for us to look acquisitively at the Parliamentary system. The Presidency is rooted in our deepest political traditions, and in other branches of executive endeavor it has strengths that surpass the Prime Minister's. Indeed, some thoughtful Britishers, restive under the limitations of their political system, are gazing admiringly at the Presidential system. In seeking to improve the Presidency's performance in legislation, we shall need to stay within the confines of the Presidential system, with its accompaniment of a strong Congress. Within such limitations what can and should be done?

We ought by constitutional amendment to provide that the President, the Senate, and the House of Representatives be elected simultaneously for a common term of four years. Historic data establish that we could well expect that elections so arranged would produce a President and two houses of Congress better attuned in party and policy outlook than their present uneven election permits. The President and the houses of Congress would be the product of and would reflect a common public mood, a political advantage that is precluded in the present arrangement. The adoption of this proposal would remove the timing of elections and the terms of office as mechanisms of the checks-and-balances system that contributes importantly to legislative-executive deadlocks. The proposal would avoid the traditional Congressional election at the President's mid-term, when the entire House and one-third of the Senate are chosen, an event that tends to work against the interest of the national majority and the President. The mid-term election is apt to concentrate on local, rather than national, issues, and to lower the President's party strength in Congress, with damage to his prestige at home and abroad.

The Constitution leaves it to the individual houses of Congress to arrange their internal organization and working procedures. These, it has been argued, can be used by the dominant minority in the legislative houses to frustrate the will of the national majority and the President as a champion of it. It is clear enough that Congress requires reorganization to enable it better to reflect the national majority. Just as the Presidency has been affected by recent amendments to the Constitution, so conceivably could Congress, but to specify legislative organization and procedure in the Constitution would be against our traditions and would create rigidities, causing difficulty for Congress to adjust to subsequent change and need.

It would be better for Congress to use its present constitutional power to reorganize itself. Admittedly, history tells us that Congress is little inclined to self-reorganization, although on several occasions it has brought itself to the effort. In the era following World War II, the most notable of these were the limited reorganization in 1946, alterations in the make-up of the House Rules Committee in 1960, and alterations in its powers in 1965.

From the standpoint of both the President's needs and the interest of a national popular majority to see its will effected both through the Presidency and through Congress, it is clear enough what the reorganization of Congress should center upon. The seniority principle, by which committee chairmen are chosen, and which provides chairmen who in too great numbers oppose the national majority and the President, especially on social and economic measures, deserves reconsideration. Various proposals have come forward as substitutes for seniority, and any one of them would bring improvements for the prospects of the President and the national majority. The chairman, for example, might be chosen by a majority of the membership of his committee. There might be voting by secret ballot, rotation among senior members, election by the party caucus. Also, there might be removal of the chairman at age 70 by a majority vote of the committee after a single term. (The national majority and the President suffer most from elderly chairmen.) Part of the chairman's great impact turns upon his ability to use his committee powers arbitrarily. To curb abuse, the setting of meeting dates, agenda, and other procedures might be done by majority vote of the committee in lieu of the chairman's decision. A committee "bill of rights" might well enable a committee majority to terminate debate after reasonable discussion, and thus on occasion rescue Presidential measures that are caught in committee bottlenecks and may languish for years in committee and never come to the floor to be voted on. Medicare, after its proposal by President Kennedy, was bottled up in the House Ways and Means Committee for almost three years before it came to the House for a vote.

The President's program, which is often blocked by procedural delays, might be helped by reducing the size of the majority required to bring measures bottled up in committee to the floor. In the Senate, the majority leader might well be authorized to offer a motion designating any bill, including those in the President's program, as a major item of legislation. The motion's adoption would require the committee to which the bill had been assigned to report it to the Senate within 30 calendar days. Quorum calls, employed to bog down action, might, through new procedural rules, be reduced or eliminated. Electric voting machines might step up the tempo of legislative processes, with benefit to the national majority and the President. The Senate filibuster, from which the President has suffered repeatedly, might be reduced by easing the rules for closure of debate. Although such a goal has been repeatedly fought for with only slight gains, it is a battle worth renewing.

If the treaty power were revised to require the approval of only a majority of Senators present, rather than the present two-thirds, the President would be less vulnerable to pressures for concessions and reservations in the treaty's development and approval. The President should be given, as some of our governors are, the item veto for appropriation bills. The item veto would equip him with a substantial new bargaining strength that he could employ widely to advance his policy enterprises on Capitol Hill. He could conceivably engage in a kind of "log-rolling," exchanging his acceptance of appropriation items for support of his own measures by legislators individually and in blocs. The item veto might bring the President to a point of a truly commanding influence in legislative affairs.

The President might also be given a power possessed by governors in four states, the power of an "amendatory" veto. Under the procedure, the executive can return a bill without his signature to the house where it originated, with suggestions for change that would make it acceptable to him. The legislature first considers the question of accepting the changes before deciding whether to pass the bill over his veto or return it to him for final consideration. The device has strengthened the governor's hand in shaping legislation and would doubtless do the same for the President.

The President might fare better in legislation if he increases his strength as the party leader. One of the more promising trends in his favor has emerged in the Kennedy-Johnson era in the increasing identification of the President's legislative program with urban needs. Earlier Presidents have gained strength as party leaders by championing policies and programs of wide popular appeal, which leaves their party no choice but largely to go along with him. The Kennedy-Johnson legislative programs seem bent upon subordinating party and Congressional politics to urban politics. The programs are pitched to the great urban groups: economic, racial, and national. Kennedy particularly cultivated state and local party leaders who determine the selection of and the support given to Congressional candidates. The method aims to light hundreds of bonfires under congressmen and senators, fueled by an urban program and stoked by urban groups and local party chieftains. The movement of social forces strongly supports the modern Presidential formula, with the huge growth of urban population and its interest in program politics, and the growing competence of urban groups in political action —in organizing and communicating their objectives on a national scale.

To strengthen the President as party leader we might well strengthen the national parties themselves. Some time ago a committee of the American Political Science Association made sweeping proposals to this end.[10] Many of its ideas were too closely imitative of the British party system to gain any acceptance in American political life. Several of the committee's themes, however, could be adapted to the present-day needs of the President. The President might gain if more positive platforms were prepared and closed primaries were encouraged, if a national party council were created to serve the President as a kind of party cabinet, if regional party organizations were created to enlarge the perspectives of state and local organizations, if more frequent national conventions were held and were charged with the responsibility of adopting at least biennial platforms; these would tend to be responsive to the President in light of the party's tendency to support him at its general conclaves.

The national committee is growing in function and financial power and is becoming an increasingly valuable adjunct to the President in its research and public relations undertakings. The committee tends to be highly responsive to him, and gains in its competence redound to his profit. Congressional party organization has been decidedly unpromising from the standpoint of the President. The main resource of centralized

[10] American Political Science Association, *Toward a More Responsible Two-Party System* (New York: Holt, Rinehart & Winston, Inc., 1950).

party management in which the President is interested is the policy committees of the respective parties, but these have had little impact. The policy committees' best uses are service and research, education, and legislative scheduling. Occasionally they work out policy positions, significant not for their number but for their indication that they can and do materialize. The Senatorial and Congressional Campaign Committees are jealous of their autonomy and afford ample impression that they would dismiss any plan to bring them into closer association with the National Committee, which is so decidedly an adjunct of the President.

What should be done to make the national administration more responsive to the national popular majority acting through the President? At the forefront of possible actions should be the enlargement of the President's directing power over the executive branch. Ideally, the President should be equipped with administrative powers comparable to those of the business executive and the heads of other governments. Not only would the majority be better served, but the quality of governmental administration, we might well expect, would be improved. What the President needs can be simply stated: a power over personnel policy, planning, accounting, and the administrative direction of the executive branch to a degree matching his powers over the executive budget. Consistent with this theme, the independent regulatory commissions—long ago described as a "headless fourth branch of government"—ought to be abolished, since they encroach upon Presidential authority and policymaking, and hamper the capacity of the national majority to assert itself against minority interest. We would need to be watchful that an old habit of Congress, recently disavowed, does not revive—to give authority directly to bureau chiefs. The practice is still another device by which minority or special interest may defy the President and the national majority.

To cope with the ever expanding policy-making responsibilities of his office, the President should enjoy sweeping freedom in establishing and arranging his personal staff, subject only to a generous financial limit. He should be enabled to create assistants for such administrative and policy areas as he deems necessary and to arrange their duties in whatever way he considers best.

To exercise maximum influence over the executive bureaucracy, the President requires a strong dual organization. One is a personal staff, a group of assistants, with flexible assignments and responsibilities of both a program-building and action-forcing nature. The President also requires an institutional staff, such as the Bureau of the Budget, the National Security Council, and the Council of Economic Advisers. The institutionalized Presidency helps assure, as much as anything can, that the multiple specializations a problem requires will be brought to it.

To improve the President's situation with the institutional staff, Congress might well desist from its frequent habit of adding ad hoc assignments to the already heavy workload of the Budget Bureau. The additions reduce the availability of this key staff agency to the President. It would be well, in the interests of maximizing the President's freedom to arrange his staff, to drop from existing statutes governing the National Security Council the designation of several executive officers as members. The council would be more valuable to the President without this impediment to his freedom to include in the council such officials as he sees fit. There should also be added to the President's institutional staff a planning agency for social policy, the equal in that field of the Council of Economic Advisers in the economic. The nation's most urgent domestic problems are social problems, such as education, health, housing, civil rights, whose pressing needs make their representation in the President's highest councils well justifiable.

To help the President escape the sterility and resistance of bureaucracy, several expedients can be established or enlarged. He will gain if he is given the widest latitude to utilize the government contract to employ private talent in the universities and elsewhere in the private sector; to create Presidential commissions to study and report on matters concerning policy innovation. He will become more free of the confinements of bureaucracy if the interchange of personnel between public and private employment is facilitated. Personnel from private life—from the universities, the foundations, law firms, and business, might be brought into government for terms of service of two and more years in a program speciality and then return to private employment. A similar exchange might also be established for the passage of government employees into temporary assignments in private enterprise. Accommodating arrangements in both public and private employment would need to be made for mutual recognition of promotion rights, retirement benefits, and the like. The Washington bureaucracy could in these ways be regularly infused, more than it is now, with new blood, new ideas, broader perspectives, and zest for accomplishment.

Prospects for Modernization

The general prospects for achieving changes in the Presidency in the interest of its modernization are good, if we consider the many changes that have indeed been made in the office since World War II. The Presidency, it is clear, can be reached by constitutional amendment. Twice in the postwar era amendments have touched the Presidency— the Twenty-second and the Twenty-fifth Amendments making significant changes in the office. Statutes have been passed—the National

Security Act, for example—that have increased the staff resources available to meet new policy problems.

Now to consider the prospects of some of the specific proposals. The outlook for a constitutional amendment establishing the national popular election of the President is exceptionally bright. The proposal carries momentum from the Supreme Court decisions on apportionment that highlight the one man, one vote ideal. The proposal now bears the prestigious endorsement of the American Bar Association. The Association's support counted much in the adoption of the Twenty-fifth Amendment and should have similar effect for the proposed Twenty-sixth Amendment, calling for the popular election of the President. In addition, the amendment has attracted support from Senator Everett Dirksen of Illinois, the Senate Republican Leader, and Senator Mike Mansfield of Montana, the Senate Democratic Leader. The bipartisan, liberal-conservative support augurs for the proposal a bright future.

The outlook for some form of governmental financial aid for Presidential and other electoral campaigning is good. It is reasonable to expect that some action will be taken by Congress soon. The chief question is which of several possible plans should be adopted. The existence of several competing plans is probably the chief force limiting action. Delay is also encouraged by the rivalries of the sponsors of the several plans, by the fact that President Johnson stands behind the federal subsidy plan and Senator Robert Kennedy behind the tax credit proposal. In addition, wide opposition in Congress has prevailed against the Johnson plan. Republicans generally have opposed it, convinced that it would reduce the advantage they possess under existing financing. Many legislators and state and local party leaders view as dangerous the centralizing of political power in the hands of the President that the plan invites, at the expense of Congressional, state, and local party power.

"The President of the United States," Senator Clifford Case of New Jersey said in 1965, is the man in Washington "who most needs Congressional reform." [11] Despite the general bleakness of the reform picture on Capitol Hill, those interested in the subject ought not succumb to the paralysis of despair. Actually, the historical record indicates, Congress on occasion has made significant changes in its structures and procedures. The Reorganization Act of 1946 encompassed several important changes. Earlier this century the impressive powers of the Speaker of the House, which led to the parliamentary tyranny of "Uncle Joe" Cannon, were sheared in a members' revolt. In 1913, Democratic and Republican progressives united to overpower the seniority system in the Senate and to install new committee chairmen devoted to a

[11] *New York Times,* April 5, 1963.

progressive program. Working in close partnership with President Wilson, they succeeded in enacting a remarkable list of major legislation. The most dramatic of the recent struggles over changes in legislative procedures centrally involved the President. Promptly after taking office, President Kennedy set as his first order of legislative business an assault on the House Rules Committee. Thanks to the President's exertion of heavy administration pressures and the large exertions of Speaker Sam Rayburn, the Rules Committee was enlarged by three members. Kennedy was driven to the struggle by the realization that unless the committee were enlarged, and hopefully with additional votes favorable to the administration, his major measures would never reach the House floor to be voted on. Despite the administration's success in altering the committee, it still suffered occasional rebuffs in its efforts to move bills to the floor. Lawrence F. O'Brien, Presidential assistant for Congressional relations in the Kennedy and Johnson administrations, and subsequently Postmaster General, regards Kennedy's 1961 fight to enlarge the Rules Committee as a major "breakthrough" in President-Congress relations.[12] The fight signified that the President can and will intervene in matters involving the internal organization of Congress, that he and his administration were prepared to march up Pennsylvania Avenue to fight for their ideas.

In 1965, President Johnson's big year of successes on Capitol Hill, the House rules were changed in a way that was substantially helpful to the administration in bringing its measures to the floor. The House then adopted a 21-day rule which permitted the Speaker to require the chairman or any other member of a standing committee to call up for consideration a bill that had been favorably reported by that committee, and if the bill had been before the Rules Committee for 21 days without receiving a rule, or special resolution, for floor consideration. The House in 1965 made this change as part of its permanent rules and thus seemed to give it the quality of permanence instead of a duration extending only for the 89th Congress. When the 90th Congress assembled in 1967, however, one of its first acts was to abolish the change. A conservative coalition of Republicans and Democrats, whose Republican ranks had been thinned by the 1964 elections, had been substantially restored by the 1966 elections.

Equally limited has been the success of the Monroney-Madden Committee, a joint House-Senate committee, which in 1965 conducted extensive hearings on the reform of Congressional procedures. No reorganization or reform act has so far resulted, although the substantial studies and recommendations of the committee remain available for action by future Congresses and the President.

[12] *New York Times,* July 12, 1965.

The prospects for modernization of the Presidency in its administrative role are a little better, although quite spotty. Congress will not take up gladly any proposal that it desist from giving special assignments to the Budget Bureau that may detract from its service to the President. The Bureau's role vis-à-vis Congress has long been somewhat ambiguous. Legislators are prone to regard the Bureau as partly a Congressional agency, a necessary auxiliary to the work of the Appropriations Committees, what with its responsibility to prepare the executive budget. Nor is it likely, given the psychology of separation of powers, which prompts each branch, including Congress, to guard jealously its powers and prerogatives, that enactments will be readily forthcoming repealing the provision of memberships on the National Security Council. The proposal of a Presidential staff agency for social policy might be carried to success by the ever more explosive character of the nation's urban problems. Congress, however, if the past be a guide, would be naturally and strongly prone to resist the proposal. The struggle to create the principal departmental social agency, the Department of Health, Education, and Welfare, occupied several decades, owing chiefly to the reluctance of Congress to acknowledge, in the creation of a department, that social welfare was an enduring responsibility of the federal government. Sweeping rejections by Congress in the past of proposals to abolish the independent regulatory commissions bode no good for that recommendation in the future. Congress is apt to regard the commissions as its agencies and to deem any encroachment upon them as an encroachment upon itself.

The effort to improve the possibilities of movement from private life to government service has made some gains, but nothing on a dramatic scale. The President now has available an orderly roster of likely private talent that facilitates his search for staff help in the private sector. Conflict of interest laws need to be eased, but the political touchiness of that step dims the likelihood of its occurring. Private enterprises are highly uneven in adopting measures to encourage their employees to undertake limited terms of public service. No real improvement is in prospect until a new philosophy develops and catches on that one's obligations of citizenship are not fulfilled by devotion to private career and profit and faithful payment of taxes, but that a tour of duty of several years in a responsible government post is also to be taken up. Something of the spirit that brings younger citizens into the Peace Corps is needed for the older age brackets, sweetened by higher compensation than the Corps offers. Such a philosophy of public dedication goes against the grain of our tradition with its heavy emphasis of self-interest. The modernization of the Presidency, it is clear enough, is a struggle to be fought and won on many fronts.

3

THE CONGRESS

David R. Derge

Introduction

What is modernization? The usual analytical connotation of this word is movement from a traditional to a contemporary society through a complex process of institutional, behavioral, and philosophical change. We ordinarily think of the "developing" countries coming to grip with the western industrial mass society model.[1] This particular approach clearly offers less analytical value for the study of the U. S. Congress, a functioning institution in the most advanced nation in the world. Perhaps one useful connection is the directionality of modernization, which is toward adjustment to contemporary pressures on the system, although by no means are all analysts agreed that the net gain over traditional patterns is necessarily good. The price of modernization may be destruction of social and religious beliefs, family structures, or other valued items. But in any case the direction is toward the contemporary.

Modernization in the Congressional context could mean alterations in the institutional practices or behaviors of the participants calculated to produce different patterns of decision-making better suited to meet contemporary pressures. This requires us to examine the role of Congress, the contemporary pressures on Congress, and proposals for modernization (sometimes called "reform") to assist Congress in exercising its proper role under contemporary pressures.

DAVID R. DERGE is Professor of Government and Associate Dean of the Faculties at Indiana University. He has published several articles and chapters of books in the areas of legislative and political behavior and has recently turned to research on the modernization of developing countries. He has been active in state and local politics and has held elective public office. He is the holder of two awards for distinguished teaching at Indiana University.
[1] *See* David E. Apter, *The Politics of Modernization* (Chicago: University of Chicago Press, 1965), for an attempt to formulate a theory of modernization.

Throughout the analysis we will limit our discussion to institutional and behavioral problems and forego the temptation to base judgments on what kinds of policy output modernization of Congress might encourage. Much of the literature on legislative reform is explicitly or implicitly built upon distress over what laws the legislature has, or has not, passed. Froman ponders that "little criticism of Congress is heard from conservatives. It is the liberals who, upset with the substance of Congressional decisions, also criticize the process by which those decisions are made." [2] It is difficult to resist the temptation to criticize institutions from a policy point of view, but the political scientist may obscure or destroy his analytical clarity by masking his own concern over policy reform with theory or generalization.

No attempt will be made to catalog and judge the literally thousands of proposals for changes or reform in Congress. Voluminous hearings are available on these proposals and they contain exhaustive expert opinions representing all persuasions.[3] Our task here is rather to identify some of the basic issues and techniques in evaluating any modernization proposal.

1945 and After: Contemporary Pressures on Congress

The year 1945 was once appealing as a useful watershed for analyses such as this one. That was the year World War II ended, and in our traditional view of wars and world affairs a new era was to dawn and our institutions and preoccupations could again return to "normal" and focus upon domestic problems. In less than two years even the most isolationist and idealistic could see the error of this assumption. Despite the fact that we had disbanded our military machine and turned to peaceful pursuits, our enemies had not, and by 1950 we were back into hot war. In order to understand the contemporary pressures on Congress it is necessary to go back at least to the beginning of World War II and to see the ensuing quarter of a century of war—alternatingly hot and cold—as the context for democratic decision-making. For some purposes it would be appealing to go back to the political paroxysms of the early 1930's, when the stage was set for dominating domestic political trends of our times—ascendancy of the executive, changing expectations about the role of government, and centripetal movements within the federal

[2] Lewis A. Froman, *The Congressional Process* (Boston: Little, Brown and Co., 1967), p. 183.
[3] For example, *see* "Organization of Congress," Hearings Before the Joint Committee on the Organization of the Congress, 89th Congress, 1st Session (1965).

system. And how far back need we go to capture the transformation of the American system into an urban-industrial mass society? All of these have produced problems for democratic institutions, including legislative bodies.

WARS: HOT AND COLD. Wars are conducted by executives, not by legislatures. Successful prosecution of a war, which in modern times almost always calls upon dedication of the whole social system to high sacrifice and singleness of purpose, demands decision-making for which large deliberative bodies like legislatures are not well fitted. Marshaling and planning of systemwide manpower and economic resources is better done by a bureaucracy with lines of authority to a small group of leaders. War's singleness of purpose precludes debate over alternative uses of these resources and the crucial decisions are organizational, not legislative. The functional equivalent of national singleness of purpose in political party terms is legislative "bipartisanship." This is suppression of the systematic development and exposition of alternatives, and gives the Chief Executive a powerful whip to use on both parties in Congress, and eliminates effective deliberation and debate.[4]

War's secrecy and need for rapid decisions further complicate the legislature's role. At best a very few legislators can be privy to high state secrets such as strategies or weapons systems, and then under circumstances that make them coconspirators with the executive branch. The Manhattan Project, which produced the world's first nuclear weapon, is an excellent example of this. Only a handful of Congressmen knew of the existence of this project, and they carefully concealed more than two billion dollars for the project in numerous appropriations bills over several years. The constant furor over the activities and financing of the Central Intelligence Agency is another example. Every President has refused to allow effective Congressional surveillance of the CIA on the perfectly reasonable grounds that national security, to say nothing of countless lives, demand absolute secrecy in matters of international espionage.[5]

[4] Strains of the most severe sort are produced when the legislature is used as a forum for debate on national purpose during a war, and no better example exists than the "hawk and dove" confrontation in the U. S. Senate over the conduct of the Vietnam war. As a nation's involvement in war becomes more total, such debate becomes more dysfunctional until at some point it must cease. At that point the legislature's traditional role as forum for debate over broad system goals and strategies is suspended.

[5] Disclosures that rocked the U. S. intelligence community came when *Ramparts* magazine attacked the CIA for support of various U. S. student organizations in international activities. Had this revelation come through the activities of a Congressional committee or individual congressmen it is probable that Congress would find out less about the CIA in the future than it does now.

Finally, the quarter-century of war, and the emergence of the United States as the world's strongest nation, have resulted in a preoccupation with external or international affairs as opposed to internal or domestic affairs. In a sense it has made domestic policies the handmaiden of U. S. international goals, although the strongest advocates of both internationalism and neoimperialism feel even now that domestic concerns receive too much priority. Constitutionally, international policies are more clearly the Chief Executive's preserve and the same problems of war—secrecy and singleness of purpose—apply here. Congress has never been notably effective as either a deliberative body or formulator of policy in the international area, and as the American system becomes more preoccupied with international goals and ambitions, to that extent the legislature becomes moon to the executive sun. Further, the range of alternatives in international policy is drastically reduced by the need to respond to dozens of other nations, friendly and unfriendly. Certainly, in terms of control over the policy environment, domestic policies offer the richest range of alternatives, while often the United States has only a few degrees of leeway in setting its international course. Even so, to pursue the metaphor, the President is pilot and captain, and the Congress is crew.

CHANGING EXPECTATIONS ABOUT GOVERNMENT ACTIVITIES. Once it was stylish to sound the alarum about the growing role of government in our lives, but under the various titles of New Deal, Fair Deal, New Frontier, Great Society, to mention only a few, the government has clearly become owner, manager, promoter, regulator, or partner in almost every enterprise of man. It is *expected* to do these things, and herein lies a crucial challenge to legislatures. While this means an expanded decision-making role for all institutions of government, the very complexity and vastness makes it difficult for the Congress to compete with the Chief Executive and the sprawling bureaucracy needed to administer the government's multifarious concerns. Two alternatives emerge: first, Congress can try to compete with the executive branch for information and expertise sufficient to ride herd on this widened range of policy. If this becomes impossible, if Congress cannot effectively oversee and legislate, it must content itself with national debate at the more abstract level of "goals" or "purposes," leaving the execution of these to bureaucrats whom even the President has problems governing.

CENTRIPETAL MOVEMENTS WITHIN THE FEDERAL SYSTEM. In another respect, the changing expectations about government have produced centripetal forces in the federal system, with a shift of greater responsibility for basic social problems to the federal government. State and local governments have grown apace, and by some measures, faster than the national government. But in terms of *decision-making*, the net gains have been at the national level in nearly all policy areas.

Riker examined nineteen areas of government activity to determine whether the national government or the state governments were gaining ascendancy over a long time period. In all but one of the seventeen areas of activity involving the expenditure of money, the national government has progressively grown in its responsibilities.[6] This basic shift in the federal system has had a multiplying effect in the growth of the national executive branch, which for other reasons noted above has become more ascendant over Congress.

While some see Congress as the main bastion of the states against reduction to insignificance in the federal system, Riker believes the political party system performs this role.

> The decentralization of the two-party system is sufficient to prevent national leaders (e.g. Presidents) from controlling their partisans by either organizational or ideological devices. As such, this decentralized party system is the main protector of the integrity of states in our federalism.[7]

This may be so, but the impact on Congress of a shift in decision-making to the national level is an intensified conflict with the executive branch over control of government decisions shifting to the center. As Truman aptly observes, "The twentieth century has been hard on national legislatures." [8]

The Role of Congress: An Evaluation

All proposals for the reform or modernization of an institution must flow from an explicit or implicit set of assumptions about a "model" or "ideal" toward which the writer hopes the institution will move. When Congressional reform is discussed this model ranges in content and complexity from a fully developed parliamentary system to a Madisonian system of Presidential government. The proposed changes may vary in extent and degree from the virtual transformation of the Congress into a House of Commons to minor procedural changes meant to improve the work of Congress within its traditional framework. In all cases two necessary sets of questions must be answered: (1) What are the proper functions of Congress? (2) In what way can Congress be changed to improve the performance of these functions?

[6] William Riker, *Federalism* (Boston: Little, Brown and Co., 1964), pp. 81-83.
[7] *Ibid.*, p. 101.
[8] David B. Truman, *Congressional Party* (New York: John Wiley and Sons, 1959), p. 1.

FUNCTIONS OF CONGRESS: A TRADITIONAL APPROACH. Keefe and Ogul present us with an effective traditional classification of legislative tasks in a democratic system.[9] Four major functions are making the law, checking the administration, educating the public, and representing constituents, localities, and interests. Minor functions that come up irregularly or infrequently include the judicial function and leadership selection. Of course it is much less difficult to label categories of functions than it is to evaluate legislative performance of these functions. In a real sense, any representative assembly will, to a greater or lesser degree, perform the functions designated by Keefe and Ogul, and criticisms of Congress must take into account two other questions that mere classification cannot answer: (1) What are the priorities among the various legitimate functions, and demands on scarce legislative resources, and how does Congress allocate these resources? (2) In the exercise of these functions how, and to what extent, does Congress exercise initiative? Criticisms of Congressional performance often are based not upon nonperformance or usurpation of functions, but upon whether Congress is doing effectively what it sets about doing. Another set of criticisms flows from disputes over the relative balance of Congressional initiative and Presidential initiative in the performance of functions about which there is agreement.

A slightly different approach would be to ask, first, "What is Congress well fitted to do?" and second, "What is the proper balance of legislative and executive initiative or leadership?" There is probably more agreement on the answer to the first question.

Proceeding from the argument of the size and complexity of the American system, the institutional structure of the Congress, and the scarcity of legislative resources, many observers conclude that the first function the Congress is well fitted to undertake is a broader policy approach to problems, leaving the details and technical problems to administrative agencies operating under clear Congressional mandates. Thus the American Assembly urges that "Congress must retain and strengthen its capacity to bring critical political judgment to bear on the major issues of the day." [10] Perhaps in an era when a few major bills represented the work of an entire session Congress could attend to a wider range of specific provisions and attempt to predict circumstances by covering all contingencies in the law, although some would argue that even given the time a legislature is poorly fitted to administer in advance of the specific situation. But when more than 10,000 bills and resolutions, a budget more than 1,000 pages long, and increasingly tech-

[9] William J. Keefe and Morris S. Ogul, *The American Legislative Process* (Englewood Cliffs, N.J.: Prentice-Hall, 1964), pp. 8-26.

[10] *The Congress and America's Future*, Final Report of the Twenty-sixth American Assembly (New York, 1964), p. 4.

nical problems must be handled by 535 elected legislators in a few months' time, preoccupation with detail means that only a fraction of public policy can receive such close scrutiny and that even in this Congress may not be equipped with the technical knowledge or experience to make detailed decisions. What worries many congressmen about this line of argument is that despite the most careful wording of general policy and administrative mandate, the crucial issue in the execution of the law may hinge upon technicalities and details that, unless anticipated by Congress, will effectively give control of policy over to an administrator, board, or commission that is supposed only to carry out the will of Congress. If this fear is real the outcome is obvious: Congress can only hope to involve itself in depth with a few problems, leaving the vast majority to administrative technicians in the executive branch. While we may be tempted to grieve over Congressional incapacity to deal with all administrative details, the crucial function of firm control general policy and the overall direction of the system remains a high priority item. Modernization proposals aimed at strengthening Congress in this way deserve close attention.

Some relief from the fear of legislative abdication comes from a second function that Congress is well fitted to perform—checking the administration, or "legislative oversight." Legislative oversight refers to the processes by which Congress evaluates, criticizes, funds, reorganizes, and reviews the performances of executive agencies to guarantee that legislative intent is being followed. Specific techniques include the control of money through authorization and appropriations, committee investigations and hearings, the creation, alteration, and abolition of bureaucratic structures, and granting relief through private bills. The importance of legislative oversight stems from a spectacular growth in the federal bureaucracy, which now includes more than two million civilian employees in addition to a large standing military force.[11] Most observers agree that even the President and his staff may encounter difficulty in overseeing this sprawling enterprise. Granting that such a bureaucracy is not intrinsically evil or antidemocratic, it still tends toward the characteristics of all bureaucracies: self-perpetuation and growth, anonymity and secrecy, and lack of popular control and accountability.

At best Congress can use legislative oversight only as a general tool of control, with the threat or prospect of a full-scale investigation and accounting serving as a check on possible bureaucratic excesses. This causes executive agencies to *anticipate* legislative intent, and may in-

[11] An interesting discussion of the problems involved in Congressional oversight in defense matters can be found in Raymond H. Dawson, "Congressional Innovation and Intervention in Defense Policy: Legislative Authorization of Weapons Systems," *American Political Science Review*, LVI (March 1962), pp. 42-57.

clude such regularized control as constant liaison between an agency and Congressional committees concerned with its activities.[12] Yet Congress seems well fitted to this task within its limited time. The President, as head of the executive branch, must maintain a different set of relationships with his administrators, although certainly accounting and control are included in his techniques. It is certain that the courts afford important protections and curbs against bureaucratic excesses. But the procedures of the judicial system are effective only in special types of grievances and then usually only after long delays and cost.

In sum, *if* systematic external oversight of the bureaucracy of a modern industrial state is even possible, the legislative branch must provide it, and modernization proposals that facilitate this must be high on the list of priorities.

A third legislative function that Congress seems well fitted to provide is continuity and stability in decision-making. The relatively slow turnover of members, particularly those who rise to positions of leadership, encourages a depth of experience and knowledge in policy areas that the President (limited to two terms) and high-level executives appointed by him (with tenures generally shorter than his) cannot accumulate. It probably shows up most dramatically among committee chairmen and others with long service, whose experience may span decades and several administrations.[13] This is particularly important in legislative oversight because if the product of the long tenure of career bureaucrats is to be matched by equal backgrounds, apparently only Congress can provide this. Continuity and stability may offset the policy-gyration-generated political changes in the executive branch, and the natural tendency for incoming Presidents to charge off in new directions with new programs. But this cuts both ways. What is continuity and stability to some may

---

[12] Seymour Scher analyzes the problems involved in Congressional oversight of an independent regulatory commission, the National Labor Relations Board, in "Congressional Committee Members as Independent Agency Overseers: A Case Study," *American Political Science Review*, LIV (December 1960), pp. 911-920.

[13] David B. Truman provides an interesting illustration in *The Governmental Process* (New York: Alfred A. Knopf, 1951), p. 424, which merits quoting at length, "During World War II the Chairman of the House Naval Affairs Committee, Representative Carl Vinson of Georgia, was so frequently consulted by the top military and civilian officials of the Navy Department that he was known among many of the junior officers as "the permanent Secretary." His influence stemmed not only from his position but also from the duration of his contacts with the Navy and from the extent of his knowledge. He had been a member of the Naval Affairs Committee since early in the 1920's and had been chairman since 1931, so that he had had longer continuous association with the problems of the top reaches of the Department than any of the admirals or key civilian officials. . . . After the unification of the armed services following World War II, Vinson, as Chairman of the House Committee on the Armed Services, apparently established similar relations with the Army and Air Force."

seem reaction and obstructionism to others, and modernization proposals that reduce the autonomy of chairmen and committees or cause the whole institution to respond more sensitively to Presidential leadership must be viewed as rejections of this legislative contribution.

The fourth function Congress is well fitted to provide is to represent, with unmatched ability, widely diverse views and interests in the political system. The 535 constituencies represented in Congress have no analog in the executive and judicial branches, and this, added to interest-group access in various stages of the legislative process, makes it possible for virtually all legitimate interests to be heard. Obviously not all interests have *equal* access or influence, and it is commonly believed that some interests (for example, Negro, and labor, to mention only two) commonly turn more to the executive branch for redress. But the executive is not institutionally suited to provide the legislature's regular and varied representation. Modernization proposals designed to improve the quality of representation thus occupy high priority and must be carefully attended to.

FUNCTIONS OF CONGRESS: A BEHAVIORAL APPROACH. A more theoretical and behavioral approach to legislative functions is exemplified by Jewell and Patterson, who attempt to place legislative activities in the broader context of the political system.[14] They divide functions into two categories, management of political conflict and integration of the polity. Management of political conflict is a major functional responsibility because "a legislative system is deeply involved in the problems of maintaining order, of attempting to assure a relatively high degree of stability in political relationships, and of creating and sustaining substantial equilibrium in the polity." Four ways in which the legislature contributes to conflict management are the deliberative, the decisional, the adjudicative, and the cathartic. Further, the legislature "serves to integrate the polity by providing support for it" and does so through authorization, legitimation, and representation. This approach is useful in discussing modernization of Congress because proposals can be related to the functional needs of a broader system as well as specific institutional processes or responsibilities identified by more traditional classifications such as the Keefe and Ogul one used above.

Jewell and Patterson maintain that the legislative system "is more than a collection of formal rules, procedures, and organization units. It is a social system in which individuals interact in terms of normative expectations derived from both within and outside the legislature itself." [15]

---

[14] Malcolm Jewell and Samuel Patterson, *The Legislative Process in the United States* (New York: Random House, 1966). The following quotations are drawn from Chap. 1, "Legislative Functions."

[15] *Ibid.*, p. 5.

Their concept of the legislative system configuration is presented in the following chart.

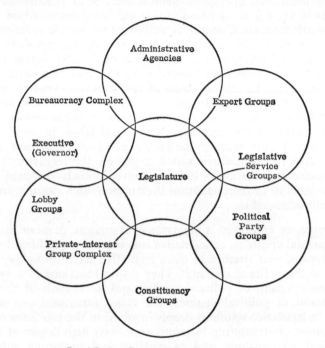

Bureaucracy Complex

Administrative
Agencies

Expert Groups

Executive
(Governor)

Legislative
Service
Groups

Legislature

Lobby
Groups

Political
Party
Groups

Private-interest
Group Complex

Constituency
Groups

Legislative System Configuration[16]

Thus, rather than viewing problems of the Congress from a strictly internal point of view, this approach requires all other participants to be accounted for:

> The keys to defining a system are the terms interaction and goals. Those who are outside the legislature enter the legislative system when they are interacting with legislators, sometimes when they are interacting with other outsiders—and when the purpose of this interaction is related to the legislative process.[17]

This broader approach, when extended to the whole political system, puts Congress in a functional relationship to a wide range of public and private groups, and national and state levels. What may seem to be intense problems when viewed in the narrow focus of Congress alone

[16] *Ibid.*, p. 6.
[17] *Ibid.*, p. 7.

become attenuated when redress has occurred in another sector of the system or, more dramatically, when what seems dysfunctional to the legislative institution is a key element in the equilibrium of the whole system. One could argue that what seems a carefully contrived reform in the base of legislative representation, bringing nearly perfect numerical equality in the size of districts, is dysfunctional to the systemwide base of representation if particular groups already enjoy disproportionate influence in the executive branch. Put another way, what may appear to establish equilibrium within the legislative institution may in fact create disequilibrium in the larger system. Thus, if equality of representation is defined in terms of the total voice or power brought to bear on the total system, the total power portrait of groups and individuals must include the executive branch, the courts, the pressure group complex, the party structure, and so on, in addition to the legislature.[18]

When some of the recurrent criticisms of Congress are viewed in terms of the processes of authorization, legitimation, and representation, what may seem objectionable on grounds of logic or policy preferences may take on another dimension when their functional significance is examined. Such practices as the seniority system, the House Rules Committee, the Senate filibuster, to mention only three, could be interpreted as institutional means to avoid becoming an executive branch rubber stamp that would jeopardize legitimation and representation.

> It is symptomatic of the essential part the legislative system plays in managing conflict that, if the legislature becomes a rubber stamp or law factory, there may be no other arena in which adequate deliberation is possible.[19]

Modernization proposals might become dysfunctional when the whole range of the external relationships of Congress is used as a measuring rod.

To use another example, some of the chelonian procedures, the ritualistic approaches to decision-making, and the obfuscation of legislative responsibility may not only be functional in terms of the survival of the Congress as an institution, but necessary aspects of what Jewell and Patterson call the deliberative and cathartic activities.[20]

> Often the legislature deliberates without making a decision in the positive sense of taking action. But the process of deliberation itself, and the rules

[18] The classic situation of treating representation *in vacuo* comes in federal court decisions of the genus *Baker* v. *Carr* (369 US 1). Here the courts explicitly limit themselves to redressing numerical inequalities among legislative districts without regard for any other components of the governmental or political systems.

[19] Jewell and Patterson, *op. cit.*, p. 10.

[20] *See* D. R. Mathews, *U. S. Senators and Their World* (Chapel Hill: University of North Carolina Press, 1960), especially Chap. 8, "The Folkways of the Senate."

under which deliberation takes place, contribute to the reconciliation of divergent interests. . . . In effect, the equivocal nature of much of what goes on in legislative systems tends to prevent the polarization of many issues: this equivocation therefore serves as a mechanism for resolving conflicts.[21]

And:

The legislature cannot accede to the demands of all interests, sometimes not even partially, but it can grant these interests a hearing—perhaps not obtainable elsewhere—and this hearing can be an important factor in the management of conflict. To discover the consequences of shutting off this safety valve, we have only to recall the demonstrations in the streets of Southern cities by Negroes who had been unable to obtain not only the policies they sought but even a hearing in state or local legislative systems.[22]

The committee power structure and fragmentation of responsibility, often hard hit by modernization proposals, find defenses in the functional analysis.

Specialization and division of labor in the legislative system facilitate the resolution of conflict. The committee structure of a legislature involved a specialization of tasks, and the tendency to accept the specialists' judgments contributes to conflict resolution.[23]

Finally, the key legislative function of maintaining a high degree of stability in the political relationships and equilibrium in the system may not be well served by the marshaling of disciplined party groups with sharply delineated policy positions reacting either as handmaidens to the President's administration program or enemies ambushing this program at every legislative pass. Jewell and Patterson warn that "both legislative deliberation and decision-making are likely, because of their functional places in the process of compromise, to be diffuse and ambiguous." [24]

Modernization of Congress

Critics of Congress, reflecting upon the performance of one or more of the functions discussed above, have developed a detailed bill of particulars against the system as it now operates and have proposed literally thousands of reforms over the past half-century. In general, Congress

[21] Jewell and Patterson, *op. cit.*, pp. 10-11.
[22] *Ibid.*, p. 12.
[23] *Ibid.*, p. 11.
[24] *Ibid.*, p. 10.

has been slow to change, but some notable alterations, such as those in the Legislative Reorganization Act of 1946 and procedural changes in the House Rules Committee and the cloture rule of the Senate, have occurred since 1945.[25] Issues involved in evaluating modernization proposals will be treated under four general categories: (1) the power structure, (2) system of representation, (3) rules and procedures, and (4) miscellaneous reforms.

THE POWER STRUCTURE. The power structure of Congress is decentralized, fragmented, and undisciplined. Under present conditions no one leader in or out of Congress, no party hierarchy, no coalition of interests, can lead and direct as the majority party in the parliamentary model is expected to do. This characteristic has led to numerous proposals designed to centralize power within the Congress and to produce either more effective leadership of the Congress by the President, or of the rank and file by Congressional leaders. Our discussion will center on the executive-legislative relationship and the internal leadership structure.

In the area of executive-legislative relations some of the proposals for modernization are engineered to enhance the role of executive by formalizing his control of the legislature, while other proposals are aimed at strengthening the legislature in its competition with the executive. The executive-legislative relationship *is* one of competition. Constitutional design creates an air of tension between the two branches and tempers this tension with a need for cooperation in order to make the machinery operate: perhaps "cooperative tension" best describes the institutional postures.

Thus one can analyze legislative reform from the viewpoint of the endless competition between Congress and the President within the constitutional framework of separation of powers. The constitutional provisions that created the arena of competition have not changed, but the competition is endless and the balance is constantly shifting. Everything having to do with one branch or the other becomes an element in this competition and may in a great or small fashion work a change in the balance. A shift in the Congressional committee system, the reorganization of the Executive Office of the President, new court criteria for reapportionment, changes in the Electoral College, alteration of the political party structure—all impact in the area of legislative-executive relations. And so it is with Congressional modernization. Thus, some observers are more concerned with the legislative-executive balance than with abstractions such as efficiency or economy or with intellectual

---

[25] *See* G. B. Galloway, "The Operation of the Legislative Reorganization Act of 1946," *American Political Science Review*, XLV (March 1951), pp. 41-68, for a detailed discussion of the contents and effects of that act.

fugues to order political institutions that seem outwardly disorderly and untidy.

Since an understanding of the assumptions of advocates of reform is necessary for an evaluation of specific proposals within a broader context, we shall examine the positions of the prolegislative and proexecutive schools of thought.

The prolegislative writers argue that a backbench Congress is unlikely to sustain a political system of divided powers and open access to places of decision-making for all legitimate social interests. Further, a weakened Congress is unlikely to withstand the already strong pressures to emasculate state and local governments by displacing their decision-making powers to the federal level (and more specifically to the executive). Congress may be the only federal institution to which state and local governments may now turn for protection, although in the final analysis the political party organization may be their last redoubt. A strong Congress is essential for the representation of the breathtakingly rich variety of interests, values, and areas that make up the nation, and it is doubtful whether an executive branch could provide this representation even through honest and deliberate efforts. Some Congressional reforms and political party reforms might shut off sections of this rich variety of interests through a strong and disciplined process transforming Congress into a rubber-stamp body. James Burnham, representing the prolegislative school, posits that

> Within the emergent managerial society the typical political form links a huge, pervasive governmental bureaucracy with a Caesarism-tending political leadership sanctioned by mass plebiscites. This combination, supported by a bureaucratized military and police apparatus, operates primarily through administrative decree while using an assembly as recording device and sounding board.[26]

Burnham typifies the point of view that holds that legislative bodies represent and protect the citizen as an individual while the executive has become an embodiment of the citizens as the masses. This leads him to conclude that

> The tie in this century and this nation between the survival of Congress and liberty is not abstract and formal but historical and specific. Within the United States today Congress is in existing fact the prime intermediary institution, the chief political organ of the people as distinguished from the masses, the one body to which the citizenry can now appeal for redress not merely from individual despotic acts but from large-scale despotic innovations, trends, and principles. The role of Congress among the nation's intermediary institutions has become more than ever critical with

[26] James Burnham, *Congress and the American Tradition* (Chicago: Henry Regnery Co., 1959), p. 337.

the continuing decline in the power of the states—a decline for which, ironically enough, Congress carries a full share of responsibility.[27]

For partisans of this school of thought the modernization of Congress must proceed upon assumptions of strengthening the body against executive domination. Reforms with the contrary effect would be considered retrogressive and threats to the survival of the system.

> If Congress ceases to be an actively functioning political institution, then political liberty in the United States will soon come to an end . . . it is impossible to have the executive unchallengeably supreme over Congress and to reduce Congress to a mere channel between the executive and masses and at the same time to have political liberty.[28]

In terms of numbers and volume of writing, the prolegislative school is in a distinct minority among political scientists and others who call for Congressional modernization.

Partisans of the proexecutive school hold that Congress has stood athwart progress toward streamlining modern government to meet twentieth-century demands, and that the only hope for democratic government lies in strong and effective executive leadership. The preoccupation of this school is with the machinery necessary for rapid solution of pressing social problems of the day. James M. Burns, a leading advocate of this school, maintains that

> The stronger the exertion of presidential power, the more liberal and internationalist it will be because of the make-up and dynamics of the presidential party. The stronger the exertion of congressional power, the more conservative and isolationist will be our national policy because of the structure of congressional forces.[29]

The executive is seen as the best vehicle for this because of his capacity and inclination to act with imagination and dispatch.

> An executive impetus and a legislation tendency confront each other at every junction. The executive impetus is to combine legislation and administrative power, to coordinate functions, to exert control from the top. . . . The legislative instinct is pluralistic. Congress and the state legislatures, under the control of legislative parties, seek to fragmentize the executive by means of individual or committee influence over administrative units, or control of specific budgetary items, or through hobbling the executive's power to reorganize.[30]

[27] *Ibid.*, pp. 338-339.
[28] *Ibid.*, p. 344.
[29] James M. Burns, *Deadlock of Democracy* (Englewood Cliffs, N.J.: Prentice-Hall, 1963), p. 264. *See also* his *Congress on Trial* (New York: Harper and Bros., 1949).
[30] Burns, *Deadlock of Democracy*, p. 262.

It is a strong executive backed by a centralized and disciplined political party system that will solve the nation's problems for, as Burns states,

> The cure for democracy, people used to say, is more democracy. A half century of hard experience has shown this cliché to be a dangerous half-truth. The cure for democracy is leadership—responsible, committed, effective, and exuberant leadership. The man and the party who take the lead in modernizing our political system, in establishing a majority party able to govern and a minority party able to oppose, will have helped put an end to the dangerous cycle of draft and deadlock in our national affairs.[31]

Burns believes that the political party system, now fragmented into four "parties" (Presidential Democrats, Presidential Republicans, Congressional Democrats, Congressional Republicans) needs reforms that would produce a dominance for the President and a disciplined, cooperative Congress:

> The Madisonion model, embodied today in the four-party system, has provided flexibility, accessibility, and representativeness in our governmental system, at the expense of leadership, vigor, speed, and effective and comprehensive national action.[32]

But in addition to the extensive remodeling and tightening of the political party system, specific corrections must be made in the institutional patterns of Congress in order to guarantee the strong and predominant executive leadership sought by this school.

> The overcoming of the congressional parties requires the curbing of the institutional buttresses of their power: the seniority system in Congress, the other minority devices such as the Rules Committee, veto and filibuster, malapportionment and one-party districts in the states, and if feasible, midterm elections for the House. It means the shaping of new party structures and procedures.[33]

A cluster of political party reform proposals central to the functioning of Congress can be found in a report entitled *Toward a More Responsible Two-Party System* issued by the American Political Science Association.[34] The American political party system is a remarkable extraconstitutional phenomenon that performs vital roles for the nation much as the spinal column does for the human body, and the party system has been described as the device that guarantees the integrity of federalism[35]

[31] *Ibid.*, p. 340.
[32] *Ibid.*, p. 266.
[33] *Ibid.*, p. 326.
[34] Published as a supplement to the *American Political Science Review*, XLIV (1950).
[35] Riker, *op. cit.*, pp. 91-101.

and the key for understanding American legislatures.[36] Thus any proposals for change in the party system must be expected to have extraordinary effects on all parts of the governmental system.

It is important to comment upon the party responsibility proposals because they are essential preliminaries for the intralegislative party discipline to be used by leaders in bringing congressmen into line with national party policies, and for the extralegislative party discipline to be used by the President to whip his Congressional party followers into line with the administration program.

The party system envisaged by this cluster of reforms is dramatically different from what now exists in the United States. It is centralized and disciplined, and features financial and policy control concentrated in the national party structure. Legislative candidates become representatives of a national party and support the national platform and candidate for the Presidency. Once elected, legislators of the President's party are obliged to give him the majorities necessary to pass his program and the other party presumably acts as constant critic of the President. A legislator who does not fit this role faces political ruin as the full force of the party structure is brought to bear against the defector, who may be removed from positions of trust, expelled from the party, and purged in the next election. The assumption is made that voters elect a "government" consisting of both executive and legislative components. The striking similarity to the disciplined parties of English parliamentary democracy is more than accidental.

It is important to point out that this cluster of proposals, in the unlikely event that they were to be adopted, could reduce the Congress to a backbench status perhaps even less significant than that of the House of Commons. Despite what we might conclude about the systemwide desirability of the party responsibility model, the emasculation of Congress must be anticipated as a consequence. Some writers maintain that only under this cluster of reforms can Congress fulfill its role, while others hold that it would reduce Congress to innocuous desuetude.

Short of complete reform of the party system along these lines, piecemeal attempts to effect such reforms may be viewed as threats to Congressional independence. For example, a current reform proposal in the field of campaign finance provides that tax benefits would be granted for political contributions provided the money goes to the national committees or a state or local committee approved by the national committee. The money would be allocated only to those state and local committees

---

[36] Keefe and Ogul, *op. cit.*, p. 485. On reform in general, these writers conclude: "Legislative reform culminating in steady majority rule would threaten established legislative ways; it would upset the traditional balance of power within the legislature; almost certainly, it would strengthen the chief executive's influence upon legislation."

meeting the tests of loyalty and doctrinal regularity approved by the national committee. If enacted into law, this proposal could quickly result in situations in which incumbent congressmen face financial strangulation by a President or national committee with whom the congressmen have differed on policy. Within the cluster of party responsibility reforms there are numerous other proposals that would pose threats to legislative independence.

The party responsibility cluster of reforms, coupled with a centralization of power within the Congress, could transform Congress into a moon of the Presidential sun. Some writers argue that this is the only proper role for Congress in these days of crisis and complex decision-making. Others fear that the price of executive domination is too high, for that price may be the passing of representative government as we know it.

Most proposals for internal reform relate to a fundamental question of the distribution of legislative power: Shall the legislative power be centralized in a person (such as the Speaker or a single party leader) or a leadership agency (such as a policy committee), or shall legislative power be dispersed among many leaders (such as chairmen of standing committees or disparate party groups)? Many internal reform proposals would affect this power distribution and most aim toward centralization of legislative power. Before mentioning specific reform proposals, it might be well to ask whether centralization of power in Congress tips the balance toward Congress or the executive in the ongoing competition discussed above. The answer seems to be that it depends upon whether the power is centralized in a political party agency or a nonparty agency.

First come the proposals for centralizing power in a party agency. The La Follette–Monroney Committee in 1946 suggested the creation of policy committees for both parties in both chambers. These committees were to exercise leadership through party channels and, in the case of the President's own party, were to provide liaison with the President. Eighteen years later Senator Joseph S. Clark went further and proposed that these committees should exercise disciplinary powers over committee chairmen, as well as rank-and-file legislators, and should serve as the apparatus for assuring the enactment of the President's legislative program.[37] Presumably the policy committee would be a command post with effective powers to guarantee the President's success, provided of course that his party enjoys a majority in both chambers. It is necessary to say that this proposal on policy committees is linked to a party reorganization that would give both parties the power to liquidate de-

[37] Joseph S. Clark, *Congress: The Sapless Branch* (Revised edition; New York: Harper and Row, 1965), Chaps. 8 and 9.

fectors within their ranks, including recalcitrant senators and representatives.

Thus, the legislative power would be centralized in a political party agency controlled in effect by forces outside of Congress. The policy committee would become functionally what the Cabinet is to the House of Commons, and the Congress would be transmuted into a parliamentary body to provide majorities for the executive's programs (or the majority party's program, if you wish). Of course, the equivalent of a vote of no-confidence would be a revolt against the party leadership in Congress—a rather extreme and dysfunctional form of behavior representing a breakdown in the system rather than ordinary procedure.

One need not belabor Senator Clark's vision of the policy committee. It is not his invention or his particular responsibility. But it does represent a *genus* of reform proposals abundant in the literature of political science and containing common elements, whether the agency is called a policy committee, a legislative cabinet, or a central council.[38] These elements are: (1) control over the legislative agendas and the flow of business; (2) effective power over all legislative groups, such as committees, subcommittees, staff, and auxiliary organizations; (3) lines of responsibility to external sources; in the case of the President's party it is a responsibility to the President for enactment of his program, which is presumed to be drawn from the party's campaign platform, in the case of the minority party the lines of responsibility are to political party committees or leaders on the national level, who may or may not also be legislators, but who act as an organized opposition to the President; (4) the power, through a centralized and disciplined party system, to inflict punishment upon the legislators who defect from the party; this punishment may range from removal from positions of importance in the legislature to liquidation at the polls in the next election.

Modern reform proposals that are tied to creation of a party leadership agency with external responsibilities to the executive and the

---

[38] Similar agencies have been proposed by Roland Young, *This Is Congress* (New York: Alfred A. Knopf, 1946), and C. S. Hyneman, *Bureaucracy in a Democracy* (New York: Harper and Bros., 1950), although I doubt that Young and Hyneman would agree with the role Clark gives to Congress in the legislative-executive struggles. Bailey sees the House Policy Committee as follows: "Adequately staffed party policy committees should be elected in both Houses by caucus. In the House of Representatives, the Speaker should chair his party's committee; the minority leader should chair the minority party's committee. The majority policy committee should assume the functions of the House Rules Committee. Both policy committees should act as the committee on committees for their party, and should perform policy and steering functions presently scattered or moribund." *See* Stephen K. Bailey, *The Condition of Our National Parties* (New York: Fund for the Republic, 1959), p. 15.

party organization include the following: stripping power from the Rules Committee, substitution of party designation of standing committee chairmen for the present seniority system, "democratizing" internal procedures of standing committees, centralizing control of the total flow of legislative business from committee consideration of referred legislation to direction of floor activities. These reforms, coupled with party responsibility reforms, would strongly tip the balance to the executive. Senator Clark foresees this when he concludes that

> It is not a Congress which says "no" so much as it is one which lacks the capacity to say "yes." Congress must be reformed because a continuing deadlock with an institution which enjoys the popularity of the American Presidency will not be forever tolerated by the electorate.[39]

The House of Commons possesses the power to say "yes" through effective management by party agencies, but the price has been high—it is not the major independent force in its nation that some expect the Congress to be in ours.

Now we may examine centralization of power in a nonparty agency. Will centralization of legislative power in a person or agency inexorably lead to executive domination of the machinery? Many think not, and some pose centralization of power in a nonparty agency as the only viable alternative. One position holds that enhancement of the leader of each chamber is an alternative. A Reed or a Cannon is seen as the alternative to executive domination or continued decentralization (and some say dissipation) of the legislature's force.[40] Thus a proposal to place the Speaker of the House on the Rules Committee and otherwise increase his power over the flow of legislative business has been made. The powers to designate chairmen of standing committees and assign members to committees would serve the same end. A similar line of reforms lies in the creation of leadership agencies composed of the chamber leader and other key leaders along the lines of a policy committee, as mentioned above, but without the lines of responsibility to the President or political party organization. The assumption is that such leadership agencies would focus the diffused powers of the Congress that now lie in leaders, committee chairmen, and informal relationships, and would bring these powers to bear sharply and forcefully in dealing

[39] Clark, *op. cit.*, p. 244.

[40] For a viewpoint supporting this interpretation, *see* James Robinson, *The House Rules Committee* (Indianapolis: Bobbs-Merrill, 1963), pp. 111-127. "The role of Congress in national decisions has gradually shifted from initiating and originating legislation to legitimating or amending bills sent to it by the executive branch. It is not inconceivable that a centralized and coordinated leadership in the House could be an important step toward strengthening Congress and maintaining the system of checks and balances" (quoted in Clark, *op. cit.*).

with the executive. Thus the President, and his vast administrative family, would be looking down the barrel of a single weapon with a small group holding the trigger, rather than facing scattered, diffused, and ineffective fire. This is an appealing argument for the partisan of Congressional parity.

But how to create such a change by reform is puzzling. The structural changes necessary for this realignment are not hard to identify: they consist chiefly of strengthening the hand of the Speaker of the House and the Majority Leader of the Senate by giving them control over the committees, legislative agenda, and the party networks, or alternatively, creating leadership groups with firm control over these and placing the Speaker and Majority Leader in strong positions of leadership of these groups. Our memories of Speakers Reed and Cannon provide us with ample practical lessons for such an arrangement, and some of the de facto arrangements of Speaker Rayburn and Majority Leader Johnson also are supportive.

But this would call for revolutionary changes in the psychological climate of Congress. Perhaps at some later time, a beleaguered, cornered, and unified Congress might deliberately create Consuls with the rank and power to compete with the President, and submit to the necessary discipline to make this competition effective. But not now. One further problem suggests itself: How can the Speaker and Majority Leader divest themselves of their party identity in dealing with a President of their own party? In a sense, centralization of power in these figures may be a way-station in the parliamentary model, lacking only the external trapping of party reform.

We can now attempt to answer the question: Does centralization of legislative power in a person or agency inexorably lead to executive domination of the machinery? It does not, but the alternative domination by powerful Congressional leaders may be as distasteful. It certainly was to the insurgents who overturned "Uncle Joe" Cannon.

Reform proposals leading to centralization of powers in the Congress will no doubt be subjected to the closest scrutiny. It is not enough for proponents to say that efficiency, economy, or streamlined organization require a particular change—they must squarely face the question of whether the proposal enhances a centralization of legislative power and if so whether the beneficiary will be the President or Congressional leaders.

SYSTEM OF REPRESENTATION. Three general areas of criticism relate to the system of representation in the Congress. First, critics attack inequitable numerical representation in the House of Representatives in terms of departure from the goal of "one man, one vote." Second, the areal representation allowing two U. S. Senators for each state is subjected to the same criticism as malapportionment in the House. Third, the responsiveness of legislators to local or parochial interests because of their electoral base in districts is abhorred. All three of these points are sometimes subsumed under one general criticism that because of the constitutional separation of powers coupled with a bicameral legislature under two different modes of apportionment, the overall configuration of Congressional constituencies, even without malapportionment, does not mirror the Presidential constituency. It is argued that this dissonance makes it difficult for the President to lead the Congress, and that the proper redress is to simulate a parliamentary system through whatever procedural and political party reforms are possible.

Much of the cutting edge of the malapportionment criticisms against the House of Representatives has been removed by the landmark Supreme Court decisions on legislative representation and application of the "equal protection of the laws" clause of the Fourteenth Amendment to district size.[41] While individual skirmishes are still being fought in numerous states, the main battle for equal representation in the House has been won, and at least in terms of district size we are rapidly approaching the ideals set out in the *Baker* decision.[42] Gerrymandering, of course, will always be possible within the "one man, one vote" requirement, and since all professional politicians are guilty of ripping the opposition by district manipulations it would be utopian to expect this kind of fair play from legislatures in redistricting decisions. The equal population district can be viewed only as a general protection against the most excessive abuses of the gerrymander. The political results of reapportionment reforms are difficult to assess. Andrew Hacker warns us that in terms of present districts, Republicans and Southern Democrats are more likely to come from the more populous and more underrepresented districts, that voters of both parties are most underrepresented when they are in doubtful or marginal districts, and that in overall terms Democrats are getting more "representation" than Republicans.[43] He warns us, incidentally, that based on roll-call analyses liberals may have little to gain from equal districting and that in general

---

[41] This principle was laid down for state legislative districts in *Baker* v. *Carr* (369 US 1), and subsequently applied to Congressional districts in *Wesberry* v. *Sanders* (369 US 186), where the Court stated: "The command of Art. 1, Section 2 that Representatives be chosen 'by the people of the several states' means that as nearly as is practicable one man's vote in a Congressional election is to be worth as much as another's."

[42] For example, a *Congressional Quarterly* calculation in 1963 revealed that, in an "ideal" reapportionment, out of 435 seats there would be six more urban seats and ten more suburban seats; there would be twelve fewer rural districts and four fewer districts classified as mixed. Quoted in Jewell and Patterson, *op. cit.*, p. 59.

[43] Andrew Hacker, *Congressional Districting* (Washington, D.C.: Brookings Institution, 1963), Chap. 4.

the policy results of redistricting will be exceedingly difficult to predict. In summary, it is clear that the courts will remain vigilant in the matter of reapportionment and that the former glaring inequities in representation are things of the past.

The U. S. Senate was never meant to provide equal representation in the sense of equal population districts. Since states as areal governmental units constitute the districts there is a dramatic variation in the number of people represented, and this has caused some discomfort among those dedicated to the "one man, one vote" ideal. According to one writer, the intention that the Senate would provide a decentralizing influence in the federal system has never materialized, and in this sense the Senate has not been as obstructionist as might have been feared.[44] It may even be, as Froman maintains, that "in general, the larger and more heterogeneous the areas represented, the more liberal will be that representation. Therefore, the Senate is often more liberal than the House of Representatives, and the Presidency more liberal than the Senate." [45] Since in political and policy terms the strongest advocates of equal representation are also the strongest advocates of liberal policies, it may not be surprising that critics of the Congress have been curiously silent about changing the system of representation in the Senate or reducing the Senate to the relative impotence of a House of Lords.

Finally, critics are distressed about the time, effort, and consequent orientation of legislators who respond to the peculiar needs of constituents and constituencies. The so-called "errand boy" functions that place the legislator as an intermediary between the people and the sometimes bewildering and remote complexity of the federal bureaucracy come in for particularly heavy criticism from those who see the precious commodity of legislative time already severely short. This is seen somewhat differently from a functional point of view, as in the "adjudicative" techniques of conflict management. "Much of the private-bill process in the national Congress is largely adjudicative in nature, in the sense that individual grievances (conflicts between individuals and authorities) are settled thereby." [46] Perhaps more distressing to those worried about localism and parochialism are the policy consequences of thinking in terms of the next election and pleasing the folks back home. This, it is claimed, gets in the way of a statesmanlike posture toward national and international problems, which should not necessarily be solved in terms of what the voters in the several districts want. The most obvious solution is to enfold the legislator in some sort of national policy context, coupled with a disciplined party system that can protect its loyal members as well as punish its defectors. In this fashion the legislator who

[44] Riker, *op. cit.*, pp. 87-91.
[45] Froman, *op. cit.*, p. 4.
[46] Jewell and Patterson, *op. cit.*, p. 14.

goes against local wishes on national matters would get some measure of political insurance against retaliatory actions.

The general criticism of dissonance between Presidential and Congressional constituencies is so intimately bound with issues of executive-legislative relationships and the proposals for political party reform that it is dealt with elsewhere in this chapter.

RULES AND PROCEDURES. In terms of the classical model of majority rule, it is now difficult for a Congressional majority to rule effectively, and minority power plays an inordinate role in decision-making. In general, this criticism holds that in the absence of streamlined rules to allow majorities to act quickly and decisively and of strong leadership to organize this action, it is possible for strongly motivated minorities to harass the majority and cause delays. Among specific targets of this criticism are the Senate filibuster, the House Rules Committee, the seniority system, power of the standing committees, and rules allowing delaying tactics. In terms of formal majority rule, only one of these gives a numerical minority the power of the negative, and this is the Senate cloture rule. Under present rules unlimited debate in the Senate can be ended only by two-thirds of the senators present and voting, giving a minority of 34 per cent (assuming that all 100 senators vote) the power to perpetually block the wishes of the remaining 66 per cent. The pro and con arguments over unlimited debate are well known, and involve the issue of the degree to which the minority must be protected against roughshod treatment from the majority.[47] The other objectionable procedural practices can be overcome by a simple majority, but in many cases the process is so cumbersome that a persistent minority can abort a less persistent majority's efforts. At this point an interesting demurrer to the majority rule criticisms should be entered. Lewis A. Froman argues that "the 'real' question being asked is not whether majorities can rule, but whether the rules and procedures favor certain groups of members and certain interests over others," and he posits that "given a decentralized Congress, and the fact that most bills generate intense feelings among only some of the members, the classic majority rule model is not of much help," concluding that "in fact, majorities, in the usual sense of that word, rarely rule . . . because majorities, again in the usual sense of that word, rarely exist." [48] Specifically excluding the Senate cloture rule, Froman concludes that "changes in the rules would not be necessary if the majority party would be able to gain control of the present rules through changes in the distribution of power within the

---

[47] See Keefe and Ogul, op. cit., pp. 231-249, for a lively analysis of the rules and consequences of debate.

[48] Froman, op. cit., pp. 212-214.

party. . . . Were it possible to make changes within the party changes in the rules would not be necessary." [49]

A functional analysis of rules and procedures in legislative conflict is found in Jewell and Patterson:

> Controversies over principles and issues are often converted into conflicts over means and thus more readily resolved. Truman has suggested how much of the conflict in legislatures focuses on struggles over procedures, technical rules of debate, the power to limit debate, committee assignments, calendars, timetables, and the like. . . . Other rules of an unwritten kind, such as the seniority rule for the selection of committee chairmen, tend to remove areas of potential contention from the realm of conflict altogether.[50]

Thus it would be a mistake to consider procedural criticisms of Congress as merely appeals for majority rule, efficiency, or some other abstract concept. Modernization proposals in this area may very well be issue conflicts in disguise or vehicles for the ongoing struggle over control of the power structure.

A similar set of objections comes from what is an apparent slowness, inefficiency, and sloppiness in the flow of legislative business. To the outsider this is chaos and gives little hope of the serious and systematic treatment he feels worthy of the nation's business. Further, he may feel that responsibility for action or inaction is difficult to fix because of the multiplicity of decentralized, competing, and conflicting legislative groups that must deal with a single bill. This leads to the characterization of the legislative process as an "obstacle course," [51] the criticism that the Congress is either refusing to act or overreacting, and the objection that Congress fails to provide innovation. These criticisms seem to be mainly the product of two forces: the decentralization and fragmentation of the power structure, which gives numerous groups and checkpoints the power to speed or slow legislation, and the responsiveness to constituency needs, which loads the Congress with heavy service demands.[52] Most writers condemn this use of precious Congressional time, but the chances of surcease are small because the services rendered to local folk often mean the difference between defeat and reelection, and Congress is often the only recourse citizens have when aggrieved

---

[49] *Ibid.*, p. 217.

[50] Jewell and Patterson, *op. cit.*, p. 12.

[51] Robert Bendiner, *Obstacle Course on Capitol Hill* (New York: McGraw-Hill, 1964), a study of legislation supporting federal aid to schools.

[52] For an interesting review of this, *see* Dale Vinyard, "Congressmen as Washington Agents for Constituents," *University of Missouri Business and Government Review* (September 1967), pp. 19-25.

with the executive branch. Localism and the ombudsman role may be the cover charge of statesmanship in a modern democracy.[53]

MISCELLANEOUS REFORMS. Proposals that do not fit into the above categories but are of sufficient interest and importance to warrant mention in a discussion of modernization include terms of office, legislative salaries, and staff aids and research services.

Proposals have been made to lengthen House terms to four years and shorten Senate terms to four years. The arguments are that a House member needs more electoral security, that preoccupation with elections takes him away from legislative business too frequently, and that the costs of a biennial campaign are prohibitive. It is also said that off-year elections may change the House party division against an incumbent President. The last argument is part of the parcel of reforms designed to enhance the executive's power over Congress. Most observers favor four-year terms for Congressmen, although the arguments for this reform are blunted for the substantial majority of House seats that involve little or no electoral competition. In order to prevent all House elections from becoming mere adjuncts of an expensive, overpowering, personality-oriented national campaign for the Presidency, some suggest staggering House terms so that only half of the seats could become vacant each two years. This would have the added advantage of guaranteeing the continuity and stability in membership that the Senate enjoys, but the determination of *which half* of the seats comes vacant *when* is fraught with political booby traps.

It is more difficult to find convincing arguments for shortening Senate terms. If they were four-year terms, and elections coincided with House and Presidential elections, one could enter the same objections to becoming mere adjuncts of a Presidential campaign. It is doubtful whether a Senator would become any less remote from his electorate in four years than he would in six, although there is little evidence that Senators do drift away from their power sources. Bailey has proposed that Senate terms be changed to eight years with half of the seats being filled every four years at the time of the Presidential election. He concludes that "the likelihood that the President would have a working majority in both Houses would be overwhelming" if this Senate change were coupled with the four-year House term proposal.[54]

Should all elections coincide, it is likely that the President would attempt to cast all Congressional and Senatorial campaigns in terms favor-

[53] Perhaps one of the most poignant examples of a legislator's debt to localism in the face of national needs is the voting record of Senator William Fulbright (Dem., Ark.), whose positions on foreign policy and many domestic policies are very liberal, but whose voting record on civil rights legislation is unmistakably Deep South.
[54] Bailey, *op. cit.*

ing his own political goals, and perhaps undertake purges. It is uncertain how successful he would be unless party reorganization centralized power at the national level. Voting studies strongly suggest that both President and congressmen ride on coattails, and that Presidential purges are often more embarrassing to the President than to Congress. There is a risk, however, and the interests of an independent Congress would probably be best served by staggering election times.

Some argue that a "clear mandate" emerges from simultaneous election of President and Congress, but the most careful voting behavior studies provide little comfort for those who view American elections as being primarily issue-oriented, or the choice of the President a rational exercise in selection of policy alternatives. It is as defensible to maintain that there would be about as many "mandates" as there were winners in the election, and it is likely that Congressional winners would hew to this interpretation. Our relatively new understanding of voting behavior provides the best argument against simultaneous elections.

Compensation of lawmakers in the United States continues to be scandalously low.[55] Probably nowhere else in our system do we expect men of the stature of Congressmen, with commensurate responsibilities and commitment of time, to serve for such inadequate salaries. The only course in the interest of Congress is to press for extension of auxiliary benefits and increase of real salaries. Among auxiliary benefits might be reimbursement for more travel back to the states and districts, special housing allowances comparable to those allowed military officers, and more generous and inclusive retirement provisions. Other institutions, such as public universities and business corporations, have found public reaction less onerous to extending the fringe benefits than to raising stated salaries. Congress might also find this true.

Most students of Congress agree that a hallmark problem is the executive's near monopoly of information-handling capacity, current intelligence, and expert knowledge, in the complex decision-making of modern government. This is dramatically illustrated by any review of the research and information-gathering operations within the executive branch, and the staff activities directed at converting information into policy proposals. These have resulted in a crushing advantage for the executive when Congress attempts to compete in the formulation of policy alternatives or criticism of the executive. Ernest Griffith states the problem well:

[55] Some of the most serious problems in legislative ethics can be traced to the low salary scale and the high cost of election campaigns, which tempt the legislator without independent income to accept political gifts for personal living expenses or to convert funds raised for political campaigns to personal use after the election. Senator Thomas Dodd (Dem., Conn.) was censured by the U. S. Senate in 1967 for just this.

The measures proposed are generally urgent; they are almost invariably far-reaching; but obscure in their derivative or secondary effects; they are often drastic in their primary impact, but in a complex and disturbing way; they are highly specialized; they may involve a multitude of principles, often conflicting; they always involve a quantity of facts for background.[56]

Some of the most significant gains in the Congressional position have been in the area of professional, permanent staff in standing committees, the Legislative Reference Bureau, and office of Legislative Counsel, to mention a few. Griffith maintains that Congress alone among the world's legislative bodies maintains some effective independent and ongoing information-gathering.[57]

It is important to maintain and greatly expand this aspect of legislative activity if Congress is to exercise "control" over executive administration of Congressional policy, rather than merely to engage in *ex post facto* "oversight." The former is more likely to assure Congress a primary role in policy formulation while the latter casts Congress in the role of historical critic more than partner. Criticism is a valuable contribution but considerably less than half of what we expect. James A. Robinson declares that "the role of Congress in the U. S. system of government has been shifting gradually away from the *initiation* of public policies toward the *legitimation* and sometimes *amendment* of policies originally devised in the executive branch." [58] Whether the hope is for a recapture of the initiation function or a creditable performance of legitimation and amendment, information is a basic element in Congressional performance.

There are several ways to strengthen the position of Congress by providing usable information and analyses. In all of these it is necessary to remember that effective staff and research services cannot be established on an ad hoc basis, but rather call for a professional operation that operates continuously and develops a permanent, first-rate staff. A first step would be a generous increase in staff support for all standing committees. While committees will vary in increases needed, Congress should err on the side of overindulgence in research and analysis for committees. This is money that enhances the capacity of Congress to fully criticize the executive and intelligently formulate alternatives to the executive's proposals, and is central to the basic function of Congress. Certain savings may be accomplished by urging the consolidation

[56] E. S. Griffith, *Congress: Its Contemporary Role* (New York: New York University Press, 1961), p. 72.

[57] *Ibid.*, p. 88.

[58] J. A. Robinson, *Congress and Foreign Policy-Making* (Homewood, Ill.: Dorsey Press, 1962), pp. 191-192.

or cooperation of counterpart staffs in the House and Senate along functional lines.

A second improvement would be creation of a Congressional staff agency that performs functions for Congress analogous to what the Bureau of the Budget provides the President: that is, an agency that takes an overall view of the operations of executive functions from fiscal and program viewpoints, coordinating and relating them to a general policy posture. Various parts of the Congressional staff effort may be doing this in an uncoordinated manner at the present time. A counterpart to the Bureau of the Budget might act as a clearinghouse, research directorate, and coordinating authority. Perhaps the Legislative Reference Service could undertake this. The head of this agency could report directly to the Congressional leadership and could be given tasks by that leadership.

A third proposal is a substantial increase in the Congressional auditing effort. This would involve both fiscal and program audit and could be a responsibility of the Comptroller General as provided in the Legislative Reorganization Act of 1946. The staff agency mentioned above might provide the leadership and coordination in this effort. Of course, the ongoing character of the auditing effort enables control as opposed to what becomes historical analysis. The La Follette-Monroney Committee made several recommendations concerning fiscal controls by Congress that might be reexamined in connection with strengthening the hand of Congress in money matters.

A fourth proposal is creation of a scientific advisory and research agency for Congress. This might be a separate effort commissioned by, and reporting to, the Congressional leadership, or could be located in the agency mentioned above. Many members of the scientific community fear that Congress will become incapable of effective decision-making in some areas dependent upon knowledge of a scientific nature and some have gone so far as to urge scientists to run for Congress and supply the professional expertise from inside. A much more reasonable solution might be to provide a high-level research group that can formulate the right questions in conjunction with congressmen to put to the executive branch and the scientific community and can evaluate the scientific information necessary for Congressional policy formulation. A well-developed Congressional agency of this sort would have been valuable in evaluating the conflicting testimonies on the Nuclear Test Ban Treaty, military weapons systems, and the vexing problems of federal support of scientific research. Unless Congress provides itself with such services on a professional, permanent, and continuing basis, it may find itself preempted in important areas of policy. John G. Kemeny states the alternatives rather more starkly when he warns that

Indeed, a layman cannot help but wonder whether most members of Congress are qualified to debate such complex issues. Perhaps we have not yet left the stage where an intelligent, hard-working Congressman can grasp the major issues of the day. But this stage too will pass. The day cannot be too far in the future when we must either stock Congress with scientists or restrict its role to the choosing of goals.[59]

Another possibility is for Congress to provide itself with scientific information by building this into its staff apparatus. But a start must be made soon since a facility of this sort is not developed overnight.

A fifth proposal is expanded research on U. S. overseas activities. Our permanent involvement in exporting millions of persons and billions of dollars overseas in connection with foreign relations seems to be well established. To mention only a few activities, AID, Peace Corps, and intelligence operations are of crucial long-range importance, and are not stop-gap programs. It is uncertain whether Congress either knows enough about the actual operations of such agencies or is able to formulate policy that relates each of them to the overall foreign policies of the United States. It is also uncertain what means would be best to guarantee Congressional involvement at crucial points. Perhaps overseas Congressional staffs with counterpart relationships to executive agencies and geographical areas would be a possibility. Thus resident staff investigators could provide continuing information, evaluation, and expertise on American overseas operations in Europe, Latin America, Asia, and Africa. Washington-based Congressional staff with existing standing committees should be expanded.

Finally, there is a proposal for minority staff and research. American legislatures are peculiar in their treatment of legislative minorities. In other systems, the minority may be relegated to the galleries and may play no meaningful role in policy formulation or management of legislative business. Of course, when and if these minorities become majorities they often fall short in experience, and lack of policy continuity weakens the legislative institution. In keeping with the meaningful role of the legislative minority, the Congress should insure adequate staff and research facilities for the minority members. "Adequate" should include at least sufficient help to support minority formulation of alternatives backed by research, and development generally of an effective "shadow government."

In summary, the money and effort invested in the collection, evaluation, and analysis of information for Congressional policy formulation pays extraordinary dividends. While research is expensive, Congress should treat itself to the same generous portion of research activities that the executive now enjoys and finds so useful.

[59] J. G. Kemeny, "A Philosopher Looks at Political Science," *Journal of Conflict Resolution*, IV (1960), p. 296.

4

THE SUPREME COURT AND
A NATIONAL CONSTITUTION

C. Peter Magrath

Shortly after the turn of the century Woodrow Wilson, writing on the unique role of the American Supreme Court, noted the special authority it derived from the supremacy clause of the Constitution, which declares:

> This Constitution, and the Laws of the United States which are made in Pursuance thereof; and all Treaties made, or which shall be made, under the authority of the United States shall be the supreme Law of the Land; and the Judges in every State shall be bound thereby, any Thing in the Constitution or Laws of any State to the Contrary notwithstanding.

The consequence, Wilson believed, had been to vest in the Supreme Court what he called "the statesmanship of control," and he continued:

> The Constitution is not a mere lawyers' document: it is . . . the vehicle of a nation's life. No lawyer can read into a document anything subsequent to its execution; but we have read into the Constitution of the United States the whole expansion and transformation of our national life that has followed its adoption. We can say without the least disparagement or even criticism of the Supreme Court of the United States that at its hands the Constitution has received an adaptation and an elaboration which would fill its framers of the simple days of 1787 with nothing less than amazement. The explicitly granted powers of the Constitution are what they always were; but the powers drawn from it by

C. PETER MAGRATH, who received his B.A. *summa cum laude* from the University of New Hampshire and his Ph.D. from Cornell University, is Dean of the College of Arts and Sciences and Professor of Political Science at the University of Nebraska. Previously he taught at Brown University. He is the author of two books on the American Supreme Court, his scholarly specialty: *Morrison R. Waite: The Triumph of Character*, and *Yazoo Law and Politics in the New Republic*. He contributed a monograph on the law of obscenity to the 1966 edition of *The Supreme Court Review*.

implication have grown and multiplied beyond all expectation, and each generation of statesmen looks to the Supreme Court to supply the interpretation which will serve the needs of the day.[1]

Wilson's statement exaggerates the Supreme Court's powers of political "control," and it is dated by the fact that the present-day Court has both expanded *and* limited the powers of government. It nevertheless contains an enduring and significant insight. Because of the interpretive work of the Supreme Court the American Constitution has served its people well as an adaptable "vehicle," capable of traversing a changing political terrain for nearly two centuries.

A National Constitution

The Court's uniqueness among judicial tribunals, both domestic and foreign, is rooted in its distinctive role as an institution whose decisions are at once legal and political. In the process of deciding public law controversies, it concurrently interprets the federal laws and the Constitution (thereby indicating the legitimate boundaries of governmental action) and influences the direction of public policy. At no time in American history has this legal-political role been more evident than today, for the modern Supreme Court has made two major contributions to the political system of the United States.

The first has been to confirm and encourage the establishment of a thoroughly national constitution that, while it recognizes a role for state and local governments, subordinates them to superior national standards. Although we still speak of the "federal" Constitution and the "federal" government, the judicial interpretations of the past three decades have endowed Congress and the President with constitutional authority to regulate virtually every aspect of the nation's economic life. Conversely, the Court, though tolerant of state social and economic regulation, has not hesitated to invalidate state laws that in its judgment conflict with federal policies or with constitutional requirements safeguarding the unhindered flow of interstate commerce. When it is recalled that the Constitution assigns exclusive responsibility for defense and foreign affairs to the federal government, it becomes even clearer why in fact if not in form we live today under a national, not a federal, constitution.

The modern Court's second major contribution has been to promote a concern for human dignity and to fashion legal protections guaranteeing individual liberties. In particular, the innovating Court of Chief

---

[1] Woodrow Wilson, *Constitutional Government in the United States* (New York: Columbia University Press, 1908), pp. 157-158.

Justice Earl Warren (1953-   ) has interpreted the Constitution so as to maximize the legally enforceable rights and liberties of racial, religious, and political minorities. It has also, in a closely related development, concerned itself with the rights and liberties of individual Americans—many of them pathetic and penniless persons who, for one reason or another, are consigned to the scrapheap of American society and appear as criminal defendants in the courts.[2]

Paradoxically, the very same Supreme Court that has endorsed a vast expansion in the constitutional powers of the federal and state governments to regulate social and economic affairs, and thereby to control the lives of its citizens, has simultaneously expanded the individual rights and liberties of all Americans. There is, to be sure, a logical inconsistency in these twin judicial developments. On the one hand, the modern Court enhances governmental powers and refuses to impose, as it once did, constitutional limitations in the name of property rights. On the other hand, it favors noneconomic liberties and limits public authority to discriminate against minority groups and unpopular individuals.

Yet logical consistency is not necessarily a political virtue, and the Supreme Court is a profoundly political institution. It is possible to argue strongly in favor of a double standard that differentiates between property rights claims and individual liberty claims. This argument emphasizes that certain freedoms (such as that of speech and press) are absolutely essential to the operation of a democratic political system; that noneconomic liberties are recognized much more explicitly in the Constitution than are property-based liberties; and that unpopular minorities and individuals who by definition have only limited access to the majority-dominated political process have a special claim to judicial protection.[3] There is, too, a certain justice in the modern Supreme Court's concern with minority rights and individual liberties. The Court's own judicial decisions expanding the powers of the federal and state government to regulate social and economic affairs have contributed to a bigness in government and a vast bureaucracy that often loses sight of the individual citizen. In an age when American society has grown into a technological giant and when its social, political, and economic units have grown correspondingly large and complex, there may be added justification for judicial intervention on behalf of human dignity.

Whatever the causes and the justifications, the Supreme Court has

[2] *See* Anthony Lewis, *Gideon's Trumpet* (New York: Random House, 1964), a case study of the Warren Court at work that focuses on the plight of one such defendant.

[3] Henry J. Abraham, *Freedom and the Court: Civil Rights and Liberties in the United States* (New York: Oxford University Press, 1967), Chap. 2.

transformed the simple Constitution of 1787 into a national constitution of governmental powers (that permit the regulation of social and economic activities) and of constitutional limitations (that assign a preferred position to noneconomic civil rights and liberties). The contemporary Court, moreover, has furthered this constitutional transformation without fundamentally inhibiting democratic majority rule. These developments are most clearly understood by examining its activities in four broad categories of decisions.

ECONOMIC AND GENERAL WELFARE POLICIES. The American Constitution today permits the federal government a free hand in regulating the nation's economic life and in promoting the general or social welfare. It was not always so. Once it was argued, and the Supreme Court often agreed, that the powers of Congress to tax, to regulate commerce, and to promote the general welfare were limited powers. They were limited, according to the old theory, because federal powers were qualified by those powers reserved to the states by the Tenth Amendment, which states in part that "the powers not delegated to the United States by the Constitution . . . are reserved to the states . . . ," and because the Fifth Amendment prohibition against the taking of property without due process of law was construed as a barrier to laws regulating business and economic relationships. Thus, during the 1930's the New Deal program of President Franklin D. Roosevelt was seriously challenged by political opponents who claimed that it was both unwise *and* unconstitutional. Until 1937 the Supreme Court seemed to concur as it invalidated a score of New Deal laws and cast judicial doubt on the adequacy of federal powers to regulate the economy in response to the crippling Great Depression.

The Court's restrictive decisions provoked a major constitutional crisis and a threat to its prerogatives that did not end until the spring of 1937, when it began to endorse the New Deal programs as completely as it had previously rejected them as unconstitutional. Under the new judicial interpretations the Constitution was perceived as an instrument to facilitate the efforts of Congress and the President to regulate the nation's economy and to promote the social welfare of its citizens. Since 1937, in fact, the Court has endorsed the constitutionality of every piece of regulatory legislation that has been judicially challenged. Laws establishing a national social security system, regulating agriculture and labor-management relations, and setting maximum hours and minimum wages for workers in interstate commerce have all received judicial approval. Their constitutional justification has been found in a few brief grants in Article I of the Constitution allowing Congress to raise taxes, regulate commerce, and promote the general welfare—seasoned by a generous reading of the "elastic" clause that authorizes Congress to pass laws "necessary and proper" to the fulfillment of its enumerated powers.

The Supreme Court, for example, has supported Congress and the President in their determination to read the sixteen-word commerce clause in the broadest possible way. It has summarized the modern constitutional doctrine in a single sentence in a decision sustaining a federal public-utility regulation based on the commerce clause: "The federal commerce power is as broad as the economic needs of the nation." [4] A 1942 decision, *Wickard* v. *Filburn*, upholding a provision of the Agricultural Adjustment Act, underscores the Justices' willingness to defer to legislative and executive judgments of what constitutes "economic need" and "interstate commerce." The commerce power, it held, was so pervasive that the federal government could regulate the wheat quota of a small Ohio farmer whose few acres of production were intended purely for his own cattle. According to the Court, the farmer's production nevertheless had an impact on interstate commerce; by growing his small quantity of wheat, he avoided the necessity of purchasing wheat from the national market.

This ruling also reveals that the Court no longer pays attention to the Fifth Amendment due-process and the Tenth Amendment reserved-powers limitations that once served to restrain federal regulation. The post-1937 Court has concluded that the vague words of the due process clause do not permit the judiciary to overrule federal economic programs desired by the legislature and the executive on the ground that they violate property rights. As for the Tenth Amendment, it has been relegated to the status of a constitutional dead letter. The formal burial took place in *United States* v. *Darby* (1941), when the Court, over an objection that Congress had overstepped the limits of the Tenth Amendment, upheld the Fair Labor Standards Act of 1938. "The amendment," a unanimous Court intoned, "states but a truism that all is retained [by the States] which has not been surrendered." [5]

Although the Supreme Court has put the final gloss on the Constitution's commerce, tax, and welfare provisions, the interpretations are merely permissive. They allow, but they do not compel, Congress and the President to undertake far-reaching programs of economic regulation and social welfare. In this sense, then, the modern Court has conferred supreme economic and social welfare policy-making power upon Congress and the President and, ultimately, upon the nation's dominant political majorities. No less significant is the broad public acceptance of this unencumbered national power to regulate, particularly when it is recalled that as recently as the 1930's a major rallying cry against the New Deal program was its unconstitutionality. Voices of dissent are, of course, still heard. One of the themes of the 1964 Republican Presidential candidate, Barry M. Goldwater, was the charge that the Supreme

[4] *American Power Co.* v. *S. E. C.*, 329 U. S. 90, 104 (1946).
[5] 312 U. S. 100, 124.

Court had wrongly expanded federal powers and whittled state prerogatives guaranteed by the Tenth Amendment. But Goldwater's views
on these issues seemed wistful, if not anachronistic, and his candidacy
was decisively repudiated by the electorate.

More revealing as an index of the degree to which a Constitution
permissive on economic and social welfare matters suits the American
political temperament is the fact that, with one minor and one major
exception, none of President Lyndon B. Johnson's Great Society legislation has been attacked on constitutional grounds. Many of the Johnson administration's proposals, which were enacted before the escalation
of the Vietnam war and before the erosion of the Democratic administration's Congressional majorities in the 1966 elections halted the progress of Great Society programs, were politically controversial. Yet the
legislation creating a scheme of medical care for the aged (Medicare),
supporting various antipoverty programs, subsidizing elementary and
secondary education, providing for the development of urban mass
transit systems, and expanding the public housing and social security
programs was all routinely accepted as within the power of Congress
to enact.[6]

The only Great Society laws to be attacked as unconstitutional were
in the field of civil rights. First to be challenged was the Civil Rights
Act of 1964, which aims to eradicate racial discrimination in such public
accommodations as cafeterias, hotels, motels, movie theaters, and restaurants. It applies to all enterprises in which either the customers or
the goods and services they receive "affect" interstate commerce. Congress voted the law despite a strong Southern filibuster that denounced
it as an unconstitutional interference with the rights of private property
and an unprecedented invasion of states' rights. Senator Goldwater of
Arizona, whom the Republican party was about to name as its 1964
presidential candidate, based his well-publicized opposition to the act
largely on the ground that its "provisions fly in the face of the Constitution."

Within a few weeks of its adoption, two cases, *Heart of Atlanta
Motel* v. *United States* and *Katzenbach* v. *McClung*, challenged the
law's constitutionality. The principal argument was that Congress had

---

[6] The minor exception to the general rule that Great Society legislation was not
charged with unconstitutionality is the opposition to provisions in the Elementary
and Secondary Education Act of 1965 for federal aid to parochial schools. The challenge here is not to the principle of an interventionist federal government or to the
idea of federal aid to education. It is, instead, based on the argument that federal
(and, for that matter, state) aid may not be given to religiously affiliated schools
without violating the principle of church-state separation enshrined in the religion
clauses of the First Amendment. This dispute, which centers on questions of individual liberties and rights, is qualitatively different from the constitutional disputes
over economic regulation and social welfare.

exceeded its authority under the commerce clause. In the first case, involving an Atlanta motel that refused to rent rooms to Negroes, a unanimous Supreme Court sustained the public accommodations provisions in sweeping terms. Justice Tom C. Clark's opinion for the Court reveals its total deference to Congress and the President whenever their legislation is tied to the commerce clause:

> It may be argued that Congress could have pursued other methods to eliminate the obstructions it found in interstate commerce caused by racial discrimination. But this is a matter of policy that rests entirely with the Congress not with the courts. How obstructions in commerce may be removed—what means are to be employed—is with the sound and exclusive discretion of the Congress. It is subject only to one caveat—that the means chosen by it must be reasonably adapted to the end permitted by the Constitution. We cannot say that its choice here was not so adapted. The Constitution requires no more.[7]

Since the Supreme Court during the last thirty years has not once found that Congress has selected unreasonable means to regulate under the commerce clause, the "caveat" mentioned by Justice Clark may be dismissed as a pro forma expression. This point is reinforced by the Court's disposition of the companion case, *Katzenbach* v. *McClung,* testing its application to Ollie's Barbecue, a family-owned restaurant in Birmingham specializing in barbecued meats and homemade pies. Ollie's Barbecue willingly served Negro take-out customers but refused to seat them in the restaurant. It challenged the application of the civil rights law to its operations by contending that the restaurant was purely local. The Supreme Court, however, had little difficulty with the case. Reaffirming the principle of *Wickard* v. *Filburn,* it noted that Ollie's Barbecue was sufficiently "in" interstate commerce by virtue of the fact that 46 per cent of the meat it purchased from a local supplier came from sources outside Alabama. Decisions such as these emphasize the Supreme Court's willingness to give Congress and the President a free constitutional hand in regulating under the commerce clause.

In a parallel development, the Supreme Court has enormously broadened state powers over social and economic affairs, so long of course as their exercise does not conflict with federal policy or burden the national economic market. Prior to 1937 the Supreme Court hampered state regulation no less than federal. Laws regulating business were frequently deemed to be in conflict with property rights protected by the due process clause of the Fourteenth Amendment. The modern judicial attitude, which is radically different, is well summarized in a 1963 decision, *Ferguson* v. *Skrupa*. Rejecting the argument that a Kansas law forbidding all persons except lawyers to engage in the business of debt

[7] *Heart of Atlanta Motel* v. *United States,* 379 U. S. 241, 261.

adjusting was a taking of property without due process of law, the Court emphasized the discretionary power of the state:

> We conclude that the Kansas Legislature was free to decide for itself that legislation was needed to deal with the business of debt adjusting. Unquestionably, there are arguments showing that the business of debt adjusting has social utility, but such arguments are properly addressed to the legislature, not to us. We refuse to sit as a "superlegislature to weigh the wisdom of legislation," and we emphatically refuse to go back to the time when courts used the Due Process Clause "to strike down state laws, regulatory of business and industrial conditions, because they may be unwise, improvident, or out of harmony with a particular school of thought." . . . Whether the legislature takes for its textbook Adam Smith, Herbert Spencer, Lord Keynes, or some other is no concern of ours. The Kansas debt adjusting statute may be wise or unwise. But relief, if any be needed, lies not with us but with the body constituted to pass laws for the State of Kansas.[8]

CIVIL OR MINORITY RIGHTS. So deferential is the modern Supreme Court toward legislative and executive policies for regulating the economy and promoting the general welfare that for a while some scholars believed that the post-1937 Justices had virtually interpreted themselves out of a significant role in the American political system.[9] Their forecasts, however, proved erroneous. With the benefit of hindsight it is now clear that the Court's relative inactivity during the 1940's was but a transitional period before its assumption of a bold new role in the American political system. The Court of today has responded generously to the demands of minority groups, particularly the Negro racial minority, that their civil rights be recognized and implemented.[10] It has reversed earlier precedents permitting public support of racial segregation and read the equal protection clause of the Fourteenth Amendment, which forbids the states to deprive any person of "the equal protection of the laws," as a total ban against all state laws and practices supporting racial discrimination.

The major symbol of this new role, and indeed its major constitutional fruit, was the decision on May 17, 1954, in *Brown* v. *Board of*

[8] *Ferguson* v. *Skrupa*, 372 U. S. 726, 731. Quotations in the Court's opinion are from earlier decisions.

[9] Edward S. Corwin, *Constitutional Revolution, Ltd.* (Claremont, Calif.: Claremont Colleges, 1941), pp. 107-117; Bernard Schwartz, *The Supreme Court* (New York: Ronald Press, 1957).

[10] Civil rights claims are most simply defined as basic constitutional rights that must be legally protected precisely because they have been denied to a particular group by the laws and customs of the community and by the actions of the public authorities. Typically, the denial is rooted in deep-seated racial or religious prejudices. The judicial recognition of a civil right is intended to be not the creation of a special privilege or favor but a compensatory right to overcome past unconstitutional deprivations.

Education, often referred to as the *School Segregation Cases*. By a vote of 9 to 0 the Court ruled unconstitutional the school segregation laws of seventeen Southern and Border states. In countless other equal protection cases the Justices have ruled that state laws and policies may not exclude Negroes (or persons of any racial category) from voting in party primaries, nor may they require the segregation of Negroes in restaurants, hotels, motels, parks, or other public facilities, or in public carriers, whether they operate in intrastate or interstate commerce. The Supreme Court further concluded that the equal protection clause renders ineffective restrictive racial covenants; these covenants, which are entered into by white owners who seek to overlay the property of certain neighborhoods with legal stipulations that it never be sold to Negroes, may not be enforced in state courts.

In 1967 the Court expanded the clause further, ruling that it had been violated when the voters of California—by the overwhelming vote of 4,526,460 to 2,395,747—approved a constitutional amendment that invalidated the state's existing fair housing laws and confirmed the right of any person to sell or rent, or not to sell or rent, his property as he "in his absolute discretion" desired. The effect of this amendment, the Court ruled, was to throw the weight of the state on the side of racial discrimination in housing, "an expression of state authority contrary to the Fourteenth Amendment." [11] The Court majority was unimpressed by the fact that the amendment had been endorsed by a 2-to-1 majority of the state's voters. Its view, very simply, is that civil rights are so basic that they cannot yield, not even to majority desires.

These civil rights decisions have had profound consequences for both the judicial institution itself and for the entire political system. *Brown* v. *Board of Education* was a decisive signal that the modern Court was willing and able to play a leading role in securing judicial and political recognition of civil rights guarantees to aid the nation's disadvantaged racial minorities. By expanding the meaning of the equal protection clause in the *Brown* case the Warren Court, as one political scientist has written, "lifted itself to a new peak of judicial power." [12] It did so by making the single most important domestic policy decision of the 1950's—that racial segregation had no rightful place in the United States. Equally significant, the *Brown* decision communicated the Court's willingness to intervene judicially on a wide range of civil rights and individual liberties issues. At the same time, it encouraged the civil rights groups and their political allies into intensified activities on aiming toward state and federal action to combat the many manifestations of racial discrimination in American life. Constitutionally speaking, the

---

[11] *Reitman* v. *Mulkey*, 35 Law Week 4475.
[12] Charles S. Hyneman, *The Supreme Court on Trial* (New York: Atherton Press, 1964), p. 198.

decision in *Brown* v. *Board of Education* had the dual effect of reversing the prosegregation rulings of earlier judicial eras and, for the first time in American history, putting the law of the Constitution squarely on the side of the nation's aggrieved racial minorities. This, in a land where, as Tocqueville long ago observed, "scarcely any political question . . . is not resolved, sooner or later, into a judicial question," was an event of monumental significance.

While the Supreme Court's holding in the *School Segregation Cases* provoked bitter political opposition for a few years, it also enjoyed wide national support. Moreover, the civil rights movement was finally rewarded in 1964 and 1965, when Congress and the President enacted two major civil rights laws. No serious observer of minority problems in the United States pretends that these laws—or, for that matter, any law—can "solve" the nation's racial questions. Yet it would be equally shortsighted to overlook their significance. The Civil Rights Act of 1964 outlaws racial discrimination in public accommodations, requires equal employment opportunities in interstate businesses, and, in effect, endorses the constitutional principle of the *Brown* decision by requiring an end to segregated schools. The Voting Rights Act of 1965 strikes decisively at all state practices that discriminate against would-be voters on racial grounds. It replaces state registration and election procedures with federal ones in all states where voting procedures and practices are racially discriminatory.

Both these landmark laws have been judged constitutional, with the Supreme Court in the happy position of placing its imprimatur on a process of constitutional and political change that it had originally stimulated. As we have already seen, in 1964 the Court upheld the newly enacted public accommodation provisions and in the process reconfirmed the fact of a national constitution and of Congressional and Presidential power to implement its provisions. In 1966 the Court's decisions in *South Carolina* v. *Katzenbach* and *Katzenbach* v. *Morgan* legitimized yet another major exercise of federal power. It sustained the constitutionality of the Voting Rights Act of 1965, which had automatically suspended state voting requirements, including literacy tests, that had been used to discriminate against Negro voters. More important, the Court staked out new constitutional ground by taking the position that Congress' power under the Fourteenth and Fifteenth Amendments extends beyond the enactment of legislation to counter explicit state racial discrimination. The two amendments confer on Congress the power to enforce their provisions, and the Court interpreted this broadly to mean that "As against the reserved powers of the States, Congress may use *any rational means* to effectuate the constitutional prohibition of racial discrimination." [13]

[13] *South Carolina* v. *Katzenbach*, 383 U. S. 301, 324 (1966); emphasis added.

Since the Fourteenth Amendment has been interpreted as reaching all forms of state-supported racial discrimination and since the modern Court consistently defers to Congressional choices as to the means used in exercising its powers, this decision expands federal power to legislate affirmatively on behalf of civil rights in a manner analogous to the federal power to regulate the economy and promote the general welfare. Congress, in other words, possesses implied power under the "necessary and proper" clause to pass any law that may assist in fulfilling a state's equal protection responsibilities. It could enact, for example, a law prohibiting private discrimination in the sale or rental of housing. Such a law could be construed as breaking down the urban racial ghettoes, thereby facilitating the states' constitutional obligation to avoid discrimination in education.

Katzenbach v. *Morgan*, upholding a Voting Rights Act provision making the completion of six years of schooling in Spanish-speaking Puerto Rican schools evidence of literacy, illustrates the point. The provision nullified a New York English-literacy requirement and enfranchised thousands of Spanish-speaking Americans. While the Court admitted that the English literacy law did not violate the equal protection clause, it reasoned that the increased Puerto Rican voting strength in New York City would assist their drive to gain nondiscriminatory treatment in public services—which, in turn, would move the minority group closer toward attaining the equal protection of the laws. Professor Archibald Cox of the Harvard Law School, a former Solicitor General of the United States, has called attention to the long-range meaning of *Katzenbach* v. *Morgan*:

> The *Morgan* case is soundly rooted in established constitutional principles, yet it clears the way for a vast expansion of congressional legislation promoting human rights. Its chief legal antecedents are the cases of the past three decades dealing with congressional power to regulate interstate commerce. For the future the decision logically permits the generalization that Congress, in the field of state activities and except as confined by the Bill of Rights, has the power to enact any law which may be viewed as a measure for correction of any condition which Congress might believe involves a denial of equality or other fourteenth amendment rights.[14]

It should be noted, finally, that the Warren Court's concern with civil rights is at once also a concern with the dignity of individual human beings. The law of civil rights is a law, to be sure, of minority groups, but groups are composed of individuals. Early in the 1960's Mary Hamilton,

[14] Archilbald Cox, "Forward: Constitutional Adjudication and the Promotion of Human Rights," in "The Supreme Court: 1965 Term," *Harvard Law Review*, LXXX (November 1966), p. 107.

a twenty-eight-year-old Negro field secretary for the Congress of Racial Equality, was arrested by police during a civil rights demonstration in Gadsen, Alabama. In seeking release on a writ of habeas corpus she was questioned this way by the solicitor in the local court:

Q. Mary, I believe you were arrested. Who were you arrested by?
A. My name is Miss Hamilton. Please address me correctly.
Q. Who were you arrested by, Mary?
A. I will not answer a question until I am addressed correctly.[15]

She was held to be in contempt by the local court and fined $50 and sentenced to five days in jail. Miss Hamilton appealed the conviction with the argument that the addressing of Negro adults by their first name or referring to them as "boy" or "girl" were elements in the South's racial caste system. The Supreme Court accepted her case and reversed the conviction summarily, citing a previous decision that states may not racially segregate their courtrooms. Legally, *Hamilton* v. *Alabama* is a small and insignificant case. Symbolically, it demonstrates how the Court's concern with large questions of civil rights and racial discrimination embraces as well a commitment to the fundamental dignity of all human beings.

INDIVIDUAL LIBERTIES AND RIGHTS. The Supreme Court has similarly placed a high premium on the guarantees of individual liberty contained primarily in the first eight amendments to the Constitution. In broad terms it has effectively nationalized the Bill of Rights, which once limited only the federal government. This has been accomplished by finding that virtually all of their important liberties are also part of the "liberty" that the Fourteenth Amendment forbids the state governments from violating.

The Court's decisions sustaining individual liberty claims have been so numerous and so rich in implications that only a brief and partial cataloging can be given here. Thus, its view of the First Amendment guarantees of freedom of speech, press, and assembly have led the Supreme Court to invalidate state laws compelling schoolchildren to salute the flag and recite an oath of allegiance and requiring their teachers to take loyalty oaths; to overturn scores of state convictions against allegedly obscene books, magazines, and motion pictures and nullify many of the laws that authorized the prosecutions; to strike down state laws and prosecutions restricting the associational rights of individuals (in practice these have normally been directed against civil rights organizations); and virtually to immunize from libel prosecutions participants in the political process who may, in the course of their speech-making, make statements impugning the integrity of their opponents.

[15] *New York Times*, March 31, 1964, p. 1.

The Justices have been equally vigorous in defending religious liberties. They have voided state requirements that public officials take an oath to God as a prerequisite to their inauguration, recognizing that the principle of religious freedom includes the freedom to be a nonbeliever; they have declared unconstitutional local ordinances and regulations discriminating against the proselytizing activities of unpopular religions, such as the Jehovah Witnesses, who lack the social and political advantages of more conventional faiths; and they have forbidden the states from establishing prayer and Bible-reading exercises in the public schools.

This last decision, announced in the so-called *Prayer Cases* of 1962 and 1964, was close in judicial spirit to the Supreme Court's ruling in the 1943 case of *West Virginia State Board of Education* v. *Barnette*. A state, the Court declared, violated the First Amendment when it compelled unwilling schoolchildren—in this instance young Jehovah Witnesses whose religious scruples forbid them to salute a "graven image"—to salute the American flag and pledge allegiance to it. The *Barnette* opinion reflects an attitude toward the Bill of Rights that captures the essence of the modern constitutional doctrine on questions of individual liberty:

> The very purpose of a Bill of Rights was to withdraw certain subjects from the vicissitudes of political controversy, to place them beyond the reach of majorities and officials and to establish them as legal principles to be applied by the courts. One's right to life, liberty, and property, to free speech, a free press, freedom of worship and assembly, and other fundamental rights may not be submitted to vote; they depend on the outcome of no elections.[16]

A similar concern with the rights of individuals has characterized the modern Supreme Court's performance in interpreting the fair-trial guarantees in the Bill of Rights and the due process of law clause in the Fourteenth Amendment. During the past three decades the Court has reversed innumerable state criminal convictions for having been based on prosecuting techniques that, either through physical force or through subtle psychology, coerced the defendant into confessing. At first many of these reversals were tied to a general notion of procedural fairness derived from the Fourteenth Amendment. In recent years the Justices have increasingly relied on the more explicit requirements of the Fourth, Fifth, and Sixth Amendments. They have ruled that state courts may not admit evidence obtained by illegal searches and seizures or by techniques that force or trick criminal suspects into incriminating themselves. They have ruled, also, that the states must provide impoverished criminal defendants with attorneys and that confessions may not be admitted as evidence unless the suspect has been clearly warned of his

---

[16] *West Virginia State Board of Education* v. *Barnette*, 319 U. S. 624, 638 (1943).

absolute constitutional right to remain silent, to have an attorney present during interrogation, and to have counsel assigned in the event that he cannot afford his own.

All of these decisions protecting the rights and liberties of individuals limit the federal government as well. The Supreme Court, however, has trod more gingerly in First Amendment cases where the libertarian claim conflicts with Congressional internal security policies related to the Cold War and the American conflict with Communism. Over strong dissents (and in many cases by tenuous 5-to-4 votes) it has sustained the constitutionality of the Smith Act of 1940 (making it a crime to advocate the violent overthrow of the United States government or to be a member of an organization that engages in such advocacy) and of the McCarran Internal Security Act of 1950 (outlawing, for all intents and purposes, the Communist Party and prescribing severe penalties for membership in it). Nor, despite repeated invitations to do so, has the Court been willing to deny Congressional investigating committees, such as the controversial House Un-American Activities Committee (HUAC), the authority to investigate alleged subversion and to punish uncooperative witnesses for contempt of Congress.

This deference to Congress on internal security issues is nevertheless more apparent than real. For one thing, since 1957 the Court has interpreted the Smith Act as not applying to mere "abstract" advocacy of the doctrine of violently overthrowing the government. As a result, the law has become a useless—and unused—tool for prosecuting Communists. In a similar vein, it has interpreted the McCarran Act so as to make its enforcement provisions unenforceable because the procedures used violate the Fifth Amendment. In 1965, in fact, the Court even voided a section of the McCarran Act denying passports to Communist Party members; it held that the provision was too broad and too indiscriminate in its restriction on a constitutional "right to travel."

Congress' investigating committees have not fared much better. Although the Court has reluctantly conceded their right to question persons about their political activities and beliefs, it has rigorously scrutinized the contempt convictions of hostile witnesses. By insisting that HUAC conform strictly to every technicality of the Congressional procedures governing its operations and by requiring that the federal contempt prosecutions similarly hew to procedural technicalities, the Justices have managed to convey plainly their distaste for the committee's wide-ranging probes of "un-Americanism": since 1961 in six contempt-of-Congress convictions initiated by HUAC and appealed to the Supreme Court there have been six reversals.

On occasion, too, the Warren Court has leveled the ultimate judgment of unconstitutionality against federal laws regulating the liberties of individuals, a judgment unheard of today in the realm of economic and general welfare regulations. In addition to finding one of the passport provisions of the Internal Security Act unconstitutional, it has used the First Amendment to void a law restricting the delivery of "subversive" literature and has invalidated provisions of the Uniform Code of Military Justice, which provided for trial by military court martial of civilian employees and dependents accompanying the overseas armed forces, on the ground that they deprived civilians of their Fifth Amendment right to a jury trial and other constitutional protections. It has voided various provisions of the Immigration and Nationality Act of 1952 that summarily stripped Americans of their citizenship for such offenses as deserting the armed forces in wartime, leaving the country to avoid military conscription, and voting in foreign elections. Initially the Court based its decisions on procedural considerations related to the Fifth and Sixth Amendments, but by 1967 it had moved to the broad position that Congress simply lacks authority to strip any American of a basic constitutional right to citizenship.

LEGISLATIVE APPORTIONMENT. Although critics have often charged that it promotes minority and individual rights by denying majority desires and rights, the Warren Court has hardly been hostile to the basic principle of majority rule. In the early 1960's it made a bold departure from previous judicial precedents and ruled, first, that federal courts could pass judgment on the constitutionality of legislative apportionment systems and, second, that the apportionment of the federal House of Representatives and of all state legislatures must be arranged so as to maximize the representation of popular majorities. Quite simply, what the Court did was to invalidate the apportionment scheme of almost every legislature in the United States, since they overrepresented the residents of sparsely populated counties and legislative districts at the expense of the nation's cities and large suburbs.

In *Baker* v. *Carr* (1962) the Court asserted its authority to examine the constitutionality of legislative apportionment schemes. In *Wesberry* v. *Sanders* (1964) it ruled that Article I, Section 2, of the Constitution providing that federal representatives be chosen "by the People of the several States" means that members of the national House must be chosen from districts that, as much as possible, are equally weighted in population size. And in *Reynolds* v. *Sims* (1964) it ruled that the equal protection clause of the Fourteenth Amendment compels the same result in the election of representatives to either branch of a state legislature.

The Court's underlying notion is that representational schemes that disregard population equality and are weighted in favor of certain geographic areas constitute "invidious discrimination." The alliterative slogan expressing this idea is "one man, one vote," and it captures nicely the essential majoritarianism implicit in the judicial rulings. Chief Justice Warren phrased it this way in his opinion in *Reynolds* v. *Sims:*

> . . . in a society ostensibly grounded on representative government, it would seem reasonable that a majority of the people of a State could elect a majority of that State's legislators. To conclude differently, and to sanction minority control of state legislative bodies, would appear to deny majority rights. . . . Since legislatures are responsible for enacting laws by which all citizens are to be governed, they should be bodies which are collectively responsive to the popular will. . . . With respect to the allocation of legislative representation, all voters, as citizens of a State, stand in the same relation regardless of where they live. Any suggested criteria for the differentiation of citizens are insufficient to justify any discrimination, as to the weight of their votes, unless relevant to the permissible purposes of legislative apportionment. Since the achieving of fair and effective representation for all citizens is concededly the basic aim of legislative apportionment, we conclude that the Equal Protection Clause guarantees the opportunity for equal participation by all voters in the election of state legislators. Diluting the weight of votes because of place of residence impairs basic constitutional rights under the Fourteenth Amendment just as much as invidious discriminations based upon factors such as race or economic status. Our constitutional system amply provides for the protection of minorities by means other than giving them majority control of state legislatures. And the democratic ideals of equality and majority rule, which have served this Nation so well in the past, are hardly of any less significance for the present and the future.[17]

So pronounced is the Court's commitment to majority control of legislatures that in a companion case it invalidated an unequal apportionment system that Colorado voters had selected in a popular referendum in preference to an alternative "one man, one vote" system. "An individual's constitutionally protected right to cast an equally weighted vote cannot be denied even by a vote of a majority of a State's electorate, if the apportionment scheme adopted by the voters fails to measure up to the requirements of the Equal Protection Clause." [18] In short, in the name of majority rule, majority rule must be denied!

Not surprisingly, the apportionment rulings have been subjected to searching criticisms in dissents within the Court, most notably by the late Justice Felix Frankfurter and by Justice John M. Harlan, and in scholarly critiques.[19] These critics have challenged the logic of the

[17] *Reynolds* v. *Sims,* 377 U. S. 533, 565-566.

[18] *Lucas* v. *Forty-Fourth General Assembly of Colorado,* 377 U. S. 713, 736.

[19] *See,* for example, the dissenting opinion of Justice Frankfurter, in *Baker* v. *Carr,* 369 U. S. 186, 266, the dissenting opinion of Justice Harlan in *Reynolds* v. *Sims,* 377 U. S. 533, 589, and the scholarly analysis by Philip B. Kurland, "Foreword: 'Equal in Origin and Equal in Title to the Legislative and Executive Branches of the Government,' " in "The Supreme Court: 1963 Term," *Harvard Law Review,* LXXVIII (November 1963), 149-157.

Court's reasoning and the accuracy of its historical interpretation of the relevant constitutional clauses. Moreover, they have severely criticized the Court for injecting the judiciary into the political questions of legislative apportionment that, they believe, are properly solved only by the people interacting with the more "political" legislative and executive branches of government. As trenchant as some of these criticisms are, there is nevertheless an elemental logic inherent in the "one man, one vote" idea. By contrast, the opponents of the reapportionment decrees must justify the idea that, for voters residing in rural areas, the operative slogan should be "two votes for me, one vote for you"—a difficult proposition to defend in a democratic political system.

In a broader sense, too, the decisions in *Baker* v. *Carr*, *Wesberry* v. *Sanders*, and *Reynolds* v. *Sims* may be seen as wisely adapting the Constitution—"the vehicle of a nation's life"—to American social and political realities in the last third of the twentieth century. Between 1900 and the mid-century, America grew into an urban nation. In 1910, 65.1 per cent of the population lived in 2,945 rural counties with populations of under 100,000; in 1960, with approximately the same number of counties, only 36 per cent of the American people lived in counties of under 100,000 population. Rurally dominated legislatures, understandably if parochially, refused to adjust their state legislative and Congressional district lines to accommodate the fast-growing cities and suburbs. Nor did they permit the revision of state constitutional provisions guaranteeing each county, regardless of population, at least one representative in many state senates.

During the nineteenth century such provisions mattered little. They favored rural counties, but most of the population lived there anyway. By 1960 the rural bias mattered a great deal. In twenty-one states votes in the most thinly populated Congressional district were worth at least twice as much as votes in the most populated district. Some of the discrepancies were even greater. Georgia's 5th Congressional District (Atlanta) had 823,680 residents; its rural 9th District had but 271,154; Michigan's 16th District (southwest Detroit) had a population of 802,-994; the 12th District in the state's northern section had a population of 174,431. State legislatures were similarly malapportioned. Los Angeles County with a population of 4,151,687 had one representative in the California Senate; three tiny counties in northern California with a combined population of 14,014 also had a senator. Overall, a study that computed the national average concluded that the average rural voter cast a vote worth double that cast by the average urban voter.[20]

The decisions of the Supreme Court are forcing, with remarkable speed, an end to this malapportionment. Within two years of the ruling

[20] Paul T. David and Ralph S. Eisenberg, *Devaluation of the Urban and Suburban Vote* (Charlottesville, Va.: University of Virginia, 1961), Vol. I.

in *Wesberry* v. *Sanders* Congressional districts had been reapportioned in twenty-one states and were in the process of reapportionment in four others.[21] Within three years of *Reynolds* v. *Sims* ninety-two legislative branches in forty-nine of the fifty states had been reapportioned in a manner close to the ideal of population equality. Where in 1960 there were only ten state legislative branches in which a majority of the representatives came from districts embracing 40 per cent or more of the state population, in 1967 there were ninety-three legislative branches in which the electoral percentage exceeded 45 per cent; many were at or just above the 50 per cent mark.[22]

Despite an apparently futile campaign by rurally oriented politicians to resist the rulings, the Supreme Court's decisions seem to have articulated a new constitutional consensus on legislative apportionment. A Gallup Poll taken shortly after the *Reynolds* v. *Sims* decision revealed that three out of five voters supported its bold conclusion. Equally significant is the speed with which federal and state courts, as well as many state legislatures, have implemented the rulings. Historically and logically the Fourteenth Amendment may not command population equality in legislative apportionment. But neither does the amendment exclude it. Within the context of a living Constitution, it seems quite reasonable to decide that the concept of equal protection requires each citizen's vote to be counted equally. There is, too, a fundamentally correct perception inherent in the Supreme Court's conclusion that severe rural overrepresentation is incompatible, not only with majority rule, but with the political needs of a complicated urban society.

Court and Constitution: An Evaluation

The Warren Court has probably been the most venturesome in American history. It has gone beyond the traditional role of negating new laws that violate old and established constitutional and political practices. By acting as a catalytic agent it has stimulated social changes and departures from established constitutional and political practices. During the Eisenhower and Kennedy Presidencies (and before the advent of President Johnson's short-lived Great Society majorities in the mid-sixties) the Supreme Court displaced the Congress, and often the President, as the most dynamic branch of American government. A cautious scholar has commented:

[21] George Merry, "U. S. Nears 'One Man, One Vote,'" *Christian Science Monitor*, February 16, 1966, p. 1.

[22] George Merry, "Reapportionment: 5 Years Later," *Christian Science Monitor*, March 25, 1967, pp. 1, 5.

. . . in the decade 1953-1963, the paramount domestic innovations in public policy can be traced more to the Supreme Court than to either Congress or the President. Surely the Court was the major *governmental* instrumentality in the complex process which brought the issue of racial discrimination to public attention and inaugurated an upheaval in American customs and laws. The precise impact of the reapportionment decisions on American political life is at present unforeseeable, but few question that it will be profound. Our standards of the permissible in literature and the other arts have altered considerably in the recent past; and while extra-governmental factors no doubt play a primary part in any such social change, the Supreme Court did more than any other public body to catalyze and legitimize this development.[23]

Such activism has inevitably produced a rich—and loud—harvest of criticism and political challenge. Yet its decisions have not been overturned, and the Court is unlikely to be shorn of its institutional prerogatives. It is inherently difficult to apply sanctions against the Court,[24] and the lessons of history suggest that the Court endangers itself only when it seeks to restrict the basic prerogatives of Congress and the President to act on major policy issues in response to the nation's dominant political forces. Historically this has occurred but twice. The first occurred in the *Dred Scott Case* (1857), when the Taney Court tried to settle the major political issue of the day by denying Congress constitutional authority to regulate slavery in the federal territories. The second occurred when the Hughes Court implied that President Roosevelt's New Deal program was unconstitutional, striking down twelve laws of Congress passed in response to the Great Depression. Both were traumatic moments in the nation's constitutional history, and both had a similar outcome: the powers of Congress and the President were successfully asserted. The Court was either bypassed and its decisions ignored (the fate of the Taney Court after *Dred Scott*), or it speedily retreated from an untenable constitutional position (the behavior of the post-1936 Hughes Court).

Neither experience is likely to be repeated. The very nature of the Court's modern decisions are not of a sort to mobilize Congressional and Presidential opposition. While frequently overruling legislative majorities (usually those of the state governments), it has avoided the fatal error of the Taney and Hughes courts—denying Congress and the President basic power to govern.

[23] Robert G. McCloskey, "Reflections on the Warren Court," *Virginia Law Review,* LI (November 1965), 1250-1251; and *see* pp. 1251-1257 for an inquiry into the causes behind the Warren Court's activism.
[24] *See* Hyneman, *op. cit.,* pp. 24-27, 48-55; Walter F. Murphy, *Congress and the Court* (Chicago: University of Chicago Press, 1926), Chaps. 1-3.

To argue this way is not to overlook the sharp controversies that have swirled around Chief Justice Earl Warren's Court. These began with its ruling in the *School Segregation Cases* and reached a peak in the late 1950's. White Southerners formed a coalition with interests angered by its defense of individual freedoms, particularly in a series of internal security cases decided in 1956 and 1957. The anti-Court coalition sought Congressional legislation to undo the decisions and to take from the Justices their jurisdictional authority to hear certain types of cases.[25] Serious as it was, the attack fell short. It failed to enlist the probably essential aid of the President, and the Court itself muted Congressional anger between 1959 and 1961 by conceding Congress' theoretical power to legislate internal security laws and to investigate subversion. (In specific cases the Court seems to have settled for a strategy of expressing constitutional unease at Congressional efforts to fight domestic communism without regard for the First Amendment by reversing convictions on narrow grounds.) The Warren Court has also been blessed in a perverse way by its enemies. It has been attacked so violently by rabid segregationists and other fanatics that persons repelled by political extremism have felt compelled to defend the Court, regardless of their views on the wisdom of particular decisions. "It is difficult," as Philip B. Kurland has observed, "not to help resist attack from racists, from the John Birch Society and its ilk, and from religious zealots who insist that the Court adhere to the truth as they know it. Responsible and respectable people are not comfortable on the same side of the barricades with these immoderates." [26]

Although its decisions decreeing an end to publicly encouraged racial segregation, reapportioning the nation's legislatures, and reforming the procedures for convicting criminals have encountered sometimes severe resistance, they have not been overturned. Quite the contrary, Congress and the President have joined in recognizing the *School Segregation Cases* as the law of the land (in the Civil Rights Act of 1964), most legislatures have been reapportioned, and, for all the cries about "court coddling" of criminals, the fair trial rulings are being implemented. The modern Supreme Court and its ambitious decisions are probably secure because they in no way challenge the ability of national majorities (or of powerful minorities) to act through and with Congress and the President on major policy questions. The Court plays no role in one of the major policy areas facing the United States—international relations —while on most issues confronting the Congress and the President it has fashioned a constitution of permissive powers. Until 1937 there were

[25] These events are described and analyzed in Murphy, *op. cit.*, and C. Herman Pritchett, *Congress versus the Supreme Court* (Minneapolis: University of Minnesota Press, 1961).

[26] Kurland, *op. cit.*, p. 176.

always doubts about the extent of federal power to regulate economic affairs and to promote the general welfare. Today there are none. Even the state governments, the most limited by the rulings of the modern Court, enjoy a far greater discretion to regulate economic affairs than they enjoyed before 1937.

The Supreme Court has nevertheless wielded its powers boldly, and it has contributed positively to many important policy questions. Their concern with freedom of speech and religion, criminal justice, race relations, and reapportionment have led the Justices to impose new limitations on the states. Yet these limitations do not thwart the basic capacity of political majorities to act. After all, the Court's decisions in favor of freedom of speech do little more than keep open the democratic political process so that all views may be heard in discussing public issues and framing their solutions. Its reapportionment rulings make even clearer the Court's desire to enhance democratic majority rule. As a matter of narrow logic it can be argued that the Court is antidemocratic when it strikes down on First Amendment grounds a state law requiring teacher loyalty oaths. As a matter of practical reality it would seem that a court that insists on freedom of speech and that decrees "one man, one vote" as the criterion for legislative apportionment is doing a great deal to make possible democratic majority rule.

The modern American Supreme Court has performed well its unique legal and political role. It has recognized that on large social and economic issues Congress and the President must lead the nation and react to its dominant political forces. It has recognized the importance of individual liberties and civil rights for a nation that professes—but does not always practice—the democratic ideals of individual freedom and racial justice. It has, finally, responded imaginatively to the political and social facts of twentieth-century American society by helping to fashion a *national* Constitution and a Bill of Rights adequate to national needs and problems—whether these be the undertaking of government programs to promote economic and social welfare, or the safeguarding of individual rights and human dignity.

The Preamble to the Constitution, written in 1787, declares that it was ordained and established in order "to form a more perfect Union, establish Justice, insure domestic Tranquility, provide for the common defence, promote the general Welfare, and secure the Blessings of Liberty to ourselves and our Posterity. . . ." The Supreme Court has contributed significantly to the fulfillment of these ideals.

5

ADMINISTRATION: THE NATIONAL SECURITY AGENCIES

G. W. Thumm

Modernization of the national security agencies includes both democratization and rationalization. First, it brings modern administrative techniques to bear on the "democratization" of national security policy by providing a system for formulating and conducting foreign affairs that will be more responsible to the electorate. (While such matters of course involve executive-legislative relations and even the substance of policy, this study will confine itself to the administrative aspects of the problem.) Second, it uses those techniques for "rationalization" through making the processes of national security more efficient by reducing conflict, confusion, and waste. Whatever the philosophical differences between the two may be, they are harmonious in practice; conflict, confusion, and waste in the determination and implementation of foreign policy deprive the electorate of effective control. Democracy requires not only that the people participate in determining policy, but that their decisions will be carried out.

While this study limits its attention to the national security agencies, many of its arguments are equally applicable to other agencies of government. It focuses on agencies spending more than 70 per cent of the 1967-1968 budget and handling complex and critical problems, primarily State, Defense, AID, and USIA.

The steps required for modernization have already been clearly

G. W. Thumm has been Professor of Government and Chairman of the Division of the Social Sciences at Bates College since 1961. From 1947 to 1961 he taught at the University of Pennsylvania, where he received his Ph.D. He was on active duty in the Pentagon from 1951 to 1953, and from 1966 to 1968 was Visiting Professor at the National War College.

The author particularly appreciates the advice and contributions of Arthur R. Day, U. S. Foreign Service, Lt. Col. Lloyd R. Leavitt, Jr., USAF, John F. Lippmann, Arms Control and Disarmament Agency, Charles E. Nelson, AID, and William C. Sherman, U. S. Foreign Service. However, the opinions and conclusions expressed herein are those of the author; they should not be taken as representing the views either of those who aided him or of their agencies.

identified, and some taken, especially in the Department of Defense. If completed, they will provide the United States with a coherent and coordinated system of planning, financing, and executing its foreign affairs programs. Whether they will be taken depends on whether adequate leadership will be provided from within and adequate pressure applied from without.

Coordination

To modernize, the Department of State must adequately coordinate the work of a number of independent, autonomous, and semiautonomous agencies. Since World War II it has lost its former virtual monopoly in the field of foreign affairs. It had to concede an increasing role to the Department of Defense as the United States became more aware of the vital nature of military power and military planning in the conduct of foreign relations. It had to yield much of its preeminence in nonmilitary affairs to the specialized organizations created to administer the major peacetime operational programs. Although in theory it remained the only policy-forming agency, the dichotomy between politics and administration proved once again imaginary. The *formal* relationships of both the principal economic aid organization (successively ECA, MSA, FOA, ICA, and AID) and the foreign propaganda organization (IIA and USIA) varied from year to year. Sometimes they were part of, sometimes entirely outside, the Department of State.[1] Their actual relationships, however, were fairly stable; their degree of autonomy was little affected by the formal structure.

Conflicts between the policies of the ad hoc agencies and the official policies of the Department were inevitable. Quite apart from any possible Parkinsonian tendency toward self-preservation and self-aggrandizement, their officials were usually so firmly convinced of the importance of their programs that they were quite likely to exaggerate the role of their agency by comparison with others; they wanted to insure the continued success of the programs in which they believed. Occasionally, factional struggles within a recipient country caused corresponding struggles within the U. S. Mission as the representatives of the various agencies tried to influence U. S. policy so as to aid that faction whose success would most help that agency's programs. Occasionally, too, the battle was carried from the embassy to Washington, where superiors continued the struggle of their subordinates. The situation was obviously intolerable.

Sometimes imaginative approaches led to ill-advised actions due to faulty coordination. Not long after Dwight D. Eisenhower became

---

[1] Burton M. Sapin, *The Making of United States Foreign Policy* (New York: Frederick A. Praeger, 1966), p. 108.

President, the Secretary of Agriculture suggested to an official of the Department of State that a good way to unload part of the U. S. wheat surplus would be to ship a million tons to perennially undernourished India. The official concurred; the shipment was made. A few months later the prime minister of Burma visited Washington; he had a query for the President. "Mr. President," he said, "we are Buddhists, and therefore we do not complain about things; but you have just ruined our rice sales to India. We would like to know what you are going to do to give us some relief in this situation." [2]

President Eisenhower sought in 1953 to cope with the problem of coordination by adding to the National Security Council structure the Operations Coordinating Board (OCB).[3] To it he appointed the Undersecretary of State (who served as chairman), plus senior officials from other agencies concerned with international affairs.

During the next few years its critics launched a number of attacks on OCB as an organization, some of which were well founded. They criticized it for spending too much time in fruitless meetings, and for issuing too many papers on too many topics. They assailed it for including in its meetings too many people from too many different agencies, some of which had only a remote interest in the policy under consideration. Particularly, the Jackson Subcommittee attacked OCB for preventing a full airing of major foreign policy issues. Instead, the Subcommittee felt, OCB deliberately sought to suppress dissent by compromising differences at low levels, then burying them by presenting innocuous reports that concealed their existence.[4]

Other observers, such as Professor Richard L. Neustadt, struck at OCB only as part of a general assault on the entire Eisenhower concept of the presidency: that of a highly institutionalized presidency, in which the President occupies a position within the Executive Office analogous to that of a military commander with his staff. These critics felt that agencies such as OCB insulated the President from the policy-forming process during its early stages when his influence could—and should—be most effective. Professor Neustadt presented their view most tellingly in his very influential *Presidential Power*.[5]

Mr. Neustadt took dead aim at Eisenhower—and hit Kennedy. He had directed his shafts at what he regarded as (1) the extreme institu-

[2] Dwight D. Eisenhower, "The Role of the President in the Conduct of Security Affairs," in Amos A. Jordan (ed.), *Issues of National Security in the 1970's* (New York: Frederick A. Praeger, 1967), p. 216.

[3] While OCB replaced the Truman-appointed Psychological Strategy Board, its functions were much broader.

[4] *See* U. S. Senate Government Operations Committee, Subcommittee on National Policy Machinery, *Organizing for National Security*, 87th Congress, 1st Session (1961).

[5] Richard L. Neustadt, *Presidential Power* (New York: John Wiley and Sons, 1960).

tionalization and excessive bureaucracy of the Eisenhower Administration, and (2) the paucity of dynamic personal leadership displayed by President Eisenhower himself. He made little impact on the Eisenhower Administration, which left office in January, 1961. However, his book was read and taken to heart by those who were to become the New Frontiersmen of the Kennedy Administration—a brilliant, individualistic, and highly undisciplined lot who needed nothing less than to be warned against overorganization. Inaugurated on January 20, President John F. Kennedy abolished OCB on February 8. But the problem OCB was to meet remained; many observers attributed the Bay of Pigs fiasco at least in part to a lack of intragovernmental coordination.

To meet the need for coordination, President Kennedy returned to the type of mechanism previously adopted by Presidents Truman and Eisenhower. In January, 1962, he created the Special Group, CI (Counterinsurgency). Its membership was basically quite similar to that of OCB. It also included the President's Special Assistant for National Security Affairs, Mr. McGeorge Bundy, the Attorney General, Mr. Robert F. Kennedy (probably in his personal rather than his departmental role), and the Military Representative of the President, General Maxwell Taylor, who served as chairman. Mr. Kennedy and General Taylor soon dropped out, and the Deputy Undersecretary of State for Political Affairs became chairman. Despite himself, President Kennedy had legitimized institutionalized interagency coordination.

It remained for President Lyndon B. Johnson to establish the most highly structured, institutionalized mechanism for coordination yet devised. In March, 1966, he replaced Special Group CI with the Senior Interdepartmental Group (SIG). As members he designated the Deputy Secretary of Defense, Administrator of AID, Director of CIA, Chairman of the Joint Chiefs of Staff (JCS), Director of USIA, and Special Assistant for National Security Affairs, and provided for other members ad hoc, depending on the topic being considered by SIG. He designated the Undersecretary of State as chairman, with full power of decision on all matters within the competence of SIG, subject only to the right of nonconcurring members to appeal to the Secretary of State himself. He further provided that in the absence of the Undersecretary the Department of State would provide another representative who would serve as chairman. In establishing SIG, President Johnson clearly went beyond either President Eisenhower or President Kennedy in assuring the primacy of the Department of State in the field of foreign affairs.

Military Input

Throughout their efforts to improve interagency coordination, successive Presidents have had to decide how to provide for the military input into the planning and execution of foreign policy. While they were able in some respects to treat military and nonmilitary foreign affairs separately, in many they could not. They realized that their commitments would be fully credible only if other nations believed that the United States would be able to fulfill them. In some way, therefore, they had to coordinate military planning with foreign policy. Also, they often found military assistance quite as useful as economic aid in such tasks as securing a U. S. presence in a country, or winning diplomatic support in the United Nations. In this the Department of Defense had an important role, both in professional-to-professional relations and in conducting military assistance programs.

The structure of the Department of Defense (DOD), and particularly the positions in that structure of the military and civilian elements, caused difficulties in determining who would provide military advice. It created a triangular relationship between JCS, the Office of the Secretary of Defense (OSD), and the three services, Army, Navy, and Air Force (ANAF), all of which became involved in varying, overlapping, and sometimes conflicting ways in the formulation of national security policy.

The Defense structure incorporating the JCS-OSD-ANAF relationship is the residue of efforts to solve earlier problems, beginning with the reorganization of 1947. After World War II those concerned with U. S. military affairs considered two major approaches to modernizing the permanent military structure. The first, backed generally by the Army and the semiautonomous Army Air Forces (the latter eager to achieve equal status for air power), proposed a single unified organization; its more extreme variants would have created a single service with a single uniform.[6] The second, backed generally by the Navy, proposed three loosely coordinated armed services, each with its own department. The National Security Act of 1947 accepted basically the Navy approach. Although every President since that time took steps leading to increased unification, only during the administrations of Presidents Kennedy and Johnson and with their backing did Secretary of Defense Robert S. McNamara, willing and eager to use his powers to the full, make DOD effectively into a single department.

Even after the Department had been effectively unified, it displayed elements of both approaches to reorganization: integration and coordination. (1) The single integrated service would have provided a single staff to plan all operations; this approach is manifested in JCS, with its

---

[6] Opponents attacked this concept as creating a "Prussian-type General Staff." As a matter of fact, the post-1871 incarnation of the Prussian General Staff was *Oberkommando des Heeres* (OKH), the Army High Command, not *Oberkommando der Wehrmacht* (OKW), the Joint Command, whose relations with OKH were a bit vague. Opposition to Hitler centered in OKH.

Joint Staff composed of personnel from all three services. Except for the Chairman the members of JCS hold two jobs, that of Chief of their respective services and Commandant of the Marine Corps[7] as well as member of JCS. Each service chief has as vice chief a four-star officer charged with actual supervision of the service so that the chief can devote his primary attention to his JCS role. Thus, JCS represents integration from within. (2) Three-service coordination would have superimposed a coordinating mechanism above the existing service establishments; this technique is embodied in OSD, created to aid the Secretary of Defense in that task. OSD represents coordination from above.

By adopting the second approach the unification procedures left in operation the already existing bureaucracies of the Army and Navy, and added one for the Air Force, plus OSD. The services compose the third side of the JCS-OSD-ANAF triangle. They retain their staffs and service functions. Even military personnel assigned to JCS and OSD are assigned by the services subject to JCS or OSD concurrence.

Because of their functions of providing and training personnel and material for the JCS-directed Unified and Specified Commands, the services are deeply involved in the programming aspect of Defense management, in which they deal with OSD rather than with JCS. This creates a second decision-making channel. ANAF participation in planning is routed through the JCS–Secretary of Defense channel; its participation in programming is routed through OSD—especially centering in the Office of the Assistant Secretary of Defense, Systems Analysis (OSD-SA)—with minimal participation by JCS. (Programs involving resource-allocation related to strategic planning are, however, submitted to JCS for comment.)

In such a situation there is likely to arise an institutional conflict that could partially divorce strategic planning from programing or resource-allocation planning. JCS may adopt strategic plans without adequate programed support, and OSD-SA may allocate resources without a well-defined plan for their use.

The position of the Office of the Assistant Secretary of Defense for International Security Affairs (ISA) also affords opportunities for JCS-OSD conflict. ISA is "the authorized Defense channel for communicating and conducting foreign policy business with the Department of State." [8] While it has its own operational functions, such as directing the Military Assistance Program (MAP), in its most important role it stands in a position within DOD analogous to the position of the Department of State in the U. S. government. It coordinates and represents

---

[7] The Commandant of the Marine Corps is authorized to sit with JCS in matters affecting the Marine Corps. Judging by his attendance at JCS meetings, there is nothing that does not affect the Marine Corps.

[8] Sapin, *op. cit.*, p. 158.

the various elements of DOD that have international security functions. It is a thoroughly integrated civilian-military organization, combining professional and some nonprofessional civil servants with military officers assigned by the services.

Since many functions of ISA overlap those of JCS, duplication and conflicts of jurisdiction are certain to arise; this is particularly true since JCS is represented directly in the SIG-IRG system.[9] Logically, a strong case can be made for eliminating ISA, combining its functions with those of JCS, and relying on the Department of State for the civilian input into foreign policy matters of defense concern. Practically, the case is not nearly so strong; ISA performs a very useful function in mediating between the more strictly military and more strictly civilian components. Under their division of labor, ISA assures Defense participation in interagency negotiations in full recognition of the nonmilitary parameters of policy, while JCS continues to make its recommendations on the basis of military judgment. JCS must compromise conflicting views to reach a judgment; however, it is thus enabled to carry its military judgment to the highest level of government rather than being forced further to compromise with and subordinate it to domestic political considerations at lower levels. While that compromise and subordination are inherent in democratic government, the fact that it exists should not be obscured beneath several levels of bureaucracy.[10]

The relationships between the service secretaries and the chiefs of the services further complicate the operation of the JCS-OSD-ANAF triangle. The administrative, programming channel runs through the service secretaries to OSD, bypassing JCS—which is composed of the chiefs of services in their other capacities. The Secretary and his principal civilian assistants often if not usually come to their posts either from outside or from some more or less distantly related post in government. Their views sometimes differ from those of their service chiefs, who arrive at their posts after a lifetime of command and staff positions in the course of which they have been steeped in the problems, policies, and doctrines of their service. Again, over a period of years the policies recommended through the ANAF-OSD channel are likely to differ from those produced through the JCS channel.

Regardless of its untidy appearance on a flow chart, the existing method of providing a military input into foreign policy planning, programing, and execution is a satisfactory expedient. It provides SIG with

---

[9] IRG: Interdepartmental Regional Group. See p. 91 for discussion.

[10] Lt. Gen. Andrew J. Goodpaster, a former Director of the Joint Staff and member of the White House staff under President Eisenhower, argues that it is desirable to maintain JCS as an "indigestible lump" in DOD for precisely this reason ("The Joint Chiefs of Staff in the National Security Structure," in Jordan [ed.], *op. cit.*, p. 232).

representation both from the Defense budgeting-programing elements centering in OSD and the planning elements focused in JCS. SIG needs both; in its operation a disagreement between the OSD and JCS members is no more serious than one between AID and USIA.

Second- and Third-Level Coordination

President Johnson went even further beyond his predecessors by incorporating into the SIG system a new institution, the Interdepartmental Regional Group (IRG) to perform the same function at the regional level as SIG at the general. He added to SIG five regional groups, each chaired by an assistant secretary of state and each composed of senior officials of the agencies represented in SIG. These officials came from the offices of their agencies concerned with affairs of their geographic region—African, European, East-Asian-Pacific, Inter-American, and Near-Eastern–South Asian. As in SIG, he made the State Department representative executive chairman; the chairman's decisions were subject only to appeals to SIG.[11]

The IRGs for the "underdeveloped" regions have been the most active. In addition to the varying attitudes of the assistant secretaries, their task will naturally be greatest where the number and magnitude of interagency programs to be coordinated is greatest: in Africa, Asia, and Latin America. The European IRG has been least active. Not only have there been fewer and smaller interagency programs for it to coordinate but, when serious problems have arisen in Europe, President Johnson has tended to rely on ad hoc missions by special representatives rather than on formally established machinery. For example, he designated former Secretary of State Dean Acheson to study the problems of NATO and former High Commissioner to Germany John J. McCloy to review our German policy. However, that SIG-IRG was not used tells us more about the methods of operation of President Johnson and Secretary of State Dean Rusk and their regard for the permanent personnel of the Department of State than about conditions in Europe.

To improve coordination at the "desk" level, concurrently with the installation of the SIG-IRG system the Department of State has begun to replace its "desk officers" with "country directors." The country directors seem to be more senior, and hence should be able to provide more mature and authoritative direction at lower levels for the country teams abroad. At least in theory, they have eliminated one level in the State Department bureaucracy; country directors work directly under the as-

[11] The appeal provision has been little-used; in practice both SIG and IRG have sought to avoid using it.

sistant secretaries. In many cases, however, a single country director is in charge of several countries; it remains to be seen whether he will have a subordinate in charge of each and become himself the intermediate level. At least, he is expected to handle more problems at the country level; his seniority may induce foreign ambassadors to deal with him rather than insist on going to the assistant secretary. In order to resolve more interagency problems at the country level, some country directors (getting thoroughly into the spirit of the times) have recruited *their* opposite numbers in the SIG-IRG agencies and organized what one wag called, "IRGlets."

President Kennedy on May 29, 1961, took steps to improve coordination in the field. In a letter to all U. S. ambassadors he told them, ". . . I shall count on you to oversee and coordinate all activities of the United States Government in [their respective countries]." He placed them in charge of "the entire United States Diplomatic Mission" including "the representatives of all other United States agencies which have programs of activities in [their respective countries]." [12] Nevertheless, the Senate Committee on Government Operations found

> To a degree the primacy of the ambassador is a polite fiction, especially where budgetary and programming decisions are concerned. Most elements of the Country Team do not, in other words, regard themselves as part of the ambassador's staff—rather they look outside the country, to intermediate headquarters or Washington, for guidance and support, and their loyalties tend to run in the same direction.[13]

SIG-IRG has had a salutary effect in facilitating coordination at the mission level. It affords an ambassador who has differed sharply with the senior representative of one of the other agencies assurance of an interagency board to settle the differences at the Washington level—and of a State Department executive chairman.

Effective Planning

Regardless of its successes in resolving conflicts arising from the execution of policy, SIG-IRG will fall short of its potential for modernizing unless it extends and improves the quality of planning and programming in the field of foreign policy. At the present time the extent and nature of planning varies from agency to agency. It is comparatively highly developed in DOD and the more strictly military areas. It tends to be fragmentary and ineffective in State and in the more strictly political

[12] Quoted in U. S. Senate Committee on Government Operations, *Administration of National Security, Basic Issues*, 88th Congress, 1st Session (1963), p. 15.
[13] *Ibid.*, p. 17.

areas. AID and USIA occupy intermediate positions. Most important, there is nowhere the integrated planning and programming the United States must have to meet its challenges in the field of foreign affairs.

Since the Department of State is the dominant agency in the foreign affairs field, it must accept responsibility for these planning and programming deficiencies. Partly they are due to the present state of the art in identifying and measuring program requirements, but they are also due in large part to its reluctance to engage in planning in a manner comparable to that of the armed forces. This reluctance stems from, among other reasons, (1) its lack of a tradition of planning; (2) its preoccupation with current developments; (3) the personal characteristics of its foreign service officers; and (4) its different relationship to its strategic environment.[14]

1. Unlike the military services, the Department of State lacks a tradition of planning; it had been able to perform its limited duties prior to World War II reasonably well without planning. The Army, on the other hand, was forced to plan. The commander who expected supplies and replacements to reach him when he needed them had to estimate what he would need, and when. He had to estimate not only the rate of movement of his supply column but his own speed of advance—or retreat—which in turn required some reasonably valid judgments as to the probability and outcome of enemy action that might affect his advance —or retreat—and the amount of supplies and number of replacements he would need. He had to *plan*. In the Department of State no such pressures existed. Embassy personnel usually "lived off the economy," that is, they procured the necessities of life locally. Except in so far as planning was to be used as a guide for broader policy purposes, it was unnecessary.

Furthermore, in sharp contrast to the military, diplomatic personnel had not been forced to plan as a training activity. The armed forces existed in peace to prepare for war. At the lower levels the drill field, firing range, or shipboard routine afforded the enlisted man and junior officer a means of training. Senior officers asked themselves how they would carry on a hypothetical campaign; they considered contingencies, wrote orders, and prepared implementing documents even though they knew their plans might never be executed. Diplomatic personnel, on the other hand, were able to train while devoting their attention to actual events. They did not have to write fictitious or hypothetical reports; they trained by writing actual ones. They dealt with real situations, not imaginary ones. In short, they did not plan—and under our policy of isolation planning was not missed.

[14] *See also* Franklin A. Lindsay, "Program Planning: The Missing Element," *Foreign Affairs*, XXXIX, 2 (January, 1961), 282-83.

Our sudden change from isolation to internationalism gave the Department of State no time to develop a tradition of planning. Now, however, it found that the circumstances within which it had to operate had radically changed. It saw resource allocations for foreign affairs and allied programs become a significant part of the total national budget. It found world leadership thrust upon it. It realized its leadership could not be effective if it merely reacted to outside developments, but its patterns of thought and behavior dating from the period of isolation continued. It had no tradition of planning, and no time to develop one.

2. The Department of State is so preoccupied with current developments that it feels forced to give a low priority to planning. Faced with an immediate problem, it naturally tends to devote major attention to meeting the crisis rather than to contemplating things that may be done in the more distant future regarding possibly more important but certainly less pressing problems. Its attitude is no longer necessary; State's personnel shortage is no longer so critical that it could not spare the manpower for planning if it saw fit. Nevertheless, if it feels a shortage at any time, it will almost certainly continue its functions of representation and reporting; it may drastically reduce planning.

3. Foreign Service Officers by temperament and inclination tend to avoid assignments to planning. They prefer to think of themselves as gifted in understanding and persuasion rather than in painstaking analysis and meticulous detailing of alternatives. Even so, there are enough qualified personnel to establish a planning system if State wanted to assemble them for the purpose. They will not seek the assignment, however; they are acutely aware that the jobs that lead to recognition and promotion have usually been those in operations, not in planning. The Foreign Service Officers will not change their preferences until the Department of State changes its assignment and promotion policy.

4. The relationship of the Department of State to its strategic environment is different from that of the Department of Defense. Military planning is fairly simple and direct in its purpose. Department of State planning must deal with complex and frequently poorly defined purposes and cope with an assortment of vaguely perceived obstacles to U. S. policy. Its ends are rarely clearly defined; in fact, it may avoid clear definition because of domestic political considerations—there may be no real agreement within the nation as to the end to be achieved.

State Department planning is more affected than Defense by changes in governments or governmental personnel—our own or others. Its policies are far more intimately related than those of the Department of Defense to the goals and style of a particular President or a particular secretary. It may find its policies disrupted by elections or revolutions in foreign countries in which it has very little influence. Such events may also affect Defense policy, as in the case of President Charles de Gaulle's impact on NATO and U. S. plans for the defense of Europe, but such examples are less frequent and usually less extreme than in the area of State's primary interest.

INSTITUTIONAL FACTORS. In addition to the factors just discussed, the Department of State has been reluctant to enter into interagency planning for reasons having to do more with the nature of institutions than with planning.

1. State desired to protect its preeminence in the field of foreign relations. With some justice, it feared that the kind of interagency planning that could be useful, and which planning advocates demanded, would permit its institutional rivals—Defense, AID, USIA, CIA, etc.—to help form policy rather than merely implement State-formed policy. Such a situation would decrease State's importance. However, it is no longer so concerned about this possibility as formerly; having become accustomed to competition in the field of foreign affairs, it has adjusted accordingly. Furthermore, it has found that when its representatives present a cogent and well-prepared position the other agencies are usually quite willing to accept its leadership. Its remaining fears are largely allayed by its enhanced position in the SIG-IRG system.

2. State suspected that plans adopted would be ignored rather than implemented. It saw both the planning process and the implementing process as interagency negotiations in which each agency fought for its own institutional interests just as nations struggled on the international scene; it noted that "not all negotiations terminate in settlements and the course of conflict is therefore marked by the postponement of disputes and by truces as well as treaties." [15]

In each process the outcome would reflect the relative bargaining power of the participating agencies just as a treaty reflects that of the participating nations. However, sometimes an agency might regard a mere plan as not important enough to warrant exerting its real strength; the plan adopted therefore would not accurately mirror the balance of forces. When time came to execute the plan that agency might take the decision more seriously; the decision on action to implement would more accurately reflect the true balance, and would differ from the plan. Sometimes the relative strength of agencies would change between the time of planning and the time of implementation. In either case, the plan would not be followed. This possibility decreased the aura of permanence and credibility that would make plans most valuable.

3. Planning would decrease the responsiveness of the Department to changes in official policy. From the standpoint of the statesman, this

---

[15] Warner R. Schilling, "The Politics of National Defense: Fiscal 1950," in Warner R. Schilling, Paul Y. Hammond, and Glen H. Snyder, *Strategy, Politics, and Defense Budgets* (New York: Columbia University Press, 1962), p. 22.

disadvantage is inherent. He likes to "keep his options open." He wants to be able to adjust national policies quickly and easily to sudden changes on the international scene. He finds that planning makes this more difficult.[16] When a situation develops similar to that foreseen by the plan, his subordinates may react immediately—without waiting for his decision or instructions. To the outsider, this is a major value of planning. To the subordinate, it is desirable; it increases his responsibility and sense of accomplishment. To the statesman, it restricts his freedom of action; parts of his former decision may already be in process of execution by his subordinates. Thus, planning is far more popular at lower echelons, whose inhabitants like predictability, than at the top, where statesmen sometimes find a bit of unpredictability positively useful in dealing with other countries.[17]

NATURE OF PLANNING. The planner must engage in four related activities, each of which may be virtually a continuing operation. (1) He must develop an estimate of the problem—he must gather information, analyze it, identify its crucial elements, and interpret the results. (2) He must establish his goals—he must recognize his (or his nation's) value structure, identify and distinguish between ultimate and instrumental values, determine his immediate and long-range objectives, and both choose among conflicting and establish priorities among competing goals. (3) He must select appropriate means to achieve the goals established. (4) He must allocate resources to implement the means selected —he must select the types of resources necessary and appropriate for the purpose, and establish further priorities among those means competing for the same resources. While with regard to any given planning operation the stages of his activity may be distinct, in the process as a whole they tend to merge; each affects the others, and the process of execution —if it is executed—affects them all.

There are three major kinds of planning: (1) strategic planning, (2) contingency planning, and (3) resource-allocation planning.

STRATEGIC PLANNING. Strategic planning is that type in which major attention is given to establishing and preparing to attain broad national goals or objectives. In the Department of Defense it appears primarily as the Joint Strategic Objectives Plan (JSOP), prepared by JCS, and the Draft Presidential Memorandum (DPM), prepared by OSD-SA. (While the latter is a resource-allocation document, it independently considers objectives.) The State Policy Planning Council (S/P) bears chief responsibility for planning in the Department of State; it produces National Policy Papers (NPP) for regions and individual states,

[16] See Schilling, op. cit., p. 12.

[17] For a discussion of the value of unpredictability, see Thomas C. Schelling, *Arms and Influence* (New Haven: Yale University Press, 1966), especially pp. 99-125.

and a number of "thinkpieces" on various topics. Generally, U. S. strategic planning is inadequate. That in Defense is too narrowly based on Defense sources and considerations, and that in State is too limited in scope and concept. Thus far S/P has been less a strategic planning agency than a "gadfly" to force people to face up to the things they already knew.[18]

CONTINGENCY PLANNING. Contingency planning is that type which prepares to deal with fairly specific situations that may arise at some time in the not-too-distant future. Some officials erroneously argue that it is useless; it cannot cover all possible contingencies, so that when a situation does arise it is most unlikely to develop in the precise form anticipated by the plan. As a practical matter, however, contingency planners will not attempt to prepare for all contingencies; rather they will identify a few of the more likely and more serious ones (or, for training purposes, merely typical ones) and prepare for them. So long as they anticipate the broad outlines of the actual development, their preparation will reduce the time required to react to the contingency. They can entrust minor adjustments to those executing the plan.

The greatest value of contingency planning is in the process rather than in the plan produced. Planners find the depth of analysis and discipline required in preparing the plan like that of preparing for a computer simulation or a game-theory matrix: valuable whether or not the product itself is a contribution. State-Defense planning for the Berlin Crisis, a too-rare demonstration of what State can do when it does feel planning relevant and important, provided an example. By six months of planning it provided Washington, Bonn, and Berlin with a large number of people who had learned to think roughly alike concerning its problems. Had it become necessary, they would have found it far easier to react promptly and effectively. However, the Department of State can derive these benefits only when the personnel engaged in planning are also those who would be engaged in operations. This is not the case with most S/P planning; State could easily do this, but unfortunately has done very little.

RESOURCE-ALLOCATION PLANNING. Resource-allocation planning is that type which determines the amounts of resources to be used in carrying out each of the various programs. Since the planner expresses his plan formally in a budget, it is inherently action-oriented; it makes action possible or impossible by granting or denying resources. As in the case of strategic planning, Defense is more advanced in this area than State, but here too it lacks adequate input from outside Defense. In order to reunite action policies with declared policies the United States must pro-

[18] George Allen Morgan, "Planning in Foreign Affairs: The State of the Art," *Foreign Affairs*, XXXIX, 2 (January 1961), 272.

vide for greater participation in military planning by the nonmilitary agencies (especially State), and it must develop resource-allocation planning in the nonmilitary field as effectively as it has in the military. Such planning is now applicable to most areas of foreign policy, and particularly in the area of economic assistance.

The planner must include in resource-allocation planning all agencies spending money to implement foreign policy. At the present time no single paper brings together all such expenditures for his review, nor even those offering different ways by which he can achieve the same objective. He must be able to develop a combination of means to secure the best results. His most useful technique in doing this is the Planning, Programming, and Budgeting System, which uses as its tool "Systems Analysis."

The Planning, Programming, and Budgeting System (PPBS)

Impressed by the success of the system of financial controls introduced into the Department of Defense by Secretary McNamara and his Comptroller, Charles J. Hitch, President Johnson decided to extend it to other departments and agencies. On August 25, 1965, he so informed his Cabinet and the heads of the affected agencies.[19] A few weeks later the Bureau of the Budget submitted more detailed instructions,[20] which became the formal outlines of the Planning, Programming, and Budgeting System (PPBS).

While the order of the President and Bulletin 66-3 were major advances in national financial administration, they had limited impact in the field of foreign affairs. The situation in that field was far more complex than that in Defense. Mr. McNamara's task would have been comparatively simple, even for one with far less personal force and ability. As the single responsible official, he had applied PPBS to the three services under his own authority. For example, he treated the Air Force's Strategic Air Command and the Navy's Polaris submarine force as a mission unit; both were charged with strategic bombardment—and had only to match resource-allocation to targeting.

The Secretary of State had no comparable authority in the general field of foreign affairs, nor, for that matter, did anyone else except the

[19] See Order of the President, "Introduction of New Governmentwide Planning and Budgeting System, Statement by the President to the Members of the Cabinet and Heads of Agencies, August 25, 1965," *Weekly Compilation of Presidential Documents*, I, 5 (Monday, August 30, 1965), 141-42.

[20] "Planning-Programming-Budgeting," Bureau of the Budget *Bulletin*, No. 66-3 (October 12, 1965), with Supplement (February 21, 1966).

President himself. His relationship to such spending agencies as AID and USIA, not to mention the programs under ISA, was quite different from that of the Secretary of Defense to ANAF. The Peace Corps and CIA were each *sui generis*.[21] Not only did he find AID and USIA administratively and budgetarily autonomous; probably even more than ANAF they had their own clientele, their own supporters in Congress, and their own boosters outside. Even after the establishment of SIG-IRG his authority remained tenuous; some even feared conflicts between SIG-IRG and PPBS.[22] Secretary Rusk appointed a committee under the chairmanship of Charles J. Hitch to study the budgeting problems in the field of foreign affairs and to make recommendations.

In October, 1966, the Hitch Committee recommended creation of an integrated, multiagency Foreign Affairs Programming System (FAPS) covering all major nonmilitary budgets in the foreign affairs field except that of CIA, exempted for security reasons. FAPS was a logical extension of the concept set forth in Bulletin 66-3, designed to meet the peculiar conditions in the field. Whereas Bulletin 66-3 had required each agency to set up its own system, the Hitch Report called for a single combined PPBS covering different agencies with related missions.

The Latin American IRG reacted quickly, reflecting the enthusiasm of Assistant Secretary Lincoln Gordon. On November 30, 1966, it directed the country team of each country under its supervision to prepare a "Country Analysis and Strategy Paper," and to submit it to IRG during March and April, 1967, for review and approval. When it had approved each paper, it would then direct the country team to submit a detailed program designed to implement the approved strategy. These programs were to be forwarded during the period May–September, 1967, in time to be used in preparing the budget for fiscal year 1968–1969. For Latin America, the IRG-sponsored submission would replace the analytical and policy sections of the previously separate submissions of AID, Defense, USIA, the Peace Corps, and the Department of State's Cultural Affairs Program.

For several reasons FAPS should not be expected to succeed in the

[21] The AID program, for example, was "prepared according to one calendar schedule, with a special frame of reference and a unique agency jargon and format, while documents covering overseas program proposals and budget requests on other activities—information, military assistance, educational, cultural and scientific exchanges, peace corps, agriculture including food for peace, health, financial matters, and intelligence collection, as well as the more traditional reporting, representation, negotiation, and participation in international organizations—emerge each according to some other schedule, often with equally special terms of reference and varying degrees of geographic focus, making unnecessary use of unique language, and probably employing specialized formats and arrangements of data" (R. Glynn Mays, Jr., "Companion Tools for Foreign Affairs Management," *Foreign Service Journal*, XLIII, 9 [September 1966], 18).

[22] Mays, *ibid.*, p. 17.

general field of foreign affairs to the extent that it did in the Department of Defense. Two of these are the differences in the degree of U. S. control and the comparative role of nongovernmental activity.

Unlike the Secretary of State, in his programming the Secretary of Defense deals primarily with matters subject to U. S. control. Only in his military assistance functions—a minor part of the DOD budget—and in reconciling NATO force levels does he have to reckon with the vagaries of foreign governments (Even here the Secretary of State is *legislatively* responsible for the military assistance program.) The Secretary of State on the other hand deals primarily with matters outside direct U. S. control. He may promise foreign aid or threaten to withdraw it, but even if he does his promise or threat is only one of the factors a foreign government will take into consideration in making its decision. In the same way, however much he may prefer a regional approach to economic development, special factors often require him to treat each country in most respects as a separate unit. In such cases he can hope only to keep his programs from interfering with each other, and perhaps eventually to harmonize or integrate them.

The Secretary of State is also more concerned than is the Secretary of Defense with attempting to control or influence the actions of private, nongovernmental agencies. By their investment and labor policies, corporations with foreign interests may either improve or exacerbate relations between the United States and the host country. The work of private charitable organizations as a supplement to or a substitute for governmentally sponsored relief programs may effectively serve the ends of U. S. foreign policy—or it may not; for example, private aid to Israel may infuriate the Arab states even as it strengthens Israel.

Since he cannot readily control such private action by direct legislation, the Secretary of State must as best he can exercise his influence indirectly. He may recommend to the Congress tax benefits or investment credits; he may arrange to sell to private organizations U. S. surplus food or equipment at bargain prices; he may hinder or promote "bridge-building" through the activities of private business men or cultural organizations by modifying passport regulations, licensing requirements, credit controls, and the like. But his weapons are usually less definitive than those available to the Department of Defense.

Congress plays as vital a role in making it possible for the Secretary of State to control direct expenditures as in helping influence private action. Customarily it makes appropriations for the civilian agencies only for specific purposes stated in the appropriations act. It has rarely permitted administrators to transfer funds from one foreign program to another. If it really wants FAPS to be effective it will have to modify the degree of its control so as to permit the Secretary of State (or SIG) to group programs into packages and thus permit the use of systems analysis. The success or failure of FAPS within its inherent limitations will depend largely on the effectiveness with which it can incorporate an adequate program of systems analysis.

Systems Analysis

Systems analysis is a procedure that applies the economic concept of marginal utility as a tool in making decisions on programs involving the allocation of resources. "[It] is intended to present decision-makers with a systematic and comprehensive comparison of the costs and benefits of alternative approaches to a policy goal, taking advantage of techniques variously described as operations research or cost-effectiveness studies. . . . It is no substitute for experience and judgment." [23] The systems analyst assumes that each additional increment of resources applied to any program should produce a return at least as great as any alternative use of that increment. His task is to provide the decision-maker with a way by which the value system of the electorate may be made more effective. He attempts to increase the amount of rational determination in the process of resource-allocation planning, and thereby to decrease the role of negotiation and bargaining.

In order to do this, first, the systems analyst must group the multitude of foreign programs into "families" having identical or similar objectives. He then answers the question, "Which program, or how much of each of several programs, is most 'cost-effective,' that is, which will accomplish the most in terms of the objective for the least cost?" At this point systems analysis makes its first major contribution to the modernization —democratization and rationalization—of national security policy procedures: It requires policy-makers to be specific in stating the goals or objectives of a particular program. For example, precisely what do they expect to achieve by their proposed program of economic aid to Ruritania? Do they really intend to raise the standard of living of the Ruritanian people? Or to make it less likely that traveling American VIPs will be jeered or stoned? To induce the Ruritanian government to vote with the United States on a critical issue in the United Nations? To maintain a wide variety of contacts with Ruritanian officials and people for intelligence purposes? For good will? To enable Ruritania to defend itself militarily against a Soviet attack? Or to pay rent for a U. S. air base or communications center in Ruritania? Unfortunately, policy-makers frequently seek (successfully) to avoid stating their objectives with

[23] U. S. Senate Subcommittee on National Security and International Operations, *Memorandum*, 90th Congress, 1st Session (1967); quoted in *New York Times*, August 8, 1967, p. 9; admittedly some of the attitudes expressed in the statement seemed pre-Cambrian.

sufficient clarity to enable the value of their program to be measured and compared with alternative ways of achieving their objectives. If their programs are to be subjected to systems analysis, they will have to state those objectives explicitly. And that will be a real contribution.

Second, he must adapt or develop techniques by which he can determine with reasonable accuracy the costs of the constituent elements of the various programs in each family. He must include not only the initial cost but the continuing cost over the entire period of anticipated U. S. support—not only the cost of building a radio station, but of maintaining and operating it (including keeping the landlord happy).

Third, he must consider other possible ways of attaining the same objectives, and determine their costs.

Fourth, he must develop techniques by which he can measure the prospective effectiveness of each program or alternative. He must deal with three problems in his measurement. (1) He may find that statistics are unreliable or unavailable, in which case he cannot help the policy-maker until an adequate statistical system is developed. (2) He may find that the anticipated benefits of a program are difficult to measure because they are intangible: to create good will, to build understanding, to secure cooperation. He must avoid ignoring them or minimizing their importance simply because he cannot adequately measure them; his greatest temptation is to overemphasize the measurable at the expense of the nonmeasurable. At the same time, he will look for methods by which the currently nonmeasurable will become measurable. (3) He will find that many projects merge U. S. resources with those of the recipient country, or feature joint or parallel action toward a common end. In such cases allocating its proper share of the results to the contribution of each participating country is extremely difficult; a marginal increment of U. S. resources may produce a disproportionately large or disproportionately small increase in output. He must urge further research by those qualified to provide him with that data.

By this time the systems analyst will have developed an input-output model that translates resources into inputs and results into outputs. Obviously, his model will deal only in quantitative terms, although the quantities may be comparative rather than numerical. As he uses his model, he continuously tests it against the real world and modifies the model so that its predicted results approach ever more closely those actually experienced when programs are carried out. He may or may not put his model into a computer; by computer simulation, however, he can use the blinding speed of the computer to try out various modifications in the assumptions built into the model and vary the combinations of inputs to determine the most effective mix. If he cannot fix quantities definitely, the computer permits him the luxury of a series of runs using different values for x and y, and to determine at what point the program ceases to be "cost effective."

The systems analyst will make his recommendation to the policy-maker on the basis of the input-output relationship: cost effectiveness. He must leave to the policy-maker such decisions as what goals are to be sought, how to allocate resources among programs having different rather than similar objectives, and, generally, all choices based on value judgments rather than on objective criteria.

Whatever his recommendation, the systems analyst will meet opposition from those whose programs have suffered as a result of his analyses. In any case he will be accused of neglecting the nonmaterial, nonquantifiable factors which in fact are beyond the scope of systems analysis and fall within the responsibility of his superior, the decision-maker. If he has recommended an alternative that he himself pieced together or originated he will be accused—sometimes correctly—of biased judgment.

No amount of systems analysis can relieve the top-level decision-maker of the necessity of using his own judgment in deciding how to allocate resources between programs designed to achieve different objectives, or in dealing with programs that attain one objective at the cost of interfering with the attainment of another. His systems analysts may tell him that a textile mill will contribute more than a steel mill to solving a country's balance of payments problem. They are unlikely to tell him whether on balance U. S. interests would be better served by in the process strengthening a communist-dominated textile workers' union rather than a neutralist steel workers' union—not to mention giving feed grains to reduce the country's imports. Such questions must remain political decisions.

Modernization: Evaluation and Prospects

By his creation of SIG-IRG and authorization of the Hitch Plan, President Johnson established the framework for a comprehensive system of coordinated planning, budgeting, and executing national security policy, but its future success or failure depends on the leadership of the Secretary of State. He now has most of the authority he needs to discharge his responsibility. National Security Memoradum 341 assigned him primary authority in the field of foreign affairs "to the full extent permitted by law." [24] SIG-IRG equipped him with much of the ma-

---

[24] Previously enacted legislation had assigned certain functions to other officials; for example, the Secretary of the Treasury continued as chairman of the National Advisory Council on International Monetary and Financial Policies. Military forces operating in the field are also exempt from the authority of the Secretary of State.

chinery he needed; full implementation of the Hitch Plan would give him financial control. To exercise it he has only to identify the activities within each department or agency to be brought into the system; he may then initiate the program in so far as budgeting is concerned. (He may still require Presidential support in dealing with a recalcitrant department or agency.) His Latin American IRG is already providing him with a pilot project. The same structure can coordinate planning and programming.

To operate effectively this kind of system, the Secretary needs an assistant secretary of state for planning, programming, and budgeting (ASPPB). Under ASPPB jurisdiction the Secretary should place general responsibility for strategic, contingency, and resource-allocation planning, and for budgeting over the entire field of foreign affairs except for U. S. military expenditures. In many respects similar to the OSD-SA staff, the ASPPB staff would combine the skills of Foreign Service Officers and systems analysts. The assistant secretary himself would sit with SIG, and one of his principal subordinates with each IRG. Civil-military coordination in planning would be simplified by the existing representation of JCS in SIG-IRG.

In strategic and contingency planning, ASPPB should relieve S/P of its task of preparing specific plans such as the NPP and country plans. To replace them, he should establish coordinated requirements for each regional and functional bureau according to which they would prepare plans of that type. He would be directly responsible for preparing general strategic and contingency plans. S/P then could assume a role similar to that of the Council of Economic Advisers; it would concentrate on detached analyses and projections, and on increasing contacts with the world outside government. The Department of State should adopt a firm personnel policy providing for continuing rotation between regional, functional, and ASPPB planning units and key political and economic jobs in the department and allied agencies. After a tour of duty in plans, key personnel would be assigned to important substantive jobs, and vice versa.

In resource-allocation planning and budgeting, ASPPB would make cost-effectiveness studies of programs proposed, submitting his findings to the appropriate IRG, SIG, and the Secretary of State. His role would be advisory only; IRG would have the task of approving or disapproving consolidated budgets for each country or multicountry program.

In the field all budgets for programs for a particular country should be placed under the jurisdiction of the ambassador. While the local SID or USIA mission would prepare its program and budgetary request, it would be subject to the ambassador's approval; the ambassador would forward a consolidated budget to Washington. To do this each embassy should be provided with a trained PPBS officer—but responsible to the ambassador, not to ASPPB. The position of the ambassador vis-à-vis the field missions, and that of the Secretary of State vis-à-vis the other agencies would become analogous to that of the Secretary of Defense in his dealings with ANAF: the operating agencies would submit programs for approval and operate them, but resources would be centrally allocated. The other agencies would resist this more than the supervision established by the Kennedy Letter of 1961, and Congress might feel more control was passing from its hands. Some steps, however, can be taken if the President and Secretary of State see fit.

During 1966 President Johnson took the steps necessary to establish SIG-IRG and FAPS. At the time of this writing it is still too early to appraise their success. Both require vigorous leadership from the Secretary of State and his principal subordinates, which for the most part they have not yet received. No doubt Secretary Rusk has found the burden of Vietnam added to the normally heavy load of his office too heavy to permit much additional activity. Undersecretary Nicholas deB. Katzenbach, a particularly important figure because of his post as chairman of SIG, came to State from the post of Attorney General; he probably preferred to familiarize himself with his general duties before assuming leadership of the new program. Katzenbach moved with all deliberate speed, but by the end of 1967 appeared to be taking an interest in SIG-IRG, at least. He could not, however, carry the entire load personally.

To date Secretary Rusk has failed to give any official the authority and responsibility to act for him or the Undersecretary in implementing these programs. At one time he seemed to be doing so; he announced the appointment of Thomas C. Schelling, Professor of Economics at Harvard, as Assistant Secretary. Partisans of the new systems assumed he had chosen Professor Schelling to oversee installation of the Hitch Plan, and were keenly disappointed a few weeks later when, for no announced reason, he resigned without having taken up his duties. They heard rumors that he had been disappointed in the support he was promised from his superiors; equally serious, that the House Appropriations Subcommittee in one of its fits of penny-wisdom had reduced the budget for his prospective office from the requested $500,000 to zero.

If they are given a chance, SIG-IRG and FAPS will be effective steps in modernizing the national security agencies—and in providing an example for the rest of the national administration. SIG-IRG, with its interagency structure and the leading role of the Department of State, is well designed to permit the President and Secretary of State to plan and manage foreign affairs. FAPS for the first time offers a real prospect of rationalized budgeting in that field. But they will not contribute unless they are used, and they will not be used unless the Secretary of State provides the necessary leadership. They require more careful attention from him in appointments, for Undersecretary, Deputy Undersecretary, Assistant Secretaries, and Country Directors will carry increased responsibilities. And they will require backing both from him and from the President of the United States in carrying out those responsibilities and in dealing with Congress.

They are not yet receiving it.

6

POLITICAL PARTIES

Murray S. Stedman, Jr.

All modern political systems, authoritarian as well as democratic, contain a political party subsystem. To be sure, the differences in function, operation, and purpose among the various subsystems are vast. Yet it is inconceivable that a modern state could exist without some kind of party organization. Interest in this aspect of politics has resulted in the development of a sizable *corpus* dealing with comparative party systems as a field of comparative politics.[1]

The Condition of the Party System

In writing the Constitution in 1787, the Founding Fathers went to great lengths to prevent domination of government by popular majorities. In this respect, the Constitution is not only a preparty document; it is antiparty. Nonetheless, legislative parties were formed in Congress during Washington's administration, and national mass parties came into existence during the Jacksonian era. For all of their prominence during the rest of the nineteenth century, the parties attracted little systematic interest on the part of political philosophers either in the United States or in Britain.

As a result of the rapid advances in social research during the middle decades of the twentieth century, many of the earlier deficiencies in the study of political institutions have been overcome. Analysis of parties has especially benefited from the political behavior approach.[2]

---

[1] On this subject *see* the pioneering study by Maurice Duverger, *Political Parties* (New York: John Wiley & Sons, Inc., 1954; the original French edition appeared in 1951). *See also* Aaron B. Wildavsky, "A Methodological Critique of Duverger's 'Political Parties,' " *Journal of Politics*, XXI (1959), 303-18.

[2] Invoking the term "political behavior" does not, of course, guarantee that particular problems will automatically be solved or even clarified. For some caveats,

THE CHARACTERISTICS OF AMERICAN PARTIES. Even within the United States and the other major democracies, the notion of a political party tends to be, as Frank J. Sorauf has noted, "out of focus." [3] This is largely because the party systems stress different functions. In the democracies the most commonly shared function is that of mobilizing voters behind candidates for public office. Indeed, this is the dominant concern of the major American parties.

A second function of the party is to propagate its ideas and programs, in other words, act as a teacher. As a third function, the parties in the democracies organize, in varying ways, the policy-making machinery of their governments. Lastly, the parties engage in a series of activities that are not overtly "political," for example, the distribution of food packages to the needy at Christmas.

The tone, the style, of a party system is determined by which of the various functions that might be performed are actually stressed in practice. So far as American parties are concerned, the focus is clearly on the electoral function, and it is this emphasis that distinguishes them from the major parties in the other democracies.

Moving from functions to characteristics, we can identify particular features of the American party system that justify calling it unique. A convenient listing of eight such characteristics was developed by Robert A. Dahl.[4] In summary form, the attributes identified by Dahl are these: (1) a two-party system; (2) variability of effective competition between the parties throughout the country; (3) diffusion and decentralization of control; (4) low cohesion (that is, the parties do not show a high degree of solidarity when it comes to voting in legislatures); (5) ideological similarity and issue conflict (that is, the parties do differ on issues, but not in ideology); (6) differences in party followings (this has two aspects: each party draws from every population stratum, but each party also has specialized followings); (7) durability; (8) variability in party support (in national elections, majorities now favor one party, now another).

CHANGES DURING THE LAST TWO DECADES. In looking back over the years since the end of World War II, it is possible to discern these principal changes that have occurred in the landscape of the American party system:

_____

see the papers of a symposium published under the title *The Limits of Behaviorism in Political Science* (Philadelphia: The American Academy of Political and Social Science, October, 1962).

[3] The discussion of party functions follows the analysis in Frank J. Sorauf, *Political Parties in the American System* (Boston: Little, Brown and Company, 1964).

[4] Robert A. Dahl, *Pluralist Democracy in the United States* (Chicago: Rand McNally & Co., 1967), pp. 213-38.

1. The parties are becoming more competitive as the number of one-party states and one-party Congressional districts declines.[5]
2. The South has become increasingly competitive in Presidential and Congressional elections as the Republicans continue to gain strength.[6]
3. The rise of "independent" citizens' groups, such as Citizens for Johnson-Humphrey, has weakened the role of regular party organizations in Presidential campaigns.[7]
4. Minor parties and locally competitive third parties have been disappearing.[8]
5. At the state level there has been a decline in job-oriented parties and an increase in issue-oriented parties.[9]
6. Big-city political machines have declined in power and in some cities have been dramatically overthrown. There has been an accompanying decline in urban politics based on European immigrant groups.
7. The widespread and increasing use of nonpartisan elections in local politics tends to atrophy the state organizations.[10]
8. Television has become a prime factor in shaping the popular images of candidates. The four televised debates between Kennedy and Nixon in the 1960 presidential campaign amounted to a revolutionary innovation in candidate-projection and image-building.[11]
9. The Old Left, consisting of doctrinaire Marxists, has been dying out. The so-called New Left derides ideology, praises "participatory democracy," and could serve as a rallying point for other "alienated" groups.

The above list is not meant to be inclusive. To it could be added various alterations in national party machinery or such innovations as

[5] On this point, see Paul T. David, "The Changing Political Parties," in Continuing Crisis in American Politics, ed. Marian D. Irish (Englewood Cliffs, N.J.: Prentice-Hall, Inc., 1963), p. 48. See also Stephen K. Bailey, "Our National Political Parties," in Political Parties, U.S.A., ed. Robert A. Goldwin (Chicago: Rand McNally & Co., 1961, 1964), p. 19.

[6] Lazer offers the interesting comment that developments in the South are primarily significant because they reflect the transformation on a national scale of party politics. See Henry Lazer, The American Political System in Transition (New York: Thomas Y. Crowell Company, 1967), p. 159.

[7] This point is strongly made in Hugh A. Bone and Austin Ranney, Politics and Voters (New York: McGraw-Hill Book Company, 1963, 1967), pp. 130-31.

[8] Sorauf, op. cit., pp. 32-35.

[9] See John H. Fenton, People and Parties in Politics (Chicago: Scott, Foresman & Company, 1966), pp. 90, 105, 116.

[10] See the comments on "no-party systems" in Fred I. Greenstein, The American Party System and the American People (Englewood Cliffs, N.J.: Prentice-Hall, Inc., 1963), p. 73. Bifactional politics is not an adequate substitute for two-party politics, as Allan P. Sindler has demonstrated in "Bifactional Rivalry as an Alternative to Two-Party Competition in Louisiana," American Political Science Review, XLIX (September, 1955), 641-62.

[11] There is a brief discussion of the Kennedy-Nixon debates in Bone and Ranney, op. cit., pp. 37-38. A Gallup poll taken after the first debate indicated that the debate assisted Kennedy materially. An effective television personality is now considered an invaluable asset in running for office.

the creation in the House of Representatives of the Democratic Study Group.[12] The principal point is that the political landscape has, indeed, changed during the last generation, and change continues.

THE SIGNIFICANCE OF RECENT CHANGES. Few would question the judgment that the developments of the last twenty years have affected political behavior and political attitudes in the United States. But whether the party system as a whole has been seriously altered is a very different kind of proposition. For parts or elements of the system to change or evolve is one thing; it is altogether different for the totality to metamorphose. In the latter case what is at stake is a new relationship between the party system and the other institutions in the political culture.

From this elevated top-of-the-mountain view, it seems evident that the American party system has remained in a fairly consistent relationship with the other institutions that make up the political environment. In the years immediately following World War II the emphasis of the parties was centered on the electoral function, and there it remains. There has been little disposition on the part of the parties to engage seriously in the other functions that are in fact undertaken by the European mass parties.

When examined in terms of the characteristics listed by Dahl, the party situation is somewhat different. Under the specific categories various long-term trends can be observed, for example, differences in party followings. Yet the general characteristics that define the party system have remained, overall, fairly constant during the last generation. The specific changes have not affected, that is to say, the relevance of the categories themselves.

It can be taken, then, as an obvious and established fact that the party system itself has not undergone any revolutionary transformation. Yet it would be a serious mistake to underestimate the very real significance of the changes that have occurred and are occurring. In 1942 E. E. Schattschneider could write: "Decentralization of power is by all odds the most important single characteristic of the American major party; more than anything else this trait distinguishes it from all others." [13] By the mid-1960's this observation had lost a good deal of its earlier germaneness. Returning to the list of particulars previously examined, two overriding trends can be highlighted: the increasing competitiveness of the parties and the continuing nationalization of issues. Both of these trends point in logic and in practice toward an increasing centralization of the parties. It is therefore no longer accurate to

[12] For an excellent account of the Democratic Study Group, see John Bibby and Roger Davidson, On Capitol Hill (New York: Holt, Rinehart & Winston, Inc., 1967), pp. 156-67.
[13] E. E. Schattschneider, Party Government (New York: Holt, Rinehart & Winston, Inc., 1942), p. 129.

consider the national parties merely a coterie of state organizations. The national parties have embarked on the road from federalization to nationalization. Though the distance to be traversed is considerable, the direction of march is quite clear, and so is the momentum.

ASSESSMENT OF THE SYSTEM. Fred I. Greenstein has suggested three basic questions that may be asked regarding any American political institution. Does the institution contribute to the degree to which the political system is democratic? Does it foster, or does it hamper, the stability of the system? Does it affect the adequacy of governmental policy-making? [14] He subsequently applies the criteria of democracy, stability, and policy-making to political parties. By these standards he found that the parties are least satisfactory as they relate to policy-making, that they have in fact encouraged political stability, and that they have been most effective in providing for popular control of leaders.[15]

How one evaluates the American party system depends in large part on which of the criteria devised by Greenstein are to be stressed. Critics of the national parties have focused their attention on the criteria of popular control of government and policy-making. Defenders of the parties as they are have stressed the criterion of political stability.

Going beyond this, Edward C. Banfield argues that a political system is an "accident" and that it is mostly "luck" if it works at all. He asserts: "To meddle with the structure and operation of a successful political system is therefore the greatest foolishness that men are capable of." [16] But this weighted statement is unduly pessimistic, for the historical record does not support anything like this degree of determinism.

It is the thesis of this study that American national parties are moving steadily toward increased centralization, which means that they are becoming more and more Presidentially oriented and dominated. The eventual development of strong Presidential parties is, therefore, not in question. The real issue is what kind of Presidential party will triumph. There are two possibilities—a personalized and temporary Presidential party, or an institutionalized and permanent one. As will be demonstrated, both from the point of view of the public welfare and also of democratic theory, it is preferable that the institutionalized party emerge as the prevailing type.

Toward a New Party System

Dissatisfied with the present political parties because they fail to meet one or more of the traditional democratic criteria, many political

[14] Greenstein, *op. cit.*, p. 2.
[15] *Ibid.*, pp. 99-102.
[16] Edward C. Banfield, "In Defense of the American Party System," in Robert A. Goldwin (ed.), *op. cit.*, p. 38.

scientists have speculated on ways to change the party system. But it would be erroneous to imagine that criticism of the existing arrangement is an academic monopoly. On the contrary, some of the strongest condemnation has come from top-level national statesmen and politicians, for example, Presidents Franklin D. Roosevelt and Dwight D. Eisenhower and Senator Barry Goldwater.

But whether practitioners or academicians, critics of the existing party system have found themselves in one of two camps. One group has advanced what is called the party-government doctrine. The other has endorsed the Presidential-party thesis. Though it is not plausible to hold to both theories at the same time, it is quite reasonable for an individual critic to shift from one position to another. In actual fact, the most famous exponent of both theories—Woodrow Wilson—shifted his support during a twenty-year period from the responsible-party idea to the Presidential-party concept. What Wilson wrote in two books on American politics has served as the basis for all subsequent discussion of party reorganization.

THE PARTY GOVERNMENT DOCTRINE. In the summer of 1884, while a graduate student at Johns Hopkins University, Woodrow Wilson completed his book *Congressional Government*. He was then twenty-eight years of age, and had returned to academic pursuits following an unsuccessful year of law practice in Atlanta. The principal emphasis of the book, first published in 1885, was the contrast between Congressional and parliamentary governments. Wilson stressed the basic difference between the two forms in his Preface: "Congressional government is committee government; Parliamentary government is government by a responsible Cabinet Ministry." [17]

Throughout the book Wilson minimized government by Congressional committees and accorded high praise to the British form of parliamentary government under a strong cabinet. In doing so, he very ably stated the case for what later came to be called the party government doctrine. A good illustration of his thinking follows immediately upon a paragraph extolling the high calibre of debates in the House of Commons:

> Our congressional debates, on the contrary, have no tithe of this interest, because they have no tithe of such significance and importance. The committee reports, upon which the debates take place, are backed by neither party; they represent merely the recommendations of a small body of members belonging to both parties, and are quite as likely to divide the vote of the party to which the majority of the Committee belong as they are to meet with opposition from the other side of the

[17] Woodrow Wilson, *Congressional Government* (New York: Meridian Books, 1956), p. 24.

chamber. If they are carried, it is no party triumph; if they are lost, it is no party discomfiture.[18]

Specifically concerning the relationship of the national to the Congressional parties, Wilson declared:

> In a word, the national parties do not act in Congress under the restraint of a sense of immediate responsibility. Responsibility is spread thin; and no vote or debate can gather it. It rests not so much upon parties as upon individuals; and it rests upon individuals in no such way as would make it either just or efficacious to visit upon them the iniquity of any legislative act.[19]

Why, in *Congressional Government*, did Wilson refrain from proposing cabinet government on the British model as the solution to the difficulties of American government—a recommendation he had made in an article only a year earlier? His stated reason for refusing to repeat his previous conclusion was that he was "pointing out facts, diagnosing, not prescribing remedies." Even so, the book, as Walter Lippmann has observed, "still points toward Cabinet Government as the remedy." [20] It also explicitly embraces the proposition that responsible, centralized national parties are far superior to decentralized parties as instrumentalities for governing.

The views of the early Wilson toward responsible party government have been echoed by latter commentators, especially by those interested in substituting a parliamentary for the Presidential regime. But the most successful exposition of the doctrine in modern times took place in 1942 with the publication by E. E. Schattschneider of a hard-hitting book entitled *Party Government*. Justly considered a classic, the work argued that ". . . party government (party centralization) is the most practicable and feasible solution of the problem of organizing American democracy." [21]

No such inhibitions or hesitations were in evidence in a brief 1950 publication entitled *Toward a More Responsible Two-Party System*, a *Report* of the Committee on Political Parties of the American Political Science Association.[22] Interestingly enough, Schattschneider was chairman of the sixteen-member committee, and he was one of the five members, but not chairman, of the actual drafting committee.

Despite the eminence of the members of the committee, its *Report*

[18] *Ibid.*, pp. 78-79.
[19] *Ibid.*, p. 79.
[20] Walter Lippmann, "Introduction" to Wilson, *op. cit.*, p. 13.
[21] Schattschneider, *op. cit.*, p. 207.
[22] Committee on Political Parties of the American Political Science Association, *Toward a More Responsible Two-Party System*, supplement to *American Political Science Review*, XLIV (September, 1950).

received a very mixed reception. It was attacked both for its specific substantive recommendations and, more significantly, for its philosophical assumptions. Critics tended to view some of the proposals, for example, the extension of House terms to four years, as suggestive rather than definitive. Therefore, ideas of this type were viewed as being negotiable, not as immovable items on a set agenda. Much more extensive, and more damaging to the committee, was the criticism that charged that the *Report* reflected an immature or erroneous understanding of democratic theory. On this score the fiercest opponents of the committee showed little mercy.[23]

Nearly twenty years after its publication the CPP *Report* continues to provoke academic interest, primarily because it serves a didactic purpose in analyzing American parties. Occasionally some of the heat of earlier criticism is rekindled as a commentator concentrates his attention on the theoretical underpinnings of the document.[24] Aside from this modest interest on the part of scholars, the doctrine of party government is today moribund. Politicians, in general, have shown a marked unwillingness to embrace the idea, while the public continues to be blissfully unaware of the doctrine's existence.

THE PRESIDENTIAL-PARTY DOCTRINE. Whether because of his admiration for President Grover Cleveland—as Walter Lippmann has suggested—or for other reasons as well, Woodrow Wilson in the years immediately following 1885 drastically changed his earlier view on the relationship between Congress and the President. By 1908 this evolution in Wilson's thinking had been completed. His new assessment was published in detail in a collection of lectures published under the title *Constitutional Government in the United States.*[25]

[23] The literature dealing with the CPP *Report* is extensive. Among the most widely cited of the critical articles were the following: Julius Turner, "Responsible Parties: A Dissent from the Floor," *American Political Science Review*, XLV (1951), 143-52; Austin Ranney, "Toward a More Responsible Two-Party System: A Commentary," *American Political Science Review*, XLV (1951), 488-99; Murray S. Stedman, Jr., and Herbert Sontoff, "Party Responsibility—A Critical Inquiry," *Western Political Quarterly*, IV (1951), 454-68; William Goodman, "How Much Political Party Centralization Do We Want?" *Journal of Politics*, XIII (1951), 536-61.

[24] For example, one recent critic says that the argument of the *Report* rests on a "naïve theory of democracy." *See* Sorauf, *op. cit.*, p. 122. Another recent critic, Allan P. Sindler, in *Political Parties in the United States* (New York: St. Martin's Press, Inc., 1966), p. 104, observes shrewdly that the real target of the committee members was the governmental system, not the party system. Another recent if brief analysis may be found in Roger H. Davidson, David M. Kovenock, and Michael K. O'Leary, *Congress in Crisis: Politics and Congressional Reform* (Belmont, Calif.: Wadsworth Publishing Co., 1966), p. 40. A sharp critique is offered by Banfield, *op. cit.*, pp. 32-36.

[25] Woodrow Wilson, *Constitutional Government in the United States* (New York: Columbia University Press, 1908; Columbia paperback edition, 1961).

The general theme of the 1908 book was that the center of governing power in the national government had shifted from Congress to the President. The implications of this power change fascinated Wilson, particularly as they pointed toward the popular expectation of Presidential leadership in matters of public policy.

A secondary but continuing theme in the Wilson lectures was the demand to increase the President's authority over his own party. While party was only one of many sources of Presidential power, it was one which ought to be developed to its full potential. In making this case for leadership by the President over his own party, Wilson made it clear that sheer aggrandizement of Presidential authority for its own sake was not the issue. What was involved was the capacity of the President to persuade members of his own party in Congress to support his programs and policies. It seemed only reasonable to Wilson that a President elected on a national program should have the machinery at his disposal to execute that program.[26]

During his eight years in the White House, Woodrow Wilson tried mightily, and with some success, to apply in practice his concept of using party as a vehicle for Presidential leadership. But his successors—Harding, Coolidge, and Hoover—subscribed neither to the precept of Presidential initiative nor to the doctrine of strong Presidential parties. Franklin D. Roosevelt revived the Wilsonian practice of strong executive leadership. Yet even he was not notably successful—except for his first two years in office—in converting titular leadership of the Democratic party into Presidential control over that party in Congress. The tradition of strong executives was continued by Truman, Kennedy, and Johnson, while Eisenhower reverted to the weak-executive concept.

As it turned out, the case for strengthening the Presidential parties has best been stated in recent years not by one of the strong Presidents but by a leading political scientist. In a series of influential books, James MacGregor Burns has propounded the thesis that Presidential government based on strong Presidentially oriented parties is necessary if government is to deal satisfactorily with modern problems.[27] This is not the place to enter into the complexities of Burns' argument, for his books are readily available. What must be noted here is that the Wilsonian thesis of 1908—that expounded in *Constitutional Government*—has been updated, elaborated, refined, and given wide current circulation by Professor Burns.

[26] On these points, *see ibid.*, especially Chap. 8, "Party Government in the United States."

[27] *See* the following works by James MacGregor Burns: *Congress on Trial* (New York: Harper and Row, Publishers, 1949); *The Deadlock of Democracy: Four-Party Politics in America* (Englewood Cliffs, N.J.: Prentice-Hall, Inc., 1963); *Presidential Government: The Crucible of Leadership* (Boston: Houghton Mifflin Company, 1965).

CENTRALIZATION OF THE NATIONAL PARTIES. The assumption that more centralization would improve the capacity of the national parties to fulfill their expected role and would therefore be a desirable development is today widely accepted. Yet the demurrer of the late Morton Grodzins, a distinguished University of Chicago political scientist, must be noted.[28] He valued localism and linked its survival to decentralized parties. In particular, Grodzins asserted that federalism makes it possible for various groups and individuals to have ready access to administrators and legislators.[29] He maintained that the ability of individuals and groups to take "multiple cracks" at the national government on behalf of local groups would be hindered by strong parties.[30]

Of the changes that have brought about shifts in the nature of social conflicts and deeply affected party politics, the following are noteworthy: the assimilation into the American matrix of millions of European immigrants; the new immigration from Latin America and Puerto Rico; the decline of sectionalism and its accompanying political-economic struggles; increasing industrialization; increasing urbanization; the Negro revolution, in its civil rights, economic, and social aspects; the growing militarization stemming from the Vietnam war.

As a result of these and related social changes, there have been profound shifts in the attitudes and expectations of the general public. Both politicians and the electorate have been moving, even if slowly, in the direction of accepting greater party centralization in the face of the changing social situation.[31]

REALIGNMENT OF INTEREST GROUPS. The relationship of interest groups to parties has a direct bearing on the degree of centralization in the parties. The functions of interest groups in American politics have been analyzed exhaustively by scholars as well as journalists, but the relationship of such groups to the parties has been less adequately examined.[32] In his celebrated *Party Government*, Schattschneider developed the thesis that the national parties and the leading interest groups were natural and implacable rivals. In a later work, *The Semisovereign People*, he amplified on this theme.[33]

In his earlier analysis, Schattschneider postulated that the future of

[28] Morton Grodzins, *"Party and Government in the United States,"* in *op. cit.*, ed. Goldwin, pp. 102-36.

[29] *Ibid.*, beginning at p. 106.

[30] *Ibid.*, p. 136.

[31] Bailey, *op. cit.*, pp. 15-19, lists the principal changes as of 1959.

[32] See Abraham Holtzman, *Interest Groups and Lobbying* (New York: Crowell-Collier & Macmillan, Inc., 1966), for an excellent assessment of the functions of interest groups.

[33] Schattschneider, *op. cit.*; *The Semisovereign People* (New York: Holt, Rinehart & Winston, Inc., 1960).

American politics would be determined by the outcome of a triangular tug of war. The participants in this struggle were identified as the national or Presidential parties, the pressure groups, and the state and local bosses and organizations. The locale of the warfare was the United States Congress. It was to the general interest of the American people, Schattschneider contended, that the Presidential parties eventually emerge as victors in the struggle.

Returning to the same subject in 1960, Schattschneider then observed that the issue had not been resolved in the preceding eighteen years. The question remained as to whether "pressure politics" or "party politics" would triumph. He repeated his earlier conviction that the party ought to be made into a principal instrument for social change.[34]

Why is it that American interest groups may properly be considered rivals of the national parties? The answer lies in the nonpartisan character of the leading interest groups. Lacking formal ties to either major party, the groups are able, theoretically, at least, to play a balance-of-power, bargaining kind of politics. They offer their support to the party that, quite simply, makes the higher bid. In this way, the interest groups, in pursuit of their own limited ends, lessen the chances for a party to pursue a consistent policy. The greater the ability of the interest groups to play one party against the other, the lesser become the party's chances to provide leadership in policy formulation. The net result of this process has been to enfeeble the major parties.

If this analysis is correct, one effective way to strengthen the major parties would be to realign the major interest groups. Ideally, there would be a relatively stable cluster of interest groups associated with each national party. As a result, there would be an approximation of the relationship between party and interest group that obtains in Britain. Clearly such a development would immensely strengthen the national parties. It would also tend to increase rationality in voting by improving the electorate's perception of the class and social basis of American politics.[35]

THE WEAPON OF FINANCE. Proponents of stronger national parties, ranging from President Lyndon B. Johnson to Professor James MacGregor Burns, have recognized the potential role of finance in bringing

---

[34] Schattschneider is very critical of the group theory of politics. See Chap. 2, "The Scope and Bias of the Pressure System," in *The Semisovereign People*, pp. 20-46.

[35] On the subject generally, see Seymour M. Lipset, *Political Man: The Social Bases of Politics* (Garden City, N.Y.: Doubleday & Company, Inc., 1960). The thesis that the American voter makes a rational choice in terms of his perceived self-interest is presented in V. O. Key, Jr., *The Responsible Electorate* (Cambridge, Mass.: Harvard University Press, 1966). Key died before the work was finished. It was completed by Milton C. Cummings, Jr.

about centralized control. In contrast, the general public has been more concerned with the rising costs of electoral contests—some $200 million in 1964.[36] Television has been especially expensive.[37]

In 1949 Burns singled out finance as a potential means for controlling party machinery.[38] Ten years later Stephen K. Bailey argued that national party financing of Congressional campaigns, by reducing a candidate's dependency on "local money," would strengthen the national parties.[39] More recently, Paul T. David has endorsed the Burns-Bailey thesis for developing more centralized parties.[40] President Kennedy appointed a commission to study the whole subject of party financing, but did not seek legislative enactment of the commission's recommendations.[41]

In 1966 President Johnson asked Congress to enact a tax-incentive plan for political contributions. Later in the same year Congress went a good deal further than the President had proposed by endorsing a plan whereby taxpayers could earmark, if they wished, one dollar each from income taxes to help pay for Presidential campaigns. Expected to raise up to $100 million per year for the parties, the law never took effect since Congress suspended its operation pending further study. A year later President Johnson presented another proposal, this time calling for direct Treasury subsidies in Presidential campaigns to cover the costs of radio and television, advertising, literature, and travel. The amount of the subsidies would be determined by Congress every four years when it appropriated funds. Major parties were to share equally, but minor parties could qualify for proportionate shares.

In Congressional debates over the poroposal it was recognized at once that President Johnson's plan, if enacted, would enormously strengthen the Presidential wing of the national parties.[42] In order to make the proposal more palatable, the Senate Finance Committee added to the measure a provision for direct Federal financing of Senatorial contests.

[36] Herbert E. Alexander, *Financing the 1964 Campaign* (Princeton, N.J.: Citizens' Research Foundation, 1966), p. 13. In 1960 the overall total for all offices stood at about $175 million. For that year total national level campaign costs were calculated by Alexander to be $34.8 million. Comparable data were not available for 1964.

[37] Herbert E. Alexander, Stimson Bullitt, and Hyman H. Goldin, "The High Costs of TV Campaigns," *Television Quarterly*, V, No. 1 (Winter, 1966), 48.

[38] Burns, *Congress on Trial*, p. 200.

[39] Bailey, *op. cit.*, p. 10.

[40] David, *op. cit.*, pp. 57-61.

[41] President's Commission on Campaign Costs, *Financing Presidential Campaigns* (Washington, D.C.: Government Printing Office, 1962), pp. 4-5. The commission was chaired by Alexander Heard, author of *The Costs of Democracy* (Garden City, N.Y.: Doubleday & Company, Inc., 1962), the leading work on party finance. Research director was Herbert E. Alexander.

[42] *New York Times*, June 12, 1967, p. 41.

Meanwhile, a parallel bill was under committee consideration in the House. There matters rested at the end of the first session of the Ninetieth Congress.

THE SHAPE OF A MODERNIZED PARTY SYSTEM. In another connection, the President's Committee on Administrative Management (headed by Louis Brownlow) used these dramatic words in its report submitted on January 8, 1937: "The President needs help." Though the Brownlow Committee was concerned with giving the President adequate staff assistance, its warning may profitably be reiterated today in connection with political parties. The President does need help if we are to avoid the development of highly personalized national political machines when he acts—in Rossiter's phrase—as Chief of Party.[43]

Paradoxically, it is precisely because the national Presidential party is institutionally weak that the President is driven to build up a highly personalized following. Given the feeble condition of the national parties, the President has little choice if he wishes to exercise—as did Truman, Kennedy, and Johnson, but not Eisenhower—strong programmatic leadership. The vacuum in leadership is filled not so much by local politicians and interest groups, as Schattschneider had feared, as it is by the President's personal following.

A personal or temporary national Presidential party—what we normally have—is characterized by the following attributes: in the President's party, a large degree of dependence upon the personality of the President; in the opposition party, an ill-defined, shifting leadership; weak party institutions; little party authority; low degree of party discipline in Congress; capricious financing; absence of long-range planning.

In contrast, an institutionalized or permanent national Presidential party would have these characteristics: the sharing of decision-making power between the President and other party leaders; permanent leadership in the opposition party; strong central party machinery; reliable and ample financing; long-range planning; a high degree of party discipline in Congress. An institutionalized kind of Presidential party would give the President a consistent and continuing base of support for his program. This is now lacking. In addition, the important decisions would, in reality, be shared decisions, in somewhat the same manner as the decisions of the British Prime Minister represent a collective judgment.

A modernized party system would have these leading features: institutionalized national Presidential parties (including a well-organized opposition party); professionalized party leadership; fairly clear programmatic differences between the major national parties; interdependence of national and state parties.

[43] Clinton Rossiter, *The American Presidency*, rev. ed.; New York: New American Library, 1960), p. 28.

A modernized party system would include the Congress, of course, as well as the Presidency within its scope of operations. It would be reasonable to anticipate a much higher degree of cooperation than is now customary between the President and his own party in the legislature. This would come about in part because the Presidential party would develop various sanctions to be used against chronic dissidents in Congress. Finally, the chances would increase vastly for the enactment into public law of the President's principal proposals.

The Pace of Development

Modernization of the American party system requires above all the strengthening of the national Presidential parties. In this process the crucial element is the centralization of decision-making power at the topmost level of the parties. In estimating both the direction and the speed of development, it is important first to compare the factors that work for change with those that favor stability.

FACTORS WORKING TOWARD MODERNIZATION. Of the factors tending to bring about party modernization, the most frequently remarked upon is social change itself. To go from the general to the specific, social change affects the political environment, which in turn affects the party system. In the impact of social change upon the political culture, the most significant development of the last two decades has been the continuing nationalization of issues and of interests. Though less responsive to social change than other national political institutions, the parties have by no means been immune, as Stephen K. Bailey has clearly demonstrated.[44] In this manner, the nationalization of issues has contributed to the modernization of the parties.

Just as the total political culture affects specific institutions, so may specific institutions, in this case, the parties, affect the total political environment. One of the earliest authorities to direct attention to this relationship was Woodrow Wilson. In 1908 in *Constitutional Government*, he predicted that the parties were about to assume a positive role in directing national policy. After commenting on the debilitating effects of the Civil War upon the health of the parties, he declared:

> But with changing generations feelings change. We are coming now to look upon our parties once more as instruments for progressive action, as means for handling the affairs of a new age. Sentimental reminiscence is less dominant over us. We are ready to study new uses for our parties and to adapt them to new standards and principles.[45]

[44] Bailey, *op. cit.*, pp. 19-20.
[45] Wilson, *op. cit.* (1961 ed.), p. 221.

Underlying Wilson's general analysis is his premise that an increase in party competition will result in an increase in party centralization. This premise remains sound even if Wilson's specific prediction was premature.[46] As has been noted, since 1945 competitiveness has gone up markedly.

Lastly, there are several intraparty trends that could affect party centralization. Of the various developments, the most interesting and the most potentially significant relates to finance. It does not take the wisdom of Solomon to realize that campaigns will become increasingly expensive. If the additional funds to meet these expenses are simply to be divided between national and local parties in the present ratio, no great power shift may be expected. But if additional funds are awarded disproportionately to the Presidential wings of the national parties, power will instantly flow in their direction. Because the stakes are very high, the battle over who controls the distribution of additional funds will be hard fought.

FACTORS RETARDING MODERNIZATION. Three principal factors operate in opposition to the construction of modernized parties. The first is "localism," which includes insulation from social change, isolation from national political trends, and the protection of vested local economic interests.

A second factor is inertia, the conviction that parties either are not or should not become instruments for social change.

Then there is a third factor that hinders the development of fully modernized parties. This is the belief that personalized Presidential parties are superior to institutionalized Presidential parties. In this view, the Presidential party is largely the extension of the personality of its leader, and its success is dependent upon elements of personality. In one form or other, both Senator Robert F. Kennedy and Professor Richard E. Neustadt hold to this view.[47]

THE PROSPECTS FOR MODERNIZATION. On balance, the trend in the American party system has been toward centralization of the national parties. Though slow, the movement has been steady. Further change seems overwhelmingly probable as the social environment of the country evolves and as the political culture reacts. A number of factors, however, could produce a very quick thrust in the direction of strengthening the Presidential parties. Among them the most likely is the centralization of finance.

[46] For a summary of the evidence on the competition-centralization relationship, see David, op. cit., pp. 53-64.
[47] See Richard E. Neustadt, Presidential Power (New York: John Wiley & Sons, Inc., 1960), for a development of this thesis.

7

THE MODERNIZATION OF
AMERICAN FEDERALISM

Charles E. Gilbert and David G. Smith

The summer of 1967 produced a number of newspaper columns like the following:

> There is one fortunate comment that can be made about the ghetto riots and that cannot be made about many of our other distresses at home and abroad: We know what is wrong and we know what to do about it. . . . Why then is the urgent and the obvious not done? The answer is that our form of government makes wise, preventive, sustained action almost impossible.
>
> Our Constitution is over-praised. Its central feature of "checks and balances" is really a host of vetoes—not unlike the veto in the UN Security Council—granted to districts and states and regions. This feature makes it very hard to get action and very easy to prevent action.
>
> It was a very clever system for inducing 13 separate sovereignties to amalgamate in 1789. And during the past century, when we were a nation of very diverse regions, it had some justifications. But today, when California watches the same TV and buys hamburgers from the same chain as does Rhode Island, it has become an impediment.
>
> The system is based on a profound distrust of strong executive power. Yet it is hard to think of a case when the Republic was menaced by strong executive action, whereas the papers each day are full of cases in which we are menaced by lack of effective executive action. The ghettos provide the most conspicuous current example.

CHARLES E. GILBERT is Professor of Political Science at Swarthmore College, where he has taught since 1955. He is the author of *Governing the Suburbs* and coauthor of *Planning Municipal Investment*. He has written numerous articles on local government, public administration, and political theory.

DAVID G. SMITH is Professor of Political Science at Swarthmore College, where he has taught since 1957. He is the author of *The Convention and the Constitution* and coauthor of *Political Science: an Introduction*. He has written widely on political theory. Professors Gilbert and Smith have been engaged in a study of administration of the social services in the Department of Health, Education, and Welfare. This essay draws heavily on that study at various points.

Contrast the British system which gives the executive, once elected, full power to carry out its program without hindrance. After a few years, the executive must go back to the people for a confirming mandate or a rejection, which then lets a different executive come in and carry out a program.

In America, the executive branch of government is the one geared and motivated to act in the interest of the whole nation. The legislative branch is really a collection of regional ambassadors, few of them from the ghettos, most of them anxious to manifest a small-minded thrift that will appeal to their well-off constituencies.

The faulty link in the circuit of American purpose is the strip of Pennsylvania Avenue between the White House and Capitol Hill. Until somebody can make that part of the circuit function, the cities will go on exploding.

Indeed, we may soon see the growth of an American Viet Cong in the ghettos and a state of permanent guerilla war developing inside our own nation.[1]

Federalism and the separation of powers have long been linked in the minds of critics of American political institutions as barriers to governmental action in behalf of popular majorities—and, in the minds of their supporters, as bulwarks of pluralism. These two forms of governmental decentralization are also connected historically and operationally in the role that states and localities play in our representative system: states in the Senate, localities in the House of Representatives, and both in the party system at large. Each form of decentralization has tended to support the other.

Political evaluations of these two institutions tend to vary with partisan vantage. The centralizing and plebiscitarian aspects of the Presidency encourage the national minority party to repair to positions in Congress and the states, from which it can rebuild. But ideological differences within and between the parties are equally important: in the years since the northern wing of the Democratic Party and the eastern wing of the Republican Party have controlled the Presidency, Southern Democrats and Republicans from the central states have collaborated in the defense of old-fashioned federalism.

Federalism is certain to be a leading issue in the "modernization" of American politics for at least the remainder of this century. Civil rights legislation and "Great Society" programs have recently altered the balance (never static) of political influence and of legal, fiscal, and administrative responsibilities within the federal system. The trend toward public action on problems once considered private, the need for delivery of complex public services to people where they live, the new mobility and growing concentration of the American population, and the probable

[1] Howard K. Smith, *Philadelphia Sunday Bulletin*, July 30, 1967.

demand for local participation in the development of programs all mean that federalism and intergovernmental relations will lie at the crux of many disputes that earlier centered on the separation of powers or the party system. Ironically, the regional and partisan divisions on this general issue are probably sharper now under a southern President than they have been since the Depression. The Republican Congressional leadership has recently declared federalism—centralization *versus* reliance on the states—to be the major issue of principle between the parties; and members of *both* parties in Congress (both progressives and conservatives) have joined in amending a number of administrative proposals so as to provide a larger role for the states in them.

In the following sections of this paper we shall attempt a selective review of some of the issues in federalism. We begin with the broad, theoretical questions and then turn to some of the details of structure.

The Functions of Federalism

If one is to evaluate American federalism it makes sense to begin with the grand issues traditionally involved in it. Even if these issues cannot be resolved—and we cannot resolve them—they help to illuminate ideologies. To simplify, let us say that two kinds of value conflicts figure in debates about federalism. These are (1) constitutional values and (2) policy values.

The *constitutional* values at issue in federalism can be broadly expressed as liberty, equality, and order (or agreement). Federalism is classically said to promote *liberty* by creating more or less autonomous centers of decision and allegiance, thus affording protection against consolidation of power. One traditional objection to this argument is that the social and economic bases of dispersion of power are far more important than the constitutional bases: that the latter add little or nothing to the former, and may even derive from the former; that, whatever the historical role of the states, they are hardly centers of popular loyalty today. Another counterargument asserts that consolidation of power is something to be furthered rather than feared, since it lends itself far better to effective, accountable public action than does decentralization.[2]

Federalism is also said to promote *equality* by providing more centers of access to government, by including more groups in the policy decisions of several jurisdictions, by adapting policies to the demands of various interests. Actually, inclusiveness may be a better term than

[2] William H. Riker, *Federalism: Origin, Operation, Significance* (Boston: Little, Brown and Company, 1964), is a harsh and trenchant criticism of federalism based in part on this point of view.

equality to describe the desideratum in this argument, since it is the opportunity for influence rather than parity of condition that is sought. Again, there is a tendency for political processes to be more broadly responsive in large governmental units than in small ones, so that national policy-making is usually inclusive of more interests proportionally than state and local policy-making is; and, if the evidence for this point is impressionistic, the theoretical basis for it is certainly plausible.[3] The second counterargument asserts that in strict logic decentralized decision-making either favors minorities, both local and national, over majorities at either level, or else it doesn't matter; and that, in the first case, it tends to undermine equality.[4]

Finally, federalism is commonly thought to contribute to political *order*, agreement, or stability in two ways, both emphasized by James Madison in the *Federalist* papers: first, by breaking the tyrannical or intolerant force of "faction"; second, by confining some irritating and divisive issues to parts of the nation instead of favoring the accumulation of issues and discords at one center and in the nation at large. Here, too, there are strong objections: that national majorities are sometimes denied the right to make policy because of our federal division of sovereignty; that impediments to majority rule imposed by federal institutions tend in themselves to foster intolerance and dissension by frustrating majorities and entrenching minorities; and that the consolidation of politics at the national level is as likely to favor a pluralistic politics of bargaining and agreement as an accumulation of divisions and bitterness.[5]

This summary statement hardly does justice to the arguments on either side, but it is full enough to illustrate a basic point: that no final assessment of American federalism in terms of its consistency with democratic political theory is in sight. Some of the issues are philosophical: they depend on definitions of "liberty" and "equality," which tend to take on different meanings on different sides of the argument. Some of the issues are entailed in empirical questions that cannot be answered conclusively: for instance, to what extent the decentralization of governmental powers promotes, and responds to, social pluralism, by which we mean a relatively high degree of group autonomy of government and of variation among group interests. Our own view is that American federalism probably makes a positive contribution to pluralism, and

[3] *Cf.* Grant McConnell, *Private Power and American Democracy* (New York: Alfred A. Knopf, Inc., 1966), and Charles E. Gilbert, "Two Academic Models for Remodeling Local Government," in L. K. Caldwell (ed.), *Politics and Public Affairs* (Bloomington, Ind.: Institute of Training for Public Service, 1962).
[4] Riker, *op. cit.*, Chap. 6.
[5] *Ibid.* See also McConnell, *op. cit.*, and, for the argument on pluralism, Robert A. Dahl, *A Preface to Democratic Theory* (Chicago: University of Chicago Press, 1956).

that it thus promotes liberty in the negative sense of autonomy and equality in the limited sense of inclusiveness; but we cannot prove it.

The policy issues in federalism are extensions of the arguments just rehearsed. Three claims are commonly made for federalism as a way of enhancing the quality of policy and improving the performance of government. The first of these is the well-known Holmes-Brandeis view that the federal system has established, in the states, a set of laboratories for experiments in public policy, and of incentives to experiment in the variation that obtains among the cultures and economies of the states. This was a more plausible argument early in the twentieth century than it is today, when disparity is a better term than variation for the relative conditions of the states, and when federal grants-in-aid dominate and constrain state policy-making in many fields. Still, we shall argue below that the pooling of grants, the use of projects grants, and the adoption of bloc grants all build on the possibility of experimentation.

Secondly, there is the closely related argument that federalism, by favoring variation in policy among several governments, provides better adaptation to the wants of populations than a single, central government can. It will be observed that this argument is close kin to the one about agreement through division of issues discussed above. If minorities or special interests are regionally or territorially distributed, then it can be demonstrated that separate sovereignties are more likely to maximize the satisfactions of these interests, although—as William Riker has pointed out—this demonstration takes no account of the frustration of national majorities or local (state) minorities.[6] On the limited test to be met in this argument a federal system is probably superior to the decentralization of policy to units of a unitary government because the former provides more independent political processes within the constituent units.

Finally, it has been said that federalism enhances governmental "efficiency" in the sense of close correspondence of policy to individual wants. The argument is not precisely the same as the foregoing one: its central point is that small governmental units provide better satisfaction of individual wants than larger ones do because voters are better able to assess the costs and benefits to them of governmental action. In this argument the assumption is that individuals act like sovereign consumers in economic theory, allocating their dollars to public or private purposes in terms of personal satisfaction; and that governments rendering discrete, clearly definable services decided on by simple political processes facilitate voter choices that are rational in this strictly economic sense.[7] On the other hand, the argument makes little allowance for complex programmatic issues, including those of income re-

[6] J. R. Pennock, "Federal and Unitary Government—Disharmony and Frustration," *Behavioral Science*, IV (1959), 147ff.; Riker, *op. cit.*
[7] The point is discussed with references in Gilbert, *op. cit.*, Note 3.

distribution; for the ways in which these are likely to be related to more complex political organization, governmental leadership of opinion, and administrative effectiveness; or for the extent to which the policies (and especially failures of governments to act) affect the rest of the nation's population beyond state boundaries. The argument tends to emphasize concrete benefits and expenditures instead of general ideals and programs. And, like the other two positions just reviewed, it also tends to discount "externalities," or the effects of state policy on the rest of the nation.

The most important abstract arguments for and against American federalism have now been summarized, however inconclusively. Our own position is that they justify a preference for federalism today, even if its historical role as a compromise measure in nation-making is no longer necessary in the United States. We would emphasize the role of governmental divisions in supporting socioeconomic pluralism; but we also note that regional variation is probably diminishing in many respects, while externalities are increasing.[8] Thus the balance of centralization-decentralization may appropriately change. Such change may well affect "federal" institutions within the central government, such as Congressional seniority, the Senate, or the Electoral College, though these institutions may still perform other important functions. We cannot analyze these questions here.

The Potentialities of the States

It is easy to confuse federalism with decentralization in general. But the fifty states are the constitutional base of American federalism. It is the states collectively that create dissatisfaction with federalism. No one objects to local governments in principle; many object to the states. Local governments promise a distinctively voluntary, broadly participative political process; but the states do not. Functions of local government must be performed within easy reach of people in their places of employment and residence; those of the states are hardly distinguishable from the nation in this respect. Critics of American federalism often strongly favor decentralization in something like local "home rule," especially for urban areas, but condemn the states for both meddling in and neglecting the affairs of local government.

The peculiar aspect of traditional federalism lies in the constitutional and political roles of the states as autonomous decision-makers and as regulators of local governments. The prospects for "modernization" of federalism depend fundamentally on the prospects of the states—which

[8] *See* the analysis of "externalities" in George F. Break, *Intergovernmental Fiscal Relations in the United States* (Washington, D.C.: The Brookings Institution, 1967).

are logically three, though each is complex and all are not mutually exclusive. First, the states may wither, not away, but to units relatively low in popular esteem and political autonomy, dwindling to little more than an administrative role within a federal system that is increasingly a legal fiction. Second, the place of the states on balance—allowing for wide variation among particular functions and individual states—may remain about what it is now. Third, the states may have an access of strength and vigor, and play a larger role, relatively speaking, in the future. We may as well say now that the last of these seems least likely.

Traditional federalism is highly and increasingly qualified in four ways. (1) It is a system of *at least three* governmental levels in which each level has some de facto autonomy. (2) These levels are closely interdependent, and interact segmentally or functionally more than they do as wholes. (3) Jurisdictional boundaries on the same level seem to be losing relevance because of the greater scale and scope of governmental functions and the growing social consciousness of "externalities." (4) The line between public and private in the development of policy and provision of services—especially in fields that are highly professionalized, or in which voluntary action is traditional, such as education, research, and social services—cannot be drawn clearly; and federalism has to be seen as itself a form of pluralism as well as a governmental system. Each of these aspects of federalism has always been part of it: the historical role of each has had growing recognition in academic analyses of federalism; the question is whether each, and all together, are gradually undermining the formal role of the states. Discussions of federalism for the last thirty years have emphasized the second aspect— broadly "cooperative" or "functional" federalism.[9] Recently the other elements have come to the fore because of two broad, somewhat contradictory factors. One is the urbanization of America, coupled with the relative orientation of state governments to rural localities, and the inadequacies of public organization in metropolitan areas or larger economic or natural regions. The other is the combination of poverty and affluence that, with the social and economic concomitants of urban living, has raised the demand for social services—health, higher education, and welfare—in which the voluntary element has always bulked large.

We thus have to inquire first about the prospects for the states in the federal system, and second, about the probable future forms of federalism more broadly construed, whatever the prospects for the states.

We begin with the observation that *local* government (usually self-

[9] The most careful, insightful analyses are those of the late Morton Grodzins, summarized in his *The American System*, Daniel Elazar (ed.) (Chicago: Rand McNally & Co., 1966).

government in some measure, especially in densely settled places), exists in all nations; and that a jurisdiction intervening between national and local exists in all *large* nations, whether they are federal or unitary. In the federal states these intermediate units tend, not surprisingly, to exhibit greater disparities among themselves in size and, in general, are larger in comparison with local government than they are in unitary states. It is unlikely that these jurisdictions are merely vestiges of government under more primitive systems of communication. Instead, they apparently function as political and administrative transformers: they help to relieve or obviate political and administrative overloads at the center; and they provide a level of appeal from and supervision of local governments that allows policies to be made in some remoteness from the pressures of local vested interests and, frequently, with greater professional competence than is directly available to local governments.

In the United States, it can be argued that one of the principal functions of the states is now, and has always been, to provide standards of performance and tribunals for appeals with respect to local government. Probably the most important of these controls are legal, administered by the courts; but legislative and regular administrative controls are also important. Given the probability of personal favoritism and social discrimination—of primitive administration and confusion of public and private ends—in localities small enough to be roughly congruent with communities, resort to the states is especially important. Direct control from the national level is all but impossible. Indirect control of localities through "states" that were merely federal administrative units would probably be less effective than the present system because the units would lack authority and would be subject to frequent intervention by the federal government. The relative independence of the states provides fifty separate structures of sovereignty for the review and control of local governmental action.

This system does not work with equal equity in all the states; it is probably accurate to describe the following as the modal pattern. State instrumentalities (apart from local governments, which are also legally state instrumentalities to some extent) exert controls over local governments. But state agencies are themselves subject to local persuasion through the local bases of state party organization and legislative representation, through the social and political connections of state judges (commonly at the county level), and through the influence of wealthy, politically active individuals. On the other hand, the state-local systems are not so independent of federal controls—fiscal and administrative controls through grants-in-aid, and legal or constitutional norms applied by the courts—but that standards of professional competence, due process, and equal protection are broadly available. At the same time, national legislation is subject to political influence from the state level in much the same way that state policy-making responds to local pressures. In states and localities whose prevailing political interests and cultures are highly resistant to the professional standards of the urban upper-middle class and to universalistic legal norms the modal pattern just described provides less effective protection for minorities; but it does provide some, as can be seen in recent federal-state clashes over public assistance administration and civil rights in the South.[10] There is also a strong possibility that the states collectively act as a balancing, bargaining, and filtering force for the mitigation of central-local conflicts—though the ways in which this function is performed are far too complex for elucidation here.[11] Federalism is a complicated way of integrating general standards and particular interests; but it does provide a balance of local autonomy with central control that would be hard to obtain otherwise in a large nation.

Discussions of federalism commonly focus on the direct activities of the states, rather than on their review and supervision of local action; though we believe that the latter contributes importantly to local democracy, which probably contributes in turn to the development and persistence of the "civic culture." So far as the administrative and regulatory activities of the states are concerned it can certainly be argued that administration and *decision-making* at the state level help to avert central overload in a central government that can hardly afford more difficulties of coordination and accountability than it suffers now. Since the late Leonard White made this point forcefully more than a decade ago nothing has happened to invalidate it; much has occurred to confirm it.[12] So we put this down as a critical potentiality of the states and explore in the following section some reasons why it has not been more fully realized.

First, however, we should examine another fundamental issue. If the states, as we believe, can play useful administrative, legal, and political roles in national life, how many states are appropriate for these purposes? The question is fundamental because, as we shall see, the territorial organization of the states may well be their principal handicap. One of the most radical suggestions for federal reform, commonly made during the Depression, has been to redraw state boundaries and reduce drastically the total number of states. Despite the entrenchment of state boundaries and identities in the Constitution, the potential complexi-

[10] For a suggestive interpretation of the variant political cultures in the several states, *see* Daniel J. Elazar, *American Federalism: A View from the States* (New York: Thomas Y. Crowell Company, 1966).

[11] The argument is developed in Paul Ylvisaker, "Criteria for a 'Proper' Areal Division of Powers," in Arthur Maass (ed.), *Area and Power: A Theory of Local Government* (New York: The Free Press, 1959).

[12] Leonard White, *The States and the Nation* (Baton Rouge: Louisiana State University Press, 1953).

ties of commingling state legal systems, and the various vested interests attached to the states as they stand—despite, that is, the extreme unlikelihood of change—it will be instructive to consider this proposal for "modernization," or "rationalization."

The usual proposal for redefinition of the states has been that they should conform to natural (economic, or geographical) regions—though many regionalists would go on to abolish federalism and make the states administrative units only. Setting aside the question of political feasibility, there are two principal difficulties with this proposal. One is how to define the "regions," since the definitions will differ according to the criteria thought appropriate. This is only to say that regions tend to be arbitrary and subject to obsolescence, not that they are impossible to create. The second problem is that this reform would tend to build certain economic differences still more prominently and irreconcilably into federal policy-making. This would seem to follow from reliance on well-defined regions; but another reason for it would probably be the small number (say, a dozen in most proposals) of constituent units in the system. American federalism today has characteristics of both direct bargaining and of indirect market processes: the large number of units in cross-cutting interests involved make direct bargaining among the states or between them and the federal government difficult except for the complex logrolling process in Congress. The federal bargaining over fiscal policies in the large British dominions illustrates this point: there it is extremely difficult to alter an apportionment formula; though the issues involved may be more clearly visible than they are in the American system, which involves more issues and politicians in federal decision-making.[13] This reasoning, and the alleged virtues of jurisdictional variation, suggests—though it surely does not prove—that it is desirable to have a larger number of units in the system than is suitable for direct bargaining: perhaps roughly double the usual proposal, or half the present number, at a minimum. No doubt, if the United States could wipe the federal slate clean, it would be wise to enlarge the states, reduce the various disparities among them, and adjust their boundaries better to metropolitan areas and natural resources. But, on the sketchy reasoning in this section, it would probably do well to keep the states in some profusion and confusion.

The Problems of the States

Having dealt so hopefully with the potentialities of the states, we should give an accounting of the problems of state government today.

[13] A. H. Birch, *Federalism, Finance, and Social Legislation* (London: Oxford University Press, 1955).

There is, however, a large, if controversial, body of doctrine on this topic; and we shall review it briefly.[14]

The structure of state government is much criticized for weak executives; fragmented fiscal procedures; insufficient professionalism in administration; legislatures that are oversized, undersalaried, malapportioned, and badly staffed; poorly administered and politically selected judiciaries; multifarious constitutional restrictions on state abilities to meet needs or respond to demands; and failures to reform local government (a critical offset to our earlier statement about potentialities). It should be recognized that many of these criticisms reflect conventional, perhaps Yankee middle-class values about sound, conservative management; but some of them also favor greater room for executive leadership combined with an upgrading of legislative capacities for control of administration, if not for policy-making. There is broad variation among states on these points today, as well as broad similarity in the sense that all state governments are based on the federal model. The National Municipal League proposal of the 1920's for cabinet or parliamentary government never took hold in the states, despite widespread local acceptance of the city manager plan; most political scientists probably agree that strengthening the independently elected governor and the responsiveness and effectiveness of legislatures are the best steps that the states could take today.[15] The conventional agreement on this point is surprising, when one reflects on the high regard that political scientists have had for the British governmental system, and on the potentialities of the states as "laboratories," but it is probably conclusive. It is relatively seldom recognized that the desired reforms of state government—at least in states deficient in "moralistic" political cultures—probably require a compromise of other values, including acceptance of some patronage as a base for political leadership and consolidation.

Thus many political scientists, following the late V. O. Key, have come to the position that political reform of the states has higher priority than governmental change.[16] Here the aim is to create "responsible"— that is, strongly organized, competitive, policy-oriented (if possible)— party systems. But party systems are hard to reform by fiat: the foregoing governmental reforms might help; removal of the direct primary might give some sanctions and incentives to party leaders; and legislative reapportionment may intensify competition. In fact, the process of ur-

[14] An excellent critical review can be found in Duane Lockard, *The Politics of State and Local Government* (New York: Macmillan, 1963). *See also* James Fesler (ed.), *The Fifty States and Their Local Governments* (New York: Alfred A. Knopf, Inc., 1967).

[15] *Cf.* Committee for Economic Development, *Modernizing State Government* (New York: Committee for Economic Development, 1967).

[16] V. O. Key, *American State Politics* (New York: Alfred A. Knopf, Inc., 1956).

banization and industrialization is slowly altering state politics in the
direction of interparty competition, and, to a lesser extent, toward
stronger party organization.[17] Recently, however, it has been argued that
this is beside the point: that state policies can be shown to vary primarily
with fiscal capacity and other economic characteristics; and that political
organization contributes little to the performance of state governments.[18]
We can only take note of this argument here, and record our doubt, on
both conceptual and statistical grounds, that the burden of argument
about the importance of state political systems has yet been effectively
shifted.

Nevertheless, the wide variation among states as to fiscal capacity is a
major problem today. The average per capita income in the twelve richest states was nearly twice that in the twelve poorest in 1960. True,
many of the most affluent states also have the most serious problems to
be met by public expenditures; but needs and resources are not highly
correlated among the states, and a few (though only a few) of the poorest states make the greatest fiscal efforts.[19] It is widely believed, moreover, that tax competition among states and tax regressivity within them
inhibit public expenditures, though there is not solid evidence for either
proposition.[20] Political scientists like to point out that the states now
raise and spend more money proportionately to other levels of government than they ever have in this century. Economists' estimates vary as
to whether the "necessary" expenditures of state and local governments
will badly lag behind available resources in the next decade or so: if
the high estimates are right, then the question arises of how the federal
government will fill the gap—whether by releasing tax sources in any of
a variety of ways, by increasing (and perhaps broadening) grants-in-aid,
or by a general distribution of federal income to the states and localities;
and the future role of the states will depend more heavily on the relative
need for such measures and the forms that they take than on governmental or political reform.[21] We should note, however, that most estimates of state fiscal capacity in the future are mildly optimistic; and

[17] *See* Herbert Jacob and Kenneth N. Vines (eds.), *Politics in the American States*
(Boston: Little, Brown and Co., 1965), especially Chaps. 1-6; and Thomas Flinn,
"Party Responsibility in the States . . . ," *American Political Science Review*, LVIII
(1964), 60 ff.

[18] Thomas R. Dye, *Politics, Economics, and the Public* (Chicago: Rand Mc-
Nally & Co., 1966).

[19] Advisory Commission on Intergovernmental Relations, *Measures of State and
Local Fiscal Capacity and Tax Effort* (Washington, D.C.: Government Printing
Office, 1962).

[20] James A. Maxwell, *Financing State and Local Governments* (Washington, D.C.:
The Brookings Institution, 1965).

[21] *Ibid. See also* Break, *op. cit.*, and Committee for Economic Development, *A
Fiscal Program for a Balanced Federalism* (New York: Committee for Economic
Development, 1967).

that federal measures of support may be used to force (or encourage) reforms of state and local government.

Finally, we should take note of the more general governmental problems of the states, of which the most serious are probably two. One is the boundary problem already referred to, which has different effects among the states: if New Mexico's problems and resources are *relatively* well contained, New Jersey's are not; and this variation no doubt creates differences (that have not been clearly identified, however) in the performances of state governmental systems. In addition, the states appear to vary in the visibility of their governments and policies to voters; though in this respect most states are probably a poor third to national and local governments—a fact that seems to reflect in some part the states' large role in the technical regulation of special interests as well as their growing role as distributors of grants to localities.[22] Neither of these functions makes them a focus of public attention; both subject state legislatures to intense lobbying.

From all these familiar observations we can derive three more general problems that complicate the prospects of federalism. The first of these problems is that of the vast socioeconomic disparities among states. There seem to be two "dualisms" in the United States that overlap unevenly: one is metropolitan-rural; the other is relative affluence–poverty. These differences—really, continua—exist both within and between states; but they serve to distinguish some states from others, and the differences are not always congruent. (Wyoming, for instance, is relatively rural and rich.) In general, the metropolitan states are the wealthier states: if they have the most dramatic problems they also command the best professional talent. They are the states where the governmental, innovative action is, and the population also, for more than 50 per cent of Americans live in one-fifth of the states. Finally, fiscal disparities and rural or urban cultures tend to be connected: the dozen commonwealths with per capita incomes of less than three-fourths the national average are ten southern states (including West Virginia) and the two Dakotas.[23] Despite the statistically continuous nature of these socioeconomic differences, special disparities in the ability to govern autonomously affect the relatively underdeveloped areas of the South, on one hand, and, on the other, the minority of states that contain (often only in part) the nation's large urban agglomerations. Southern industrial development may in time relieve the heavy southern dependence on federal aid, thus increasing the viability of the states in that area. But northern megalopolitan growth may tend to outmode the most populous

[22] We cite no evidence for this proposition, which does, however, appear in much of the literature on the states. It may be questionable; and it doubtless varies in its applicability to the fifty states.

[23] Advisory Commission on Intergovernmental Relations, *op. cit.*

minority of states, thus favoring the trend toward more direct federal intervention in urban problems as well as those of economic development.

Second, all four of the complex factors discussed in the beginning of this section—governmental organization, political patterns, fiscal capacity, and boundary problems—may help to account for the fact that most states and localities, in terms of the focus of voters, are involved in a relatively utilitarian politics of taxes and expenditures compared to the federal government's more idealistic politics of programs (to use Alan K. Campbell's terms).[24] They also mean that state politicians (especially legislative politicians) tend to be "locals" as opposed to "cosmopolitans" (in Robert K. Merton's terms) in the coalition of metropolitan politicians and federal executives. Although this is an imprecise distinction, it probably delineates a cultural alignment between a majority of states and congressmen on one hand and the politics of metropolitan America on the other.[25]

Finally, there is the unresolved issue whether the drift of legislative and fiscal response problems in the direction of the federal government could be checked or reversed by changes in state governmental and political structures. Political scientists simply disagree on this issue. Some, like the late V. O. Key, believe that the reform of state political institutions would help to restore the states. Others, like the late Morton Grodzins, believe that factors in our third and fourth categories above —fiscal and broadly administrative—make the drift irresistible.[26] Still others argue that the fiscal and policy roles of the states are still so large that "restoration" is hardly at issue. Can all three views be partially correct, as we believe they are? An analysis of trends in federal policy will help to decide this.

Trends in Federal Grant Programs

In this section and the next we shall narrow our focus sharply to the trends affecting intergovernmental relations during the last generation. The social services—principally those administered by the federal Department of Health, Education, and Welfare—will be at the center of our focus and, in the following section we shall deal with one of these —public health—to illustrate the trends on which we comment in the present section. Although these fields of policy constitute only a portion of federalism, it will be appropriate to focus on them for at least two

[24] *See* Campbell's testimony in Hearings Before the U. S. Senate Subcommittee on Intergovernmental Relations of the Committee on Government Operations, *Creative Federalism*, 90th Congress, 1st Session (1967), Part 2-B, pp. 846 ff.

[25] *Cf.* Elazar, *op. cit.*

[26] Key, *op. cit.*; Grodzins, *op. cit.*, Chap. 12.

reasons. First, these fields underwent a basic change during the Depression: the Social Security Act of 1935 redistributed to the federal and state governments responsibility for programs formerly considered state and local, primarily; it shifted the fiscal balance of federalism so that federal grants became more of a necessity than a supplement in most state programs; federal standards attached to the programs altered significantly the practice of the social services; and in time public funds (especially federal funds) substantially displaced voluntary efforts in fields where the private agencies had long bulked larger than governmental efforts. Thus it is probably correct to speak of a "new federalism" in these fields. Yet, second, the social services are changing rapidly in response to both poverty and affluence in America; and the rules of local governments and of voluntary agencies remain important for the programing and delivery of services, together with federal financing. Thus, we shall argue below that a "new, new" and a "new, new, new" federalism are now in evidence. By these we mean the direct federalism of grants to *local* governments, and the private federalism of grants to individuals and nongovernmental institutions—for example, universities, clinics, or "community action" programs. Moreover, the social services are likely to assume still greater importance in federal programs in the future. Before dealing with these developments, however, we shall analyze some trends in the "new federalism"—now "conventional federalism"—that have led to them.

Six broad trends have occurred in federalism with respect to the social services since the Depression. First, the role of federal grants has continued to grow in importance. Today they amount to more than 15 per cent of state-local general revenues for all programs (*not* just the social services), and in fifteen of the fifty states, mostly in the South and West, the proportion in 1962 was more than 20 per cent.[27] Thus the fiscal effect of federal grants, entirely apart from their stimulative effect on specific programs, is most significant in the poorer states. This is especially true in the social services because of the growing use of equalization formulas in federal grants.

Equalization, then, is a second trend, reflecting the use of measures of state fiscal capacity in the grant programs—either in the distribution formulas or in their matching requirements. Examples are the programs in hospital construction, community health, water pollution control, school lunch, aid to elementary and secondary education, child welfare, and public assistance. Most of the programs to which equalization formulas apply are administered by HEW; and the largest single grant program, that for highways, contains no such provision.[28] In most cases

[27] Advisory Commission on Intergovernmental Relations, *The Role of Equalization in Federal Grants* (Washington, D.C.: Government Printing Office, 1964).
[28] *Ibid. Cf.* Break, *op. cit.*, Chaps. 3, 4.

equalization has come at administrative initiative as a way of providing more uniform national service levels; in a few cases it has been pressed by poor regions strategically represented in Congress. So far, the general fiscal effects of equalization formulas have been slight because equalization is not pronounced in grant programs taken as a whole; but it has enlarged the federal role in particular programs without necessarily entailing more federal controls on the states. This problem of control is dealt with in connection with the following trends.

Third, grant programs have become increasingly categorized. This trend is most marked in public health, as related in the next section; but most of the social services are characterized by rather narrow categories, earmarked funds, and special projects that implement federally determined priorities. There is ample testimony from state officials that the categories bind.[29] In theory, a creative state administration could simply turn the taps on the several federal pipelines to produce its own optimal program mix; but a combination of accounting and organizational controls and categorical ceilings discourages or forbids many mixtures. The third trend is also one, however, in which there are signs of a reversal; and this will be important for the future of federalism.

A fourth trend has been toward tighter federal standards governing state performance in grant programs. The effects of formal regulations vary widely. In some cases, such as the public assistance program, proliferation of federal administrative regulations has not much altered state policy; in others, such as hospital construction allocations, more stringent federal standards have probably been effective. In the first of these illustrative cases the federal statute only allows federal regulations on matters of administrative detail rather than of general policy; in the second case the statute permits broader federal policy controls.[30] Allied factors influencing the effectiveness of federal controls are the extent to which they deal with matters of public controversy on one hand or reflect a professional consensus on the other. In most programs federal standard-setting has been a process of gradual professionalization and general acceptance of standards; those programs (such as the highway program) where federal controls are weak are also relatively unprofessionalized and most subject to state political intervention.

Closely allied to professionalism is a fifth trend: use of the project

[29] See, for example, *Federal-State-Local Relations*, Hearings Before a Subcommittee of the U. S. House of Representatives Government Operations Committee (Washington, D.C.: Government Printing Office, 1957-1958).

[30] On public assistance, see Advisory Commission on Intergovernmental Relations, *Statutory and Administrative Controls Associated with Federal Grants for Public Assistance* (Washington, D.C.: Government Printing Office, 1964). We also rely heavily throughout this discussion and the following section on our own investigations of HEW grant programs. For one report, see Charles E. Gilbert, "Policy Making in Public Welfare," *Political Science Quarterly*, LXXXI (1966), 196 ff.

grant, especially for research and "demonstration" purposes. Unlike formula grants, the project approach entails direct federal approval of specific applications. States need not avail themselves of project grants; but they are attractive to professionals, they rarely require any state matching at all, and they enable new approaches to special problems in metropolitan regions that are not well met by standardized formula grants. Project grants seem to be less a method of centralization than of federal leadership, together with the more advanced states, in program innovations and professional development. They supplement professionalism and sometimes lead to the extension of standards in formula grants.

Some grant programs are not clearly classifiable as either formula or project. The grant programs for hospital construction, community mental health centers, and higher educational facilities are examples. In these programs, and some others, a sixth trend is discernible: federal review of state decisions, sometimes to the point of final federal decision, even though funds are distributed to the states according to a general formula. Thus, instead of simply approving a general "state plan," the federal agency may approve, or disapprove, specific projects. As the quality of state plans varies (in the federal agency's estimate) so does the intensiveness of federal review; but in some cases, and especially in new programs, the latter is tantamount to central decision.

The six trends together give rise to a pair of general issues: one normative, one descriptive. The normative issue is whether the diversity and disparities among federal grant programs are desirable. Financial formulas, specificity of categories, and extent of federal standards vary in part —and apart from political considerations—because of differences or ambiguities in the intent of programs. Three major ends compete in theory: (1) equalizing the fiscal capacities of the states; (2) offsetting "external" effects of programs among states; and (3) achieving national uniformity and improving professional standards in the administration of programs. Each of these ends (and there are other possible ends) implies at least a slightly different pattern of grants. Wide agreement on one or another objective is unlikely, since the interests served by them are often inconsistent.[31] But it is possible that debate about the course of federalism will focus more directly on these issues in future.

The second question is whether the six trends discussed above amount collectively to more centralization of the federal system. This question is difficult to answer directly because the channels of power or influence and the direction of movement of influence are so hard to identify. In part, the answer depends on what programs one has in mind: even if the six trends have spelled "centralization," they have not affected all pro-

---

[31] Discussions of grant objectives can be found in Break, *op. cit.*, Chaps. 3, 4; and in Richard Musgrave (ed.), *Essays in Fiscal Federalism* (Washington, D.C.: The Brookings Institution, 1966).

grams equally; nor have all the trends been felt in all programs. More basically, centralization and decentralization require better definition than they have had in the federal context; and their political, administrative, and fiscal aspects sometimes point in different directions.

Most scholarship is inclined to deny that there has been much centralization. We may briefly note three interpretations. One is *political*: party decentralization (consequent on federalism in some part) is said to have two principal effects: first, grant programs are favored over national programs because they combine an effective, nationwide tax base with state discretion in the distribution of benefits; and, second, administration of the programs has been subject to Congressional and local political intervention. So Morton Grodzins powerfully argued; and Phillip Monypenny somewhat similarly explained the functional specificity and fiscal perversity of the major grant-in-aid programs.[32] Another interpretation is *administrative*—or its central point may be said to be that political and administrative relationships in federalism are indistinguishable. It states that professionals or specialists are leading constituents of grant programs at all governmental levels, tending to fragment (decentralize) each of the several levels, local, state, and national, while linking them in new hierarchies.[33] Thus "marble cake" federalism tends to reduce program control by elected officials, legislative and executive, to substitute informal, professional relations for the conventional divisions of federalism and the separation of powers. Still another interpretation stresses the inconsistency of *fiscal* principles. Formula grants, it is said, entail some compromise between, say, stimulation of programs and fiscal redistribution; between national uniformity and provision for local diversity.[34] No principle can be pressed very far without contravening others; and few citizens or officials hold consistent views about them. The point is that these tend to conflict so that to some extent the system reflects an adjustment among several objectives.

We lack space in this paper to sort out the foregoing arguments, or more precisely to define "centralization." Much depends on whether one views it in terms of nation vs. states, politicians vs. administrators, executives vs. legislators and specialists, popular control vs. group competition. Fiscal, administrative, and political aspects must be distinguished. Perhaps it is a fair statement that influence on policy in many programs has gravitated to professionals and administrators in the federal government *and* in the more "advanced" states. But the fact that the accuracy of this statement heavily depends on the program one has in mind

[32] Phillip Monypenny, "Federal Grants-in-Aid to State and Local Government: A Political Analysis," *National Tax Journal*, XIII (1960), 1.

[33] Grodzins, *op. cit.*

[34] Advisory Commission on Intergovernmental Relations, *The Role of Equalization*; Selma Mushkin, "Barriers to a System of Federal Grants-in-Aid," *National Tax Journal*, XIII (1960), 193.

should emphasize that "centralization" of the federal system has not gone far.

The more significant development, we think, has been the recent displacement of the now conventional "new federalism" just discussed by what we termed above "direct" and "private" federalism—which, strictly speaking, are not federalism at all! Some sources of that development can be found in the six trends in conventional federalism, others in factors discussed earlier. In the social services, at least—and here we include programs of housing and community development beyond those administered by HEW—there is now a serious question of the extent to which conventional federalism, and thus the role of the states, will be displaced by direct and private federalism.

Direct federalism has recently been the subject of a book by Roscoe Martin, and we can content ourselves with six swift observations.[35] (1) As Martin points out, it makes up less than 20 per cent of all grant-in-aid programs, though it is rapidly increasing in extent. (2) It is in some degree a response to big-city difficulties thought to be neglected by states and thus reflects the independent political role of large metropolitan centers. (3) It has never been restricted to cities, however: housing, renewal, educational, and airport grants have always been available over most of the urban-rural continuum; and the transportation and open space components of urban renewal are especially attractive to suburbanites. (4) Direct federalism is a means of putting the money more precisely on target, and may be seen as a reaction to two aspects of conventional federalism: distribution of federal funds by states as they saw fit, according to their political systems; and the growing impatience with state and local boundaries among reformers administering federal programs. (5) In most of these programs national control of local action is relatively close, though the usual federal difficulties exist of balancing sanctions and inducements, of how to treat with powerful local politicians, how to staff regional offices for program loyalty and effectiveness.[36] (6) It should be observed that while most direct federal programs require state enabling legislation for local participation, in only a minority of states has this normally led to more than pro forma state action.

Private federalism obviously involves not only by-passing the states, but making grants to private agencies or even to individuals (such as research scholars in universities). Thus it is not reflected in analyses of *intergovernmental* fiscal relations, though it is often an alternative to the public provision of services. Like direct federalism, it has grown rapidly,

---

[35] Roscoe Martin, *The Cities and the Federal System* (New York: Atherton Press, 1965).

[36] *Cf.* Scott Greer, *Urban Renewal and American Cities* (Indianapolis: The Bobbs-Merrill Co., Inc., 1965), Chap. 5.

though it lacks a clear pattern. An analysis of all of HEW's grant programs by the authors for the five-year period 1961-1966 showed it to be by far the fastest growing grant category, amounting in the latter year to more than 20 per cent of all grants.[37] Three reasons probably account for most of its growth. One is the need to command the scientific and professional resources of universities and industrial firms for programs emphasizing special skills, allied with the fact that many professionals prefer private to public employment. Thus it is closely akin to the recent, rapid growth of "government by contract" and of governmentally sponsored nonprofit corporations. A second reason is the desire to place some functions on a regional basis, coupled with the ability of private institutions to transcend governmental boundaries. The third reason is a design to build clienteles or to stimulate "participation," as with mental health facilities or the "War on Poverty." Usually the adjective "community" is attached to such programs, which seem frequently to be intended to insulate the program from competing pressures and to organize a clientele that will support and protect the program. Effective social service programs may be especially dependent on the enlistment of voluntary effort, since they commonly lack pecuniary incentives and often depend on participation of the clientele for their effects. There may also be a fourth source of private federalism in the ideological dislike of Americans for large, centralized government: like "cooperative" or "functional" federalism, private federalism has always existed in the United States.

Like conventional federalism, too, private federalism is a form of decentralization and social pluralism combined with central finance. The problems with it lie in the reasons for its increase. The support of private organizations with public funds within unique jurisdictions, and the building of special constituencies mean that programs are less broadly visible and accountable than they are in governmental federalism, either conventional or direct. Our first job, however, is not to criticize but to understand the increase in private federalism. Circumstances vary among programs—those of the Poverty Program, for example, are well known. The following case study of public health describes the progress from public to private federalism in a less controversial field.

Public Health: A Case Study

The modern era in federal-state relations for public health begins with the New Deal and especially with World War II. Prior to 1936, the Public Health Service (PHS) collected vital statistics, enforced in-

---

[37] The materials for analysis can be found in *Grants-in-Aid and Other Financial Assistance Programs Administered by the U. S. Department of Health, Education, and Welfare* (Washington, D.C.: Government Printing Office, annually).

terstate sanitation and quarantine, and provided technical assistance to state departments of public health. A departure from this traditional "layer-cake" federalism began in 1935 with Title VI of the Social Security Act, which authorized $8 million annually for training and technical assistance to state and local health work.[38] More important for the administrative history of the contemporary PHS were the experiences of World War II and anticipations of future needs for medical treatment and professional training. After the war, supervening political influence combined with administrative planning to urge the PHS toward a new pattern in federalism.

The postwar program put forward by the PHS mixed old and new conceptions of federalism. New Deal "cooperative" federalism was represented by a strengthened frame of public services: support for local public health units in cities and counties and grants for categories of need not met by fee-for-service medicine—such as mental illness, TB, and care for the chronically ill. "Private" federalism was represented in the famous Joseph Mountain–Thomas Parran "Integrated Hospital System." [39] This scheme for regional hospital complexes and service areas was intended to make medical care broadly available, to integrate specialties efficiently, and to insure continuing improvement in the health professions. Local health units and categorical support for weak program areas would strengthen the "continuum of care" in varieties of medicine not profitable for private practice.

Technical trends were probably more important in postwar policy than politics. One such trend—thanks to the PHS itself and to "wonder drugs"—was the sharp decline of communicable disease. Scientific and medical interest turned increasingly toward the chronic, killing, and crippling diseases such as heart disease, cancer, arthritis, and the like. Professional sophistication also increased rapidly after the war, marked by more specialization and by interest in clinical and basic research. By and large, the PHS and other leaders in health foresaw the first of these developments, but not the rapid shift toward specialties or the impact of the postwar "information explosion" upon medicine.

Technical and professional developments favored a move toward "private federalism." So did the politics of the period. More specifically, the debacle of the Ewing Plan ("socialized medicine") and its defeat left the PHS politically weak. A new surgeon general from the National Institutes of Health (NIH)[40] and the mood of the Eisenhower era also

[38] Edwin E. Witte, *The Development of the Social Security Act* (Madison: University of Wisconsin Press, 1962).

[39] *Wartime Health and Education*, Pt. V, Subcommittee on Education and Labor, U. S. Senate, 78th Congress (1944), pp. 1173-1207.

[40] The Institute (later Institutes) was originally a research organ of the PHS exclusively. After World War II, the NIH developed an extramural program of grants and became the primary government support for biomedical research.

tended to move programs away from vigorous and active involvement with state and local governments toward less contentious relations with the professions, the medical schools and hospitals, and the local "community."

There were two important developments in PHS grants policy during the twenty-year period since the war. The relative importance of different grants to the states changed radically: decline of the general health grant; the absolute and relative increase in categorical grants; and finally, the growing importance of project and research grants relative to both of the preceding kinds. Secondly, biomedical research and research training increased vastly, relative to other programs, and ultimately displaced them as the main elements of PHS program development. The first change related especially to the more traditional Bureau of State Services (BSS); the second, to the National Institutes of Health.

Before reviewing the first of these developments—the decline of the general health grant—it is worth commenting that this grant was initially conceived and was administered as a way of strengthening state public health programs as whole entities. The grant was especially popular with the state officers. They could use it to pay administrative costs, support local health units, or fund projects of their own choosing to give "visibility" and popularity to public health programs.

The general health grant fit a traditional conception of public health as largely governmental rather than private and a "cooperative federalism" that emphasized a hierarchy of governments. Under Parran (Surgeon General, 1936-1948), grants policy for state aid expressed this philosophy of "cooperative federalism" faithfully: categorical support was not a *deduction from* general support, but an addition to it, strengthening the program in weak areas. After 1948, categorical grants grew at the expense of general health support, making the latter increasingly residual.

One reason for the relative increase in categorical grants was change in the sources of program support. Locally, efforts to organize a heart disease control program or build a hospital brought together small clusters of doctors, fund raisers, and health and welfare associations— not public agencies or governments. At a higher level, professional interest and associational efforts centered upon mental health and cancer, upon disease categories, and not—except for the Association of State and Territorial Health Officers (ASTHO)—upon state or local public health departments. The period was also one of changing conceptions of medical practice, yet of uncertainty about the point at which new conceptions would converge. Prudent administrative planning dictated that public health personnel both locally and in the PHS itself maintain close contact with the professions and voluntary associations in areas of categorical interest.

The trend to categories also had a political rationale that depended on both the substance of programs and unique aspects of the American political system. Public health programs cover wide fronts: scores of separate services and projects. Categorical efforts—so many kidney machines, heart control surveys, TB cases treated—can be made "visible" to legislator and public alike. Legislators like categories: they afford leverage to control programs, especially through annual appropriations. They also provide opportunities to become, for instance, Mr. Water Pollution Control or Mr. Health and thus acquire both a power base in Congress and popular support nationally and locally. By contrast, the more traditional public health—resting upon the states and localities—was supported by a fragmented constituency, out of the professional mainstream, and lacked "visibility," or was believed to lack it.

The decline of the general health grant and an increase in categorical aid expressed one pull toward "private federalism," the importance of professions and health associations for program support. The rapid increase of project and research grants relative to both other kinds of grants was responsive especially to a need for scientific research and development, facilities, and professional manpower. Since the 1950's, such grants have been used as a way to broaden and extend research and development to include basic science, building facilities, and training manpower. Also, as the distance between PHS aspirations and actual or potential state performance grew—because of changing needs and technology and because of weak federal leadership and lack of state responsiveness—the project grant was used with varying success to stimulate public or private activities or close the distance between the two.

The project grant evolved pragmatically, in response to needs or program gaps as they developed. For instance, Hill-Burton and water pollution construction money was needed by cities and regions. The formula-project grant provided a way of putting the money there. Clearing out "pockets" of VD and TB required a concentrated, short-term effort in a particular area and the organization of a locally coordinated attack. The terminating project grant lent itself to this job. Outpatient programs or services for the chronically ill called especially for expanding the hospital's endeavors and for joint public-private activity: thus, for project grants directed at hospital services and tying them with community efforts.

An important point about the project grant is its appropriateness for utilizing the services of professional groups or private institutions. The project grant could be funded without going through an intervening layer of government and without adhering to civil service regulations. It was awarded, typically, for a project originating in some local, professional, or scientific interest and aimed at some "problem" of public health practice or research.[41] It was judged by a panel composed of professional "peers" or of administrators and professionals combined. Project grants especially combined flexibility in the use of personnel and acceptability by professionals and scientific or medical institutions.

The project grant in service programs was an administrative device sought for by the PHS but stoutly resisted by the states, by ASTIIO, and by President Eisenhower's staff, who disliked "direct" federalism especially. Project grant authorization in most BSS programs came after 1960 and the change of administration—appropriately enough, inasmuch as the project grant is especially suited to "frontiersmanship." After 1960, project grants in community health quickly grew to rival categorical aid, completing the reduction of the general health grant to a small, residual slice of the total program.

These trends in community health, toward increasing categorization of aid and the use of project grants, illustrate changes *within* a traditional federal program in aid of the states. Much more important than these changes was the development of a *separate* approach toward ultimate delivery of service based upon the program logic of scientific research and development and centering upon the NIH.

Choice of the NIH route depended upon secular trends extraneous to government and contemporary, fortuitous circumstances. The postwar years brought interest in basic science, including biomedical science. The PHS, wanting a stronger research arm, welcomed this trend and expanded NIH over the years.[42] Without President Eisenhower's contribution, however, the NIH would likely have remained a small service agency within a traditional PHS mission. Frustration with the President's weak support, Marion Folsom's energy and interest in health, the opening of a path through two appropriations committees, and administrative capability in the NIH combined to encourage a path of least resistance: the route of private federalism, of subsidy to science, the universities, and the professions.

The major "breakthrough" came in 1956, ratified by the President's Health Message of that year. In the message, research came first, with an emphasis upon "basic research." A second item, support for Health Research Facilities ("regional nonfederal centers"), assigned NIH a responsibility for the "crippling and killing" disease categories and strengthened the alliance of the NIH and the universities and research centers. Support for the training of nurses and public health specialties was a weak third to this trinity of science, facilities, and health manpower, but it established the principle. The practical effect of legisla-

[41] *Cf.* T. D. Weldon's distinction between "problems" and "difficulties" [*The Vocabulary of Politics* (London: Penguin Books, 1953), pp. 75-83].

[42] Donald C. Swain, "The Rise of a Research Empire: NIH, 1930 to 1950," *Science*, CXXXVIII (1962), 1233-1237.

tion during 1956 was to give approval to an expanded NIH research mission and to assign to the Institutes a large and undetermined future responsibility for health resources and operational activities related to medical research and development.

The interplay of Congressional appropriation, the visibility of the "big categories" represented by the Institutes, and broadened NIH programs, produced spectacular results. In a period when domestic services were faring badly, NIH appropriations increased by approximately $100 million a year to top $1 billion. The budget request for 1965 was $1.1 billion. By contrast, the total of *all other* PHS programs, including community health, Hill-Burton, environmental health, the medical services and government hospitals, was $600 million.

The NIH's rapid growth and great popularity invite comment, particularly with respect to the strengths of "private federalism" in biomedical science. For one item, the NIH provided subsidy with few strings attached. Furthermore, the grants went especially for research and traineeships in medicine and biomedical sciences, fields with a traditionally low rate of investment except for the bread-and-butter of training and service. Finally, effective program organization—through national advisory councils, study sections, and committees of university administrators, scientists, and government officials—coincided almost perfectly with effective organization for political support and Congressional lobbying. The private federalism of the NIH rested—and rests— upon a powerful and legitimate constituency: of able, energetic people in frequent communication, sharing a common goal and interest, and capable of advancing their cause indirectly through universities and professional associations or directly, with access to the "corridors of power," at the cabinet level, with congressmen and senators, and the President himself.

NIH programs have continued since 1960 to grow not just in authorization and appropriation, but in scope and jurisdiction as well. In the latter categories of change, four items deserve brief mention.

A decisive step in extending research and development toward eventual delivery of services was the establishment of large-scale support, especially after 1959-1960, for categorical and general clinical research. In 1957 Congress authorized bricks and mortar. Beginning with 1959, funds were earmarked to train manpower and provide block grants to medical schools and clinical centers for program support. Inasmuch as "research" supported facilities, manpower training, and treatment costs —especially, for instance, in program projects—research and development became in fact a device to provide the manpower (educate it) and to deliver services (albeit selectively) to patients.

To compensate for some of the side effects or "externalities" produced by heavy investment in research, the NIH also assumed a responsibility for the general welfare of the research institutes, medical schools, and university departments involved in biomedical research. To fulfill this responsibility, the NIH has sought increased payment for indirect costs, funds for instrumentation and special research resources, and block grants for general research and the general medical sciences (as distinguished from the clinical specialties).

A third area of NIH program expansion was manpower development. This responsibility included training of health manpower generally, though mainly under the guise of research training. Also, support for training was used for wider purposes. For instance, development and career fellowships—similar to five-year and tenured academic appointments—both developed scientific manpower and provided a source of "hard money" (reliable income) for the institutions. With respect to some of the clinical fellowships, and especially the National Institute of Mental Health (NIMH) traineeships, the responsibility assumed was even larger: transforming the conception of practice while training the manpower to implement the new conception.

In broad, inexact terms, NIH program development from 1956 to 1966 could be viewed as supplementing a scientific research and development mission with clinical (applied) research, and support for facilities and manpower development. The ultimate step, completing this hugely successful experiment in "private federalism," was to go "operational." The NIH took this step in 1965 with two programs: staffing grants for the Community Mental Health centers, supervised directly by NIMH; and "regional medical programs" (originally, Heart-Cancer-Stroke), designating the path of the region, the medical "multiversity," and the clinical research team toward improved medical services to the patient.

As a comment upon the relative ascendancy of "private" over "public" federalism, these same years brought little new responsibility for the traditional branches of the PHS. For instance, few believed that the PHS should administer Medicare, the most important health legislation in a generation. The other most important health service programs— mental health and the regional centers—were made NIH rather than BSS responsibilities.

Some of the factors that have encouraged "direct" federalism were also at work in the public health field—hard-core needs concentrated in metropolitan centers; and antiquated state administrative systems, made even more conservative by categorically fragmented programs, and parsimonious traditions of public expenditure in health and welfare.

The shift toward "private federalism" both in more traditional BSS programs, and independently of these, through NIH extramural grants, depended mainly upon factors extraneous to politics; upon changing patient populations, trends within the health professions, the excitement and challenge of science, and the internal politics of the biomedical constituency itself.

Private federalism has also created its own new-style "pressure groups" with an enormous potential for innovative leadership and mobilization of political resources. Old-style public health officers denounce the NIH, the Lasker Foundation, and the biomedical constituency; but they are disarmed by their good works. One PHS official commented, in retrospect, "They beat Eisenhower when no one else could." The constitutional implications of the comment are worth pondering.

Private federalism probably tends to increase some disparities between public and private programs and rich and poor. It tends in the first instance to afford opportunity mainly to the competent and resourceful, and to benefit for the longer run primarily those able to implement new discovery and to attract and hold trained manpower. The rich may not get richer and the poor poorer, since many institutions and public authorities with modest resources can through disproportionate effort do well for themselves. However, the less well-endowed community or institution tends to share less in the total grants package and especially less in the livelier aspects of health and medical developments. In concrete terms, elite universities and well-established medical complexes, California and Michigan and New York City, do well while others do less well. Universities, hospitals, and professional groups have often benefited enormously, public programs have often got less, and been out of the "mainstream"—more in backward states and cities, but also everywhere.

Some of the rancorous controversy over Medicare and its implementation indicate other issues that "private federalism" creates: disputes over the public-private balance in programs; implicit regulation of one profession by another; conflicts of interest. Private federalism also tends not only to create but to obscure just such issues, particularly in the initial stages of program development.

This historical account would be misleading without a recognition that administrative leaders and—in this case the PHS—are mindful of undesirable aspects of private federalism. With respect to the PHS, for example, the new Surgeon General has taken two important steps. One is abolition of most categorical grants to states and an attempt, through encouraging "comprehensive planning," to strengthen state public health programs. Another is the assertion of the authority of the Surgeon General's Office over the NIH, with the implication—not yet an accomplishment—that the NIH will tend increasingly to become a "health" rather than a "science" agency. Both of these measures would tend to limit "private federalism" and take an important step toward a larger public role. Whether the established trends and the existing categorical and professional interests will prove too powerful remains to be seen. In any event—and this is another important aspect of "private federalism"— the struggle will be largely a secret one, over issues understood mainly or only by administrative or professional "insiders," and the decision itself ultimately in the keeping of a few men, many of whom will not be in government at all.

Conclusion: The Prospects for Federalism

Earlier we inquired whether the states are likely to have a new access of public functions, political authority, and fiscal resources; to decline; or to maintain their present place in the federal system. And we noted that there is disagreement about the extent of their present role. Some final considerations on this point will also help to illuminate the prospects of the states.

We can begin by considering intergovernmental fiscal relations under conventional federalism. Here the question is whether the secular, proportionate growth in state taxation and expenditures is a fair measure of the states' autonomy and importance.[43] The answer depends on the politics and administration of intergovernmental fiscal relations as well as on ratios of taxing and spending. Specifically, it depends (1) on whether state policies and administration are severely constrained by federal matching requirements and by the standards attached to federal grants, and (2) on whether state grants to local governments (a large share of state outlays) are accompanied by effective state policies and standards. No one has carefully assessed the evidence on these points. All one can say is that it varies according to the program and the state in question. Moreover, definitive study of the question depends on the measurement or comparison of influence, which is extremely difficult— as our earlier remarks about trends in centralization or decentralization suggest. The central question is that of the extent to which the federal and state governments can establish their own policies and standards for grants to the states and localities, respectively; or, conversely, of the extent to which they are influenced by state and local pressures. The federal system is so complex that no one has produced a general answer; and there are few definite answers for given grant programs. We record our impression that the influence of granting governments on grantees is growing because of the larger fiscal impact of grant-in-aid programs, and that minor administrative regulations attached to grants tend increasingly to constrain state and local governmental action. Neither of these trends is dramatic, however, and both are offset to some extent by

[43] It is frequently taken to be so. Cf. Martin, op. cit., and Fesler, op. cit., Chap. 4.

the legislative influence of lower levels of government on the policies of the granting agencies, especially at the state level.

A second issue pertaining to state autonomy and importance is that of the reach of federal regulatory and enforcement policies. To the extent that federal statutes dealing with, say, racial discrimination in education, housing, and employment displace state action the role of the states will be diminished. In this field there is wide variation among the states today; and the principal danger to state autonomy, given a growing national effectiveness of groups favoring action, seems to be that the inaction of some states will lead to more federal regulatory legislation and direct federal enforcement of it. The politics of race has altered the federal system periodically for a century, and especially in the last decade; matters long considered "municipal" in constitutional law are now regulated by federal law. A large extension of federal social regulation, following the growth of federal economic regulation earlier in the century, would further undermine the constitutional position of the states and their political role in social policy, leaving the states with the regulation of professions and small business primarily; but it is probably fair to say that the states have not nearly reached this residual position yet.

A third question is whether direct remedial action, as well as regulation, by the federal government is likely to reduce the states' functions further, or at least alter their proportionate role in the federal system. This prospect seems likely in several fields that overlap state boundaries, or in which interstate fiscal disparities are important, and, in which public demand is relatively intense. In these fields the federal government has so far acted through a combination of regulatory policies and grants-in-aid. The question is what form these will take; specifically, whether they will use the conventional federal system.

In this connection we have discussed two new forms of federal action: direct federalism and private federalism, evident in the social services. It is appropriate to add a third pattern, which might be termed "regional federalism," common in economic development and natural resources. One example is the Appalachia Program, in which a federal-state commission allocates funds over 373 counties in 12 states. Another example is contained in recent legislation to establish federal commissions in federally designated "air sheds" for the control of air pollution. Federal, federal-state, and interstate agencies, established on a regional basis, have a long history in these fields as well as in transportation. The prospect is for more of them; and the question is how they will be organized. The original proposals for Appalachia legislation in 1965 and the Air Quality Act of 1967 (to stick to our two examples) called for by-passing the states almost entirely in planning, regulation, and enforcement; but amendments in Congress (and the protests of some

Democratic governors in the case of Appalachia) led to a substantial role for the states in the former program and a residual, rather than initial, federal regulatory and enforcement authority in air pollution. Nevertheless, further pressure toward direct federal action in these fields is predictable.

Thus a possible pattern for the federalism of the future is one in which the states will gradually be supplemented, displaced, or confined to their current activities, while new programs of social remedies and physical amenities will be administered by different forms of federal partnership (direct, private, and regional); and in which federal regulatory statutes, largely enforced through the federal courts, erode a little further the constitutional base of the states. Such a system would be highly pluralistic and also highly complex: it would consist of a number of spheres of interest and of influence, functionally and geographically defined—a medieval confusion of corporations, commissions, and professions, all somewhat autonomous, few subject to direct popular control. It would recreate at the level of the nation, and thus on a larger scale, the public organization that now obtains in metropolitan areas. The states would serve as fiscal conduits for many established programs and as regulatory jurisdictions over many private and local governmental affairs; but their roles in policy would be much diminished.

The alternative prospect is for continued reliance on the states as the basic intermediate level of government with a considerable measure of political, fiscal, and administrative autonomy. There are incipient federal policies that point in this direction, too: the recent movement away from categorical grants toward broader block grants in public health and welfare; the reconsideration of some federal accounting and organizational controls in the social services so as to allow states to combine grant programs more adaptively and creatively; and the proposals to enlarge state financial resources through a federal tax credit or —more certainly and considerably, if possibly less autonomously—by a return to the states of a significant share of federal taxes.[44]

Which alternative is likelier? There are strong political forces in the federal government—mainly in the newer agencies, staffed with a new generation of professionals—that favor the first alternative. Those supporting the second course tend to be located in the old-line agencies and in Congress. And those in Congress are divided between conservatives who favor the states as they stand and "progressives" who would attach further sanctions and incentives to federal grant programs in order to encourage governmental reforms, political initiatives, and administrative professionalism in the states.

[44] *Cf.* Walter W. Heller, *New Dimensions of Political Economy* (Cambridge, Mass.: Harvard University Press, 1966), Chap. 3; and Joseph A. Pechman, *Federal Tax Policy* (Washington, D.C.: The Brookings Institution, 1966), Chap. 9.

The issue will not, of course, be settled wholly within the federal government. Its outcome will be influenced by the conduct of the states —not only the active minority containing a majority of the population and national wealth, but the conservative majority and especially those in the less well economically and politically developed areas of the nation. Moreover, it is easy to overlook the strong interests and traditions that attach to the states, although many of these tend to favor state inaction and thus indirectly to promote federal action through new forms.

Nevertheless, had the Vietnam war not intervened, the Great Society programs that were in the planning stage before the escalation of the war would probably have forced the issue of the future course of federalism; and it seems likely that the issue would have been resolved in the direction of the first alternative mentioned above. The thesis of this essay—to state it in extreme form—is that the complexities of the first alternative (even though some of them are inevitable) do not add up to a politically responsible form of political modernization for America, and that the constitutional structure of federalism is worth preserving for its relative clarity and accountability and despite its inconveniences. This is to say that the given system, which is difficult to change fundamentally, is to be preferred over the most likely alternative, which will not achieve the centralized and accountable system sought by critics of American federalism. But the preservation of the basic federal pattern will probably require substantial and imaginative reforms, or "modernization," of state and local government and politics, as well as a federal policy designed to support and encourage such modernization. Thus this essay only sets the stage for another, more challenging task: the devising of the appropriate reforms and policies.

8

LOCAL AND STATE GOVERNMENT

Clyde D. McKee, Jr.

We are being asked to probe into the soul of America.
—Governor Otto Kerner

The fuse between political thought and governmental action must be shortened. Sparks of contagious conflict are gnawing at the very foundations of American government. In 1965 the arrest of a Negro high school dropout for drunken driving touched off the riot in Watts. Six days of turmoil in Los Angeles left 35 persons dead and 900 injured. Moving across the nation, the ghetto of Hough in Cleveland erupted a year later. And during the first half of 1967, Buffalo, Boston, Newark, and Cambridge, Maryland, were hit. The "American Tragedy" in Detroit left 39 dead, about 3,000 arrested, and an estimated $1 billion in property damages. In July, 1967, the Associated Press reported that 68 cities in 24 states had experienced major damage to persons and property from civil disorder. These statistics do more than challenge the wisdom of the programs associated with the Great Society. They cry out that something is basically wrong in America, that attitudes towards government and the structure and procedures of our basic political institutions must be changed.

Evaluation

DE FACTO V. DE JURE. The transition from "negative" to "positive" government occurred in the United States at the national level in 1937. This basic transformation in the relationship of government to society

CLYDE D. McKEE, JR., PH.D., Assistant Professor of Government at Trinity College, was Training Coordinator and Acting Director of the Foreign Administrators Training Program, University of Connecticut. As a student of the political institutions of local and state government, particularly local political parties and the council-manager form, he has served as both professional consultant and elected official.

is well documented by a number of decisions of the United States
Supreme Court. Economic prosperity and victory by the Allies in World
War II placed career administrators and elected officials in a new light.
They had status, prestige, and, most important, a mandate to initiate
and expand governmental authority. The idea that "government is best
when it governs least" was repudiated forever—but only at the national
level. The "layer-cake" and grid conception of the American federal
system continues to serve as spark gaps for governmental inaction. It
is only when problems reach the crisis stage—double sessions for suburban schools, impoverishment in Appalachia, death and destruction in
the urban cores, and deadly pollution of our human environment—that
the need for positive government at the local and state levels is recognized.

The conceptual cleavage between positive government at the national
level and negative government for cities and states can be traced to
inherent weaknesses in American constitutional law and political theory.
The United States Constitution makes no provision for local government. But the theory of American government is based, in large part,
upon the Lockean-Jeffersonian doctrine, which gives localities the right
of self-government by direct democracy. By definition, political parties
are excluded.

American political theory fosters an obsolete concept of political responsibility. The Lockean-Jeffersonian doctrine emphasizes the judicial
rather than the legislative and executive functions, so much so that
today councilmen, mayors, legislators, and even governors tend to re-
semble judges as they pass judgment upon proposals that they should
have initiated. But it is traditional for the burden of initiative to be
placed outside established political institutions. This tradition grew out
of the social contract. Having lost its revolutionary heritage, the concept
of the social contract with its distinction between society and government provides convenient theoretical justification for the suburban-
urban style of living at present so characteristic of American society.
Thus, while lacking constitutional legitimacy, the Lockean-Jeffersonian
doctrine now occupies a comfortable niche in the entire lower half of
the federal concept.

The strength of the political institutions of local and state government
has been sapped also by the Dillon-Cooley dispute, which has been
with us for a century. In 1868, Judge John F. Dillon of the Iowa Supreme
Court wrote:

> Municipal corporations owe their origin to, and derive their powers from,
> the legislature. The [municipal corporations] are, so to phrase it, the mere
> tenants at will of the legislature.[1]

[1] *City of Clinton* v. *Cedar Rapids and Missouri Railroad Company*, 24 Iowa 455
(1868).

Although constitutionally sound, this decision broke with the Lockean-Jeffersonian doctrine. But the bias was soon to be reversed. Three years later, Michigan Judge Thomas M. Cooley wrote a decision in which he said:

> The state may mould local institutions according to its views of policy; but local government is a matter of absolute right; and the State cannot take it away.[2]

The Cooley doctrine holds that from time immemorial local governments have exercised the right of self-government, that this right is inherent, inviolate, and more fundamental than a written constitution. But the United States Supreme Court has indicated on a number of occasions that the Cooley doctrine is not the law of the land.

Legally, the Dillon Rule controls the actions of every city and town in the United States. In 1911, Judge Dillon published his treatise on the law of municipal corporations.[3] It is the main source for the local law director's shibboleth: constant advice to the chief executive and city council that "the city is a creature of the state." In abbreviated legal language this means that a local government as a municipal corporation can exercise only that authority "granted in express words" by the state government; or powers that are "necessarily or fairly implied"; or those powers that are "indispensable" rather than "convenient." When the authority of political institutions at the local level has been tested in court, the burden of proof has been upon the government. Legal rather than political justification has ruled the issue. When the basis of local authority is in doubt, power is denied.

As every veteran mayor, city manager, and councilman knows, the Dillon Rule has cut the heart out of local government's ability to grasp with imagination, enthusiasm, and perseverance its most pressing problems. As Adrian has indicated, this legal doctrine prevents a city from regulating billboards for purposes of aesthetic design; blocks it from financing parking lots out of a parking meter fund; checks legislation for smoke abatement; precludes enactment of ordinances prohibiting the construction of gas stations in commercial areas for reasons other than safety; and creates a tangle of legal problems for a city anxious to experiment with solutions for physical and human deprivation. There is an obvious need to rework the theory of public law so that legislative, executive, and judicial authority is restored to parity. Judges should not be able to overrule councilmen on political issues.

---

[2] *People ex rel. Le Roy v. Hurlbut,* 24 Michigan 44 (1871).

[3] *See* John F. Dillon, *Commentaries on the Law of Municipal Corporations,* 5th ed. (Boston: Little, Brown and Company, 1911). For an excellent discussion of the law of municipal corporations, *see* Charles R. Adrian, *Governing Urban America* (New York: McGraw-Hill Book Company, 1961), p. 171.

The Dillon-Cooley dispute may be compared to the disputes resulting from the paradoxes of Zeno in the fifth century B.C. For some twenty-two hundred years Zeno's concepts successfully frustrated the understanding of motion in a universe divisible into many parts—Achilles never caught the turtle; the arrow never hit the target; and the three chariots never completed the race. Political theory must now provide a similar formula for the basic institutions of government. The place to begin is with dynamic constructs for interaction and process. American society will explode before it will wait twenty-two hundred years.

SOURCES OF RESISTANCE TO MODERNIZATION. Just as the Dillon-Cooley dispute has frustrated philosophical and legal reform, the polished doctrine of the National Municipal League obstructs structural reform. This evaluation of the League's present influence, however, should in no way disparage the achievements of this organization during the first half of the twentieth century. Quite the contrary, these achievements must be understood because they now serve as major impediments to the evolution and transformation of those political institutions that should be most responsive to the will of the people.

Since the turn of the century, the National Municipal League has assumed that effective public administration at the local level is more a technical problem than a problem of politics. To eliminate the function of political process, a reform movement was designed to end corruption, increase efficiency, and to make government more "democratic." In pursuing these objectives, the League and a number of less influential organizations championed adoption of such devices as the petition, initiative, recall, and referendum. But during the past twenty years these techniques have been either ignored or they have been used to obstruct experimentation, innovation, and the implementation of programs to attack recognized problems.

Leaders of the early reform movement believed that government could be made more democratic if it were made more visible. Therefore, steps were taken to shorten the ballot so that candidates for elected offices could become known to the voters. At the same time, citizens' associations and research bureaus were established to investigate and to report what local governments were actually doing. Candidates for local offices were forced by the good government groups to take defined positions on matters of public policy, to commit themselves in relationship to past activities of the board or commission upon which membership was sought. These efforts were as successful as the goals were commendable.

But the public has paid a price for the success of the reform movement. Sometimes by accident and sometimes by design efforts to make government more democratic by making it more visible isolated candidates and drove them out of politics. Unable to sustain themselves under the attacks of the League, local units of the national political parties folded their tents and abandoned the areas of contest. Experience has shown that there are relatively few citizens in our society who have the initiative, resources, and vanity to enable them to circulate petitions in their own behalf, win nominations, and then wage successful campaigns. The reform movement destroyed partisan functions of recruitment, screening, and financial support for political contenders. In a number of municipalities responsibility for these political activities fell upon the citizens charter committee. But democracy involves choice among alternative candidates and political programs as much as it does visible government. The citizen charter committee as a political institution has been so effective within the nonpartisan framework in putting its endorsed slates into office that it has driven opposing slates out of political contest. Therefore, the nonpartisan doctrine currently sustains the practice of one-party government throughout much of America, and an important feature of democracy has been lost.

Just as contests among candidates were eliminated, local governments were isolated and insulated politically. The doctrine of insulation has become an illogical part of America's political theory. The basis of this doctrine is the assumption that the goals of democracy in terms of self-government and direct participation are best served if the activities of local political institutions are made separate and distinct from the political activities of the institutions at other levels. For the past half-century state legislatures have been under constant pressure to adopt provisions enabling local governments to exercise home rule, to provide for the nonpartisan ballot, and to schedule local elections at times different from state and national elections.[4]

There is some evidence, however, that these provisions have had undesirable side effects. Citizen interest, measured in terms of voter participation, usually declines under nonpartisan elections. Local officials in need of national and state resources frequently lack interpersonal relationships necessary to acquire these resources for local purposes. The doctrine of insulation also encourages inefficient and ineffective government in that it precludes examination of governmental services to determine optimum levels for policy execution. But the advantages and disadvantages of this doctrine must be carefully weighed.

[4] Although there is no authoritative definition for nonpartisan elections, the term is generally used to indicate the absence of party labels from the ballot or voting machine. It also usually means that local political parties have no procedural advantages in the nominating process. Connecticut is perhaps the best example of a state that has structured its political institutions and procedures to give the national political parties maximum opportunity to exercise responsible party government at both the state and local levels.

The National Municipal League is now in the position of the Federalists at the end of the third decade of the nineteenth century. The objectives of the movement have been achieved. Almost 50 million Americans in the United States live under council-manager government.[5] It is the majority form for communities with populations exceeding 10,000 persons. Sixty-four percent of *all* communities with more than 5,000 persons use the nonpartisan election. The figure rises to 84 per cent when only council-manager forms are considered. Most cities have adopted or are in the process of adopting the executive budget, "business-like" accounting and auditing procedures, and merit and classification systems. Patronage has been eliminated, except in the appointment of architects, lawyers, appraisers, and insurance brokers; namely, those services in which discretion rather than competitive bidding is recommended. To make the efforts of the old reform movement complete, many of the objectives of the National Municipal League have been taken over by the national government and are being forced upon local and state governments as conditions for receipt of federal aid. National standards have been particularly effective in modernizing local and state personnel and accounting practices.

THE POSITION OF THE STATES. Viewed in the light of the early reform movement, the position of the state governments is somewhat paradoxical. Starting from a constitutional position of great strength, the states were reduced to political impotency. To understand this transformation, it is necessary to grasp the position of the states within the federal concept. The United States Constitution gives authority *to* the national government but takes it *away* from the states in the form of specific limitations. Because the states have always had authority no constitutional grant was necessary. In constitutional theory, therefore, the residual powers made state government the stronger half of the federal relationship.

But the history of state government is a history of the erosion of this position. State government as a composite of political institutions withered partly because it was too responsive to public pressures. Internal and external forces formed alliances, became entrenched, and caused hardening of the state's political arteries. The focus of these forces was the state constitution as an instrument for granting authority. As John Buechner has indicated, "most state constitutions today are old, contradictory, lengthy, poorly written, and often inadequate for modern state government." [6] This condition exists despite the efforts of such

---

[5] *The Municipal Year Book* (Chicago: International City Managers' Association, 1966), p. 74.
[6] John C. Buechner, *State Government in the Twentieth Century* (Boston: Houghton Mifflin Company, 1967), p. 54.

reform-minded groups as the National League, the National League of Cities (formerly the American Municipal Association), the League of Women Voters, the Chamber of Commerce, various taxpayers associations, and most recently the Committee for Economic Development. The achievements of these groups at the state level are in marked contrast to their accomplishments at the local level.

State government can be modernized only if we understand why political institutions at the state level have been so successful in withstanding change. Based on the frequency of constitutional conventions and enactments of new constitutions, the period of resistance extends from the end of World War I to 1962, when it was broken by the Supreme Court's decision in *Baker v. Carr*. Prior to this period there were three major phases of intensive charter writing: during the 1850's, when the values of frontier individualism were written into the fundamental laws of the states; during the reconstruction period immediately following the War between the States; and during part of the old reform movement, from the 1890's through World War I.[7] This use of fundamental law for the pragmatic expression of attitudes has never been part of the constitutional history of our national government.

State government was the target of various reform movements. Although it can be shown that these movements differed significantly from the movement that focused on the political institutions at the local level, these movements at the local and state levels had one thing in common. The achievements of both now serve as sources of resistance to change.

State government has been immune to the doctrine of the National Municipal League mainly because the theory of nonpartisanism is essentially incompatible with the popular conception of American federalism. Political institutions of the state have always been viewed as "political" rather than "administrative," although the need for competent career administrators has long been recognized. In response to the growth of Jacksonian democracy in the 1880's, direct participation of male voters was expanded; *administrative* positions were filled by election rather than appointment; and the procedures for amending many state constitutions were simplified. State constitutions became instruments for preserving rural interests and registering the influence of dominant economic interests.

The fundamental law of the states was turned into statute law. The spirit of the Dillon Rule was violated as state legislatures cooperated with the leaders of the local government reform movement. Provisions for constitutional home rule were enacted that became the conceptual

[7] See Charles R. Adrian, *State and Local Governments* (New York: McGraw-Hill Book Co., 1960), pp. 115-16.

basis for the "sectionalism," "localism," "urban-rural" split, and "metro-politan-nonmetropolitan" cleavages that have been catalogued so pains-takingly by such writers as Daniel Elazar.[8] Reappraisal of the state's political institutions by constitutional conventions composed of dele-gates selected on a basis of population rather than geographical units would have been suicidal for both the entrenched legislators and ex-ternal vested interests.

THE SITUATION AFTER WORLD WAR II. With the cessation of hostilities in 1945, the attention of American society focused once again upon domestic issues. It was natural for state governments to look rather self-consciously at their structures and procedures, which had been, for the most part, ignored since the days of the Great Depression. But the nature of this self-conscious examination emerged in terms of tradi-tional principles of government that made little provision for the dynamic social, economic, and political forces set in motion by a society recently geared for unconditional victory over a stubborn enemy.

Somewhat typical of most state legislatures was the General Assembly of Connecticut, which in 1949 created the Bowles' Commission to study the need for reorganization of state government. In 1950, this commis-sion delivered its report. In its letter of transmittal it said:

We have full faith in the American genius for self-government and in the strength of American political traditions. Better government begins at home. To enable the state government to carry its responsibilities ef-fectively, and to avoid where possible the concentration of responsibility in Washington, greater efficiency at the state level is needed. If this in-volves stronger management in the executive branch, it calls also for strengthening the General Assembly and the courts, and for new controls in the hands of the citizens. We aim to build on the separation of powers that has been the traditional protection of our liberties.[9]

Reasserting the Lockean-Jeffersonian doctrine, the Bowles Commis-sion expressed fear of strong central government. At the same time, there was real concern for improving efficiency, even if it meant chal-lenging entrenched legislators and vested economic interests. It should be noted, however, that the spirit of reform was mainly internal. In the late 1940's there was little desire to experiment with either the tradi-tional intergovernmental relationships among the branches of state government or to establish new concepts for relating the political insti-tutions of the state to those of the local or national governments.

State reform was viewed in terms of structure and organization rather

[8] Daniel J. Elazar, American Federalism: A View from the States (New York: Thomas Y. Crowell Company, 1966), pp. 182-83.

[9] Commission on State Government Organization, The Report (Hartford: State of Connecticut, 1950).

than politics. As great as the fear of central government was the fear of political parties. Respect for political parties is new in the United States. The partisan function was conceived as an adjunct to the concept of checks and balances, rather than as the heart of the political process, the source of democracy.[10] After World War II, political scientists expressed concern for the expanded authority and technological power vested in the office of the President.[11] The task of the national parties was to diffuse executive power and make it safe for democracy. Because governors and state legislatures do not possess the authority to declare war and engage society in nuclear conflict, strong, responsible party government has never been fully justified at the state level.

The crisis in national-state relations caused by the Supreme Court decision in *Brown* v. *Board of Education of Topeka* (1954) was still in the future. Also, state legislatures were not aware of the economic transformations taking place in the core cities. Therefore, reform commissions limited their recommendations to such proposals as the creation of finance departments, which combine the functions of the offices of the comptroller and the treasurer, the tax and motor vehicle departments; annual executive type budgets, prepared on a "performance" basis; establishment of requirements for revenue estimates and expenditure controls; creation of an item veto for the governor; and the initiation of independent auditing procedures.

Of somewhat lesser concern the area of governmental personnel procedures. A number of states had already followed the lead of the national government and enacted civil service laws in the second and third decades of the century. Merit systems were introduced in the 1930's; and various types of personnel manpower studies were made during the early 1940's. After 1945 there was recognition of the need for improved recruitment and classification procedures; better means for evaluating skills and performance, mainly for purposes of economy and efficiency; and new grievance procedures for improving employee relations. There was still fear, however, of establishing by organization and structure a close relationship between the career service and the political authority of the governor. Progressive action at the state level was frequently viewed in terms of elaborate structure and procedures to insulate public employees from the corrupting influence of the political parties. At the same time, a number of local charters were adopted that in-

---

[10] The concept of the political party expressed by E. E. Schattschneider in his *Party Government* (New York: Holt, Rinehart & Winston, Inc., 1942) has never been generally accepted in the United States because it challenges directly the Lockean-Jeffersonian doctrine, offering no compromises.

[11] "Toward a More Responsible Two-Party System: A Report of the Committee on Political Parties of the American Political Science Association," *American Political Science Review*, XLIV (September, 1950), Supplement V.

sulated local employees from the influence of the council and, in some cases, from the manager.[12]

In view of the fact that reapportionment was not forced upon state governments until *Baker* v. *Carr* (1962) and subsequent Supreme Court decisions, it is interesting to review the struggles of the state commissions with the issue of malapportionment. The Supreme Court had said in *Colegrove* v. *Green* (1946) that the issue of malapportioned legislative districts was a "political question" and that relief should be sought by means of the political process. Study of this process at the state level shows how naïve the Court was in the *Colegrove* decision.

It is significant that malapportionment *was* recognized by the states as a problem. This recognition is revealed in the variety of solutions that were proposed. The single-chamber proposal, known as the "Nebraska Plan," provided for approximately 100 legislators elected on a straight population basis. It seems strange now that the "one man, one vote" standard has become widely accepted that *bicameral* systems with both houses apportioned on the basis of population were considered as a variation of the Nebraska Plan.

There was real concern after 1945 about the need to recognize and preserve the divergent interests of the rural and urban areas. The technique of "population density" provided a plausible although sophisticated solution. Using census figures provided by the national government, states were districted into towns, groups of towns, or parts of towns, and a "sliding scale of population density" was proposed to give each district a single legislative representative.

Bicameral proposals incorporating the principle of representation by both population and density were also considered. This proposal, which included a senate based on population and a house based on density, was particularly favored by those who felt the need to preserve checks and balances *within* the legislative branch as well as among the branches.

The problem of malapportionment was a problem not of *what*, for solutions came easily, but of *how*. Political institutions ponderously balanced and checked against one another offered few opportunities for reformers to insert political levers against fulcrums supported by sentiment and conviction to topple entrenched bases of power. Few, if any, blue-ribbon commissions were able to reach agreement among their members as to the best solution to the problem of just representation. But rather than using the problem to gain deeper insight into the problem of state government in general, the reformers dodged the issue. They recommended that state legislatures adopt procedures for the question of representation to be settled through initiative and refer-

[12] An excellent example of such a charter is that of Hartford, Connecticut, adopted by referendum and approved by the state legislature in 1947.

endum. In short, a problem too difficult for a group of highly skilled, like-minded specialists was passed on to the people.

Criticism of state governments for their inability to reorganize their power structures should not spoil the significant changes that were recommended and, in a number of cases, instituted. The members of the political institutions of the state governments have long suffered from lack of status in their own eyes as well as the eye of the public. Various proposals were made for increased compensation for legislators; improved office facilities; better legal, financial, and research assistance; and annual sessions, with no fixed date for adjournment. Perhaps even more significant but less publicized was action by state legislatures abolishing conflicts of interest and dual office holding, a traditional source of corruption of the worst type.

The state judiciary had long been the target of great criticism. And, with rare exceptions, this criticism was entirely justified. The Bowles Commission did an able job of describing the problems of the state courts:

> Over the years the catalog of complaints has grown impressively long: a multiplicity of uncertain and sometimes overlapping jurisdictions, congested calendars, the delays and expense of retrials, outmoded rules, inadequate records, the absence of uniform and professional standards of judgment, the persistence of the discredited fee basis of compensation, and political connections and patronage which undermine the appearance if not the substance of impartiality.[13]

The basic theoretical problem of judicial reform in the United States has been the lack of clearly defined and well-understood procedures for relating the judicial function to political process. There has long been agreement among legal scholars and judges that a judicial system should be unified, fairly simple in design, and composed of judges who are professionally competent and capable of exercising independent judgment. There has also been agreement that a judicial system needs adequate administrative assistance. But how should judges be selected, by election or appointment? Who should be a judge? How long should a judge serve, for life or for a relatively short term? By what means should society exercise its will if there is general dissatisfaction with the courts and the quality of justice? These questions force consideration of the relationship of the judiciary to the political parties.

A judgeship has long been regarded in American society as one of the best "political plums" available. Therefore, if one tends to believe that strong two-party government is essential for democratic society, one

---

[13] Commission on State Government Organization, *op. cit.*, p. 63.

cannot ignore the need for partisan organizations to have enduring and recurring political resources, such as judgeships, to attract and hold the attention of those with talent and ambition. Many honest, capable young attorneys will serve the public for years as candidates, officials, and party workers if they feel they have reasonably good opportunities to win judgeships as rewards for faithful and loyal service. Using the Supreme Court of the United States as evidence, one can make a strong case that partisan experience is a desirable if not indispensable qualification for a good judge.

Two final observations regarding judicial modernization are necessary. First, judicial reform at the local level has been blocked by the doctrine of insulation. Towns and cities throughout the country have long enjoyed a variety of municipal courts—justice of the peace, police, juvenile, and probate, to name but a few. There is strong popular sentiment that justice is best when it is kept close to the people, particularly in cases involving domestic issues such as divorce, commitment to mental institutions, juvenile delinquency, and the settlement of family estates. But the *Model City Charter* of the National Municipal League makes no provision for the judicial function at the local level.[14] Thus, while local courts have escaped the attention of reform groups such as the League, existing courts have been protected by the doctrine that the reformers have used to insulate political institutions at the local level.

Second, all too often rule-making authority is forgotten as a vital area for legal reform. Frequently when standards for judicial conduct are found to exist at all, these are legislative rather than administrative directions initiated and supervised by the chief justice of the state's highest court. Furthermore, the concept of judicial "independence" has been interpreted to mean that local and state judges are free from supervision of any type, save that of God. In actuality, judicial autonomy has meant that lower court judges are free to perpetuate traditions of short work hours, long vacations, and the right to interject personal values into legal decisions. But little progress was made in judicial modernization: first, because reform commissions often failed to see subtle interrelations among the branches and, second, because few states possessed the political leadership necessary to reorganize the power structures associated with the existing institutions.

During the 1950's attention at the state level shifted from a reorganizational approach for its own institutions and the political institutions of local government to real concern for local problems. For the first time states became aware of the fact that towns and cities were caught between insistent demands for new and expanded municipal services and

---

[14] *Model City Charter*, 6th ed. (New York: National Municipal League, 1964).

mounting resistance on the part of property owners to increased taxation.[15]

A variety of approaches were recommended to assist the local governments. First, there were those who advocated greater state participation
in financing the costs of such major responsibilities as education and
highways. Second, others took the position that relief from the property
tax could be secured by increasing the local tax base from sources other
than real property. A third approach called for rearranging the functions of local and state government so that local political institutions
could be relieved of those administrative and financial responsibilities
that they performed either inadequately or at excessive cost.[16]

Although these proposals illustrate the awareness by state officials of
the need to assist their local governments, particularly in the area of
financial resources, there was little realization of the extent to which
problems of education, public housing, health, and highways would
intensify, nor was there understanding of the interrelationships of these
problems. Solutions were still being proposed in the light of the structures and procedures of the established political institutions, although
various study commissions had demonstrated rather convincingly that
these institutions were inadequate.

Reconstruction

NATIONAL ECONOMIC AWARENESS. At the end of the 1950's and early
in the 1960's two significant changes took place that were to have great
impact upon the political institutions of local and state government.
First, realization of the scope and magnitude of the postwar problems hit
the business world. And second, concern for urban problems was shifted
dramatically from the state to the national level. With this nationalization of problems that had traditionally been the responsibility of the
local and state governments, significant changes took place in the attitudes of large business corporations towards the affairs of government,
partisan politics, and political process in general. The broad concept
of the public-private relationship began to evolve.

In 1957, the Committee for Economic Development (CED) made a
major policy decision to concentrate its attention upon two important
areas of interest: first, the economic development of regions and localities of the United States, and second, the complex problems of our

[15] Commission to Investigate the Relationship Between the State and Its Subdivi-
sions, *State and Local Governmental Relationships in Connecticut* (Hartford: State
of Connecticut, 1954), p. 7.

[16] *Ibid.*, p. 8.

urban-metropolitan areas.[17] To implement this policy, CED commissioned two research papers, one dealing with "the changing economic functions of the central city" and another treating "the efforts of local governments to maintain orderly community life in the midst of great changes which surround them." [18] In many respects these decisions marked the revival and application of political-economic theory to the problems of local government.

For the first time, urban problems were defined in economic rather than strictly governmental terms. Businessmen wanted to know whether there was evidence that urbanization would be sustained. More specifically, for the sake of their corporate enterprises, they wanted to know how such activities as manufacturing, wholesaling, retailing, business services, and home building would be "spacially distributed *within* metropolitan areas."

Businessmen suddenly realized that urbanization had revolutionized economics. Prior to the late 1950's, there had been little concern for the "external economics of aggregation in urban areas" or the economic consequences of the "cumulative process of urban growth." The study of urban economics led to an understanding of the need for cooperative rather than antagonistic relationships between the public and private spheres of activity. For example, the theory of urban renewal was just beginning to be understood by local officials and private developers.

The pattern of urban development began to be defined with scientific accuracy, particularly in such areas as home building and retailing. It was noted that of the 13 million dwelling units erected in nonfarm areas between 1946 and 1958, approximately 11 million, or 85 per cent, had been located outside the central cities.[19] Businessmen expressed real concern about labor markets for expanded production. Based on studies made in the late 1950's, they were fairly confident that a hard core of economic activity would be tied to the central city.

> Certain types of activities . . . show little inclination to deconcentrate. Business and governmental services requiring face-to-face relationships or dependent upon a large pool of female labor continue to exercise a strong preference for office space in the core of large metropolitan areas. In

---

[17] The Committee for Economic Development is composed of 180 leading businessmen and educators. CED has two basic objectives: (1) To develop through objective research and discussion, findings and recommendations for business and public policy which will contribute to the preservation and strengthening of our free society, and to the maintenance of high employment, increasing productivity, and living standards, greater economic stability and greater opportunity for all our people. (2) To bring about increasing public understanding of the importance of these objectives and the ways in which they can be achieved. See CED's *Guiding Metropolitan Growth* (August, 1960).

[18] *Ibid.*, p. 1.

[19] *Ibid.*, p. 17.

eight leading standard metropolitan areas about 80 per cent of all employment in finance, insurance and real estate in 1956 was in the central cities.[20]

The Supreme Court had decided the *Brown* case the year before, but few realized the impact that this decision would have upon the civil rights movement in general and urban development. Within five years a number of state office buildings and insurance companies were being located in the suburbs. In the early 1960's the New York Stock Exchange shook the business world when it considered moving to Greenwich, Connecticut. Women were afraid of the city, and men disliked the traffic.

Relatively little research had been done by government on the relationship between the personal values of Americans and urban-suburban development. Research by business filled the void. It was noted that the strong desire for low-density living on the part of families with children had led many to choose a suburban home. The single-family dwelling surrounded by a shaded green moat has long been an important part of the American dream. Congress responded to this dream by adopting new policies for mortgage insurance, which favored suburban development. The pump was primed. The national government had made the move out of the core cities both possible and attractive; now the local, state, and national governments had to face intense demands for improved highways, schools, sewers, incinerators, and recreational facilities in the suburbs. And with the exodus of middle-class whites from the core cities, the needs of the urban centers increased and the tax resources declined.

Only the national government had the financial ability to respond to these demands. In the decade of the postwar period the expenditures of local governments had tripled. For more than a half-century the property tax as a source of local governmental revenue had been declining in terms of percentages of total revenue from all sources. In the late 1950's federal officials recognized that one of the reasons local demands were not being met was that local institutions were not designed to provide optimum services at minimum costs. For example, such functions as welfare administration, highway units, and health agencies require a base of 20,000 to 30,000 persons to achieve economies of scale. Second, the national government recognized that it had much to learn about the urban environment, particularly metropolitan politics.

NATIONALIZED URBANISM. The Advisory Commission on Intergovernmental Relations (ACIR) was created by the first session of the 86th Congress and approved by the President in September, 1959. ACIR

[20] *Ibid.*, pp. 17-18.

began immediately an extensive and intensive research program to probe the mysteries of the urban environment. United States senators, governors, mayors, state legislators, and selected members of the President's Cabinet demonstrated that they were willing to work together with able administrative and technical assistance to seek solutions to enduring local problems. From the start the national goals were prescriptive as well as descriptive.

Between January and June, 1961, ACIR published eleven reports. Nine were devoted to the areas of taxation, grants-in-aid, investments, and constitutional and statutory restrictions on the borrowing power of local governments. Although ACIR demonstrated its interest in such other areas as the structure, organization, and planning in metropolitan environments; reapportionment of state legislatures; and factors affecting voter reaction to governmental reorganization, the target of study was clearly finance. The Committee for Economic Development had dramatized the influence of the urban movement upon business practices, stressing the need for a new theory of political economics; ACIR now gave full recognition to the fact that financial capability is the heart of the political institution.

Unlike the political institutions at the national level, which are shaped mainly by political and administrative forces, local institutions are often the direct result of outmoded constitutional provisions affecting revenue and expenditures. To free these institutions from their legal bondage, which can be traced to the economic crisis of the 1870's when local governments issued "railroad aid" bonds, the ACIR established basic premises and made specific recommendations. These recommendations were based on recognition of the constitutional authority of the states over local governments, but stressed the need for "intensive review and major changes" in the legal provisions affecting municipal finance.[21] States were encouraged to give maximum powers to local governments with regard to indebtedness; to vest legal authority to issue bonds in the local governing bodies, subject only to a permissive referendum, the results determined by a simple majority vote; and to make available technical and advisory assistance for long-term debt, with little "red tape."

But more important for the theory of modernization is the scheme of values and political convictions developed by the Commission. The most important value, which is prominent in nearly all federal grant-in-aid programs, is that of local self-reliance, or, for want of a better phrase, the Cooley conviction. Although urbanization has been nationalized, the federal government has consistently followed the policy of assuming that local initiative can and must be preserved, *even if it*

---

[21] Advisory Commission on Intergovernmental Relations, *State Constitutional and Statutory Restrictions on Local Government Debt* (Washington, D.C.: Government Printing Office, 1961), p. 3.

has to be recreated. There is some evidence that the national requirement for local self-reliance is realistic for only those communities large
enough to justify a corps of highly skilled career administrators. A number of states are beginning to realize that initiative for modernizing
local and state institutions is essentially the responsibility of the state
government.

In 1962 the national government created the basis for a new theory of
American local government. In a section entitled "Concepts Relating to
Local Government," ACIR developed the key ideas of this theory. First,
the Commission cut into the Dillon-Cooley dispute. It said:

> The picture of local government has been clouded by the legal distinction
> between governmental and corporate power. Also, municipal corporations
> have been thought of as having ability to do business or provide services
> as a corporation, without general concern for the source of the power
> authorizing the business or service.[22]

Next, the Commission recognized that one of the best ways to study a
political institution is to view it in terms of its relationship to conflict
and values, which revolve around "the distribution and use of governmental power." The three values in which the Commission expressed
particular interest were "liberty," "equality," and a relatively new concept
called "welfare values."

The functions of local government were then related directly to these
three main values, to which the ACIR added the "sustaining function."

> Sustaining functions are the housekeeping, financial, and revenue-raising
> functions and are subsidiary to liberty, equality, and welfare functions.
> When local government functions were dominantly liberty-oriented, sus-
> taining functions were minimal and naturally administered in a manner
> comparable to liberty functions. Sustaining activity has increased along
> with the volume of welfare activity and has inherited the brunt of the
> conflict surrounding welfare values.[23]

To demonstrate the application of these functions within specific governmental context, the Commission applied them to the government of
Mercer County, N.J., and the city of Phoenix, Arizona. But ACIR did
not go far enough.

In developing its theory the Commission may be criticized on two
counts. First, it failed to realize the full implications of its thoughtful
analysis of local political institutions. It should have driven its theory
to its logical conclusion and written a modern definition for political

[22] Advisory Commission on Intergovernmental Relations, *State Constitutional and
Statutory Restrictions Upon the Structural, Functional, and Personnel Powers of
Local Government* (Washington, D.C.: Government Printing Office, 1962), p. 13.
[23] *Ibid.*, p. 16.

institutions at the state as well as the local levels. Second, there is evidence that the Commission could not break out of the doctrine of insulation. It failed to realize that the values, functions, and conflicts of local political institutions can no longer be described in terms of geographical boundaries. The very fact that extensive state and federal funds are involved requires a new definition of political institutions that accounts for these resources. To correct this deficiency the following definition is offered:

> A political institution is a process constructed around a function, service, or problem deemed by society to be too vital to entrust to private discretion. As a process it usually includes appropriations and expenditures of public funds, definitions and descriptions of public interest, designations of authority, areas of jurisdiction, and sometimes the application of sanctions for the enforcement of its will.[24]

In 1966, the Committee for Economic Development reasserted the need for modernization of our basic political institutions. CED saw three alternative courses of action:[25]

1. Continuation of "functional government," which implies an extension of federal standard-setting, decision-making, and administrative controls—"with heavier transfusions of federal funds directly or through state channels."

2. Expansion of administrative mechanisms of state government to supersede local authority, gradually taking over one function at a time.

3. Drastic revisions of existing patterns of local governments to encourage local policy decision-making and to permit effective management of local affairs.

As one might guess, CED strongly recommended the third alternative, mainly because it offered the greatest possibility for preserving "the fundamental values of local self-government."

The Committee failed to realize that this third option no longer exists. Local self-government in the traditional sense has not been possible since 1945. Rather than selecting an outmoded solution from within the layer-cake grid conception of the American federal system, CED would have done better to create a fourth alternative, which would have combined the advantages of the first three. An attempt to describe such an alternative will be presented later in this essay.

In its study of the political institutions of state government, the Com-

---

[24] E. E. Schattschneider was perhaps the first scholar to define a particular institution as a "process." In his *Party Government* (New York: Holt, Rinehart & Winston, Inc., 1942), he said, "The Party becomes, therefore, a process formed about the elections" (p. 61).

[25] Committee for Economic Development, *Modernizing Local Government* (New York: Committee for Economic Development, 1966), p. 14.

mittee finally recognized the need to abandon the concept of insulation. It said:

> There is some advantage in linking state and local elections with national contests. All levels of government are increasingly involved in the administration of the same functions.[26]

But it could not abandon completely the National Municipal League's doctrine of nonpartisanism to the extent of wholehearted endorsement of responsible two-party government.[27] While stressing the need for structural factors that would encourage the development of substantive issues within the confines of the political systems of state government, the Committee still laid the basis for recognition of the legitimate function of the national political parties in the affairs of our basic political institutions. Regarding the modernization of the legislative, executive, and judicial branches of state government, the CED had little more to say than was said by the more progressive state commissions in the early 1950's. There was one significant change, however. In 1967, the problems of state, like those of the urban areas, were nationalized.

CONCEPTS AND TRENDS IN MODERNIZATION. Since 1945 the focus of modernization has been upon existing political institutions rather than upon efforts to create entirely new ones. But a few important institutions and forms have been seriously considered. In November, 1966, Mayor Lindsay of New York announced that he was considering substituting an ombudsman for the Civilian Complaint Review Board, which had been rejected by the voters. Although the ombudsman has become increasingly popular in Northern Europe, it has received relatively little support in the United States.[28] Justification for the legislative appointment of an individual to serve as special guardian of individual rights is perhaps best found in those states in which the legislature meets every two years for a short term. Such an appointment, however, cuts deeply into the traditional responsibilities of both the legislative and executive branches to hear complaints against administrative officials and to investigate them thoroughly and impartially. In healthy political systems the function of the ombudsman is provided by the minority party.

The two most popular forms of local government in the United States are the mayor-council form and the council-manager plan. In

[26] Committee for Economic Development, *Modernizing State Government* (New York: Committee for Economic Development, 1967), p. 18.

[27] For a good but slightly dated description of the theory of party government, see Austin Ranney, *The Doctrine of Responsible Party Government* (Urbana: University of Illinois Press, 1962).

[28] The ombudsman became part of the Constitution of Sweden in 1809. It has spread to Finland (1919), Denmark (1955), New Zealand (1962), and Norway (1962).

1965, more than 51 per cent of all cities of more than 5,000 population were governed by mayor-council government. But since 1915 the manager plan has been recommended by the National Municipal League in its *Model City Charter*. Each form has its advantages and disadvantages. The mayor plan offers the best possibility for dynamic leadership from an elected chief executive who can use the public mandate to attack knotty urban problems. On the other hand, the manager plan enables a community to receive the services of a career administrator who is professionally trained, experienced, and capable of giving continuity to complex governmental programming.

In the early 1950's a hybrid form was introduced; namely, the mayor-administrator plan. After initial success in San Francisco, the plan has been adopted by such large cities as New York, Chicago, and Philadelphia. With the abandonment of the nonpartisan doctrine that problems at the local level are inherently administrative rather than political, this hybrid form is spreading down toward the smaller communities and out from the core cities into suburban territory. Unlike the ombudsman plan, it facilitates responsible two-party government.

EXPLORATION OF THE PARA-LEGAL: A CASE STUDY IN MODERNIZATION. Written constitutionalism has made America the most legalistic country in the world. Therefore, it is difficult for us to consider techniques for modernization that are not firmly based on constitutional or statutory authority. But the residual powers for the states are even older than our constitutionalism. The reason the residual doctrine is nearly extinct in American political theory is that it has always been inherently alien to government by law rather than government by politics. This essay has discussed a number of techniques and proposals for modernization that have been tried, evaluated, and found deficient. Thus let us revive the concept of residual powers for the entire lower half of the federal scheme, recreate one of America's greatest traditions, and put it to work immediately for modernization.

The social contract was always meant to be a political rather than a legal agreement. The three agreements: man with his fellow man; society with the public decision-makers; and, finally, society and government with Ultimate Reality—are all political agreements, implying vast residual authority among all participants. But somehow when the word was written as law, the law became sovereign, and the judicial function became the dominant political institution in American society. Unlike other countries, all branches of American government—legislative, executive, and judicial—and all levels, particularly the local, have been permeated by the judicial function. It is now time for the political function to reemerge. New covenants must be made with the American people. These covenants must be political and be made *outside but not contrary to existing law*. They must lead rather than follow the law.

Because the concept of the para-legal is difficult for Americans to grasp, it is perhaps best illustrated by a particular local example. The State of Connecticut has the usual variety of constitutional and statutory provisions for controlling the political activities of its towns and cities: laws regulating taxing, borrowing, investments, and auditing procedures; requirements and restrictions for municipal incorporation; provisions and enticements for consolidating functions, services, and even governments; requirements for minority representation of political parties; corrupt practices act; optional nonpartisan or partisan election; and even an optional party level for voters. Because politicians strike out if they do not thread carefully through these legal needle holes, they have seldom seen the potential for innovative political activity that lies *outside* these check points. A recent experiment in Connecticut demonstrates that it is possible to change the complete structure, procedures, and administration of a local government without making a single change in either the laws of the state or the ordinances of the local government.

This experiment took place in the town of Old Saybrook: population about 10,000 persons; located on 16 square miles of land at the mouth of the Connecticut River; governed for some 300 years by the selectman–town meeting form of government, to which an independent board of finance was added in the 1920's in response to the reform movement of the National Municipal League. As a result of (1) federal mortgage policies, (2) the construction of the Connecticut Turnpike, (3) the trend for industries to seek low-tax, low-density, suburban environment, and (4) a plateau of economic affluence that has made the single-family dwelling a realizable part of the American dream, Old Saybrook's population jumped 111 per cent between 1950 and 1960.

Various attempts were made during this period to modernize Connecticut's political institutions. For the most part, they were consistent with the recommendations of both the Advisory Commission for Intergovernmental Relations and the Committee for Economic Development. Some additional steps were also taken. During 1964 and 1965 Connecticut's major political parties cooperated in reapportioning the state legislature, drastically reducing membership in the House of Representatives. The tradition of responsible party government was introduced into the state government of Connecticut in 1959 and had been tested by the most difficult of political problems, namely, malapportionment. But the doctrine of insulation and the Cooley conviction persisted. Other steps were taken.

The Connecticut Development Commission had been made a sophisticated substitute for county government, which was abolished in 1960. This commission designated Old Saybrook part of an eleven-town planning area, called the Estuary Planning Region, one of fifteen such regions in the state. But the doctrine of self-reliance required local initiative by the member towns, and the planning region was never formed into a productive agency. Each session of the state legislature enacted local tax and grant-in-aid inducements for planning education, and public health, but these went unnoticed for lack of local leadership and initiative. The 1967 session of the state legislature reorganized Connecticut's administrative and political structure, establishing a politically oriented Commissioner of Personnel and Commissioner of the newly created Department of Community Affairs. A new clean-water task force with money and political muscle cited some 82 of Connecticut's towns and cities for pollution, giving each a limited time to correct violations under threat of court action. The state had set an example for the local governments.

In the spring of 1967 Old Saybrook had a political crisis. The new chairman of the Democratic Town Committee faced up to the fact that his party had never won an election in the history of the town; that the Republicans outnumbered the Democrats more than 4 to 1; that he and his campaign committee were faced with the task of finding 23 candidates for local offices ranging from the top position of first selectman, through the board of education, down to constables; and that there were no funds in the party treasury. The party's nominating caucus was less than a month away (July 10).

At this point the party chairman sought the advice of the writer, an assistant professor of government, who had for some years been active in various local activities. First, this consultant told the committee that it had little hope of winning the next election; voter registration was too imbalanced. Second, he offered the committee a radical plan, which he defended on the grounds that it would give the party considerable publicity, aid in the recruitment of candidates, serve as a vehicle for an exciting campaign, and, if the party were victorious, be a technique for immediately modernizing the government.

The plan called for the creation of a "demonstration mayor–council–executive assistant form," which would be superimposed upon the existing form. Because the Connecticut Home Rule Law sets forth exact requirements for adoption of a local charter, the proposal had to be completely para-legal.

The Democratic Party had to make clear distinctions between "legal" and "political" candidates. The plan had three basic steps. First, the party had to endorse two candidates for the office of first selectman and board of selectmen. These candidates then had to declare that they were candidates for the newly created offices of "mayor" and "deputy mayor" that would be established if the party won the election on October 2. Next, the candidates had to pledge to the party members in caucus assembled and then to the voters that if elected they would create a new nine-member, bipartisan "advisory council," which would have no legal authority but great political authority because both the "mayor" and "deputy mayor" would pledge to abide by a majority decision of this council on all matters legally within the jurisdiction of the board of se-lectmen, a three-man body. Third, the candidates for "mayor" and "dep-uty mayor" would pledge to give up their budgeted salaries, $10,000 and $1,000 respectively, to hire a full-time career administrator. This admin-istrator would have no legal authority but by his knowledge and ex-perience in local government be able to exercise considerable influence upon the activities of the local political institutions. For the first time in its history the Town would have the political and administrative capability to acquire available resources from the state and federal gov-ernments. The executive assistant would be directly responsible to the mayor, who would recruit him and recommend him to the council for majority approval.

As predicted, the Democratic campaign went off like a skyrocket. It received statewide attention. The party had no difficulty getting candi-dates; money poured in; issues developed; and the campaign committee was engaged immediately in the task of winning the election. The small group of party members who ran the campaign followed two basic ground rules. First, it was agreed that the campaign should be based solidly upon fundamental political principles: the need for leadership and pinpointed responsibility in the chief executive; increased representa-tion in the council; and new administrative capability in the executive assistant. Second, although it was agreed that the campaign should be hard-hitting and deal with "gut" issues, the team agreed to attack the incumbent party and administration in only those areas for which the minority party could supply immediate solutions: elimination of conflicts of interest among elected officials and town employees; improved records and equipment inventory system; improved annual report and new pro-cedures for informing the citizens of governmental activities; regularly scheduled and open meetings of the "council" based on published agendas; improved recreational facilities; uniform enforcement of zoning regulations; up-dated master plan; the creation of a "youth-in-govern-ment day"; plus other platform planks of this type. Although the plat-form was purposely designed to be financially conservative, the candidate for "mayor" had informally alerted various state officials that he would be paying them visits in the event of an upset victory.[29]

Perspective

Modernization of the basic political institutions in America has been a topic of national importance for a decade. During this period attitudes

[29] On October 2, 1967, the Democratic candidate for "mayor" came within 347 votes or 3 per cent of defeating the incumbent selectman. After the election both sides agreed that the campaign had demonstrated the need for drastic governmental reform.

have clustered around dominant concepts and doctrines. In a keynote speech delivered at an intercollegiate conference in April, 1966, Undersecretary of the Department of Housing and Urban Development Robert C. Wood identified three schools of thought that have developed around urbanization: the "Cassandra school," which looked at America's urban environment in the 1950's and found it distasteful; the "Pollyanna school," composed of urban political economists content to find rational social, economic, and even political patterns in such urban phenomena as Watts; and finally, a third school, located between the poles of the first two, with particular interest in the "impact of the orders of magnitude" facing political institutions, and disturbed by the need for enlightened critical decisions with long-term consequences.[30] But these schools tell us little about the future.

After months of hearings by the second session of the 89th Congress, President Johnson signed the Demonstration Cities and Metropolitan Development Act.[31] In looking at an act of this type, one should study first the purposes of the act, and then the appropriations available for the implementation of these purposes. The Act focuses squarely upon key urban problems: blighted areas; housing; job and income opportunities; welfare; education; public health; crime and delinquency; recreation and cultural opportunities; and transportation. It appropriates $12 million for the program in fiscal 1967, $412 million in fiscal 1968, and $500 million in 1969. Definitions and resources of this magnitude will serve as catalysts for the continuous modernization of our basic institutions. But future emphasis may be more upon new functional institutions than upon the static compartments within the layer-cake grid.

For example, the Act makes provision for "metropolitan expediters," who will be appointed by the Secretary of Housing and Urban Development to provide guidance and leadership in implementing the goals of the demonstration program. Such states as Connecticut have already responded to the leadership of the national government by creating a new Department of Community Affairs, with "regional administrators" prepared to supervise state programs.

Soon to emerge will be a new type of political institution that will be problem-oriented, funded by financial resources from all levels, and supervised by federal "expediters," state "administrators," and local "executive assistants." Cadres of this new breed of bureaucrats will provide the expertise necessary for the "civil community." If the people of Amer-

[30] *The Urban Challenge Proceedings* (Cambridge, Mass.: Massachusetts Institute of Technology, April 13-16, 1966), pp. 4-12.

[31] *Federal Role in Urban Affairs*, U. S. Senate Committee on Government Operations, Subcommittee on Executive Reorganization, 89th Congress, 2nd sess., 1966. *See also* "The Demonstration Cities and Metropolitan Development Act," Public Law 89-754, S. 3708, November 3, 1966, 89th Congress, 2nd sess.

ica are to retain control over the affairs of these new political institutions, then outmoded concepts and doctrines must be abandoned. The era of the new reform movement has been with us for a quarter of a century. It is time that we began to recognize its implications.

9

THE PROSPECTS FOR MODERNIZATION

Murray S. Stedman, Jr.

During the last quarter of a century rapid social change and an ever rising level of public expectations have resulted in the placing of unprecedented new demands upon American political institutions. As the preceding essays have pointed out, the impact of change on the institutions has been substantial. During the same period vast new social movements have arisen, and they have exerted severe and urgent pressures on the political structure. As cases in point, one need only consider the demands resulting from the civil rights movement, the antipoverty campaign, and the recent programs to improve American urban life. In trying to deal with problems of this sort, both individual citizens and organizations have looked toward government agencies at all levels for leadership as well as for remedial programs and action. In this process our political institutions have been subjected to extraordinary stresses and strains.

As might have been expected, the responses of the institutions to the new demands placed on them have varied considerably. To word the matter differently, some institutions have met the challenge of modernization more satisfactorily than others. Of the institutions analyzed in this volume, it appears that the Supreme Court and the Presidency have been the most successful in adapting their operations and philosophies to deal with changed conditions and new problems. Conversely, in my opinion, political parties and Congress have both lagged in their ability to adjust to a changing environment. (Prof. Derge would probably disagree with my judgment on Congress.)

Of the general social forces impelling political institutions in the direction of modernization, two are of outstanding significance. They are urbanization and industrialization. Closely related, these forces have been changing the social as well as the physical environment of America. On the political side, the net effect has been to nationalize problems instead of considering them as purely local or regional questions. This has been particularly apparent in the case of the Supreme Court. As C. Peter Magrath demonstrates in his analysis, the Court has permitted Congress and the President to deal with important economic issues on a national basis. At the same time the Court has in effect nationalized the protection of civil liberties.

Of the institutions at the national level of government, Congress has been the most resistant to the demands of modernization. The reasons for this are complex, as David R. Derge has indicated, but the result, in my view, if not Derge's, is a kind of parochialism that often seems anachronistic in the present age. In contrast to the President and to the Supreme Court, Congress is, of course, drawn from many individual constituencies. The President and the Court, on the other hand, represent in effect one vast constituency—the nation. If one may borrow from Rousseau without endorsing his mysticism, it often seems as though both the President and the Supreme Court embody the "general will" of the country, while Congress usually represents "the will of all." The first conception is one of the general public interest; the second is based on the sum of various private and specialized interests.

The nationalization of problems and issues has operated very strongly in the direction of modernizing political structures. Having noted this, it is wise to draw some distinctions between nationalization of issues and centralization of institutions. It is quite possible to consider problems to be national in scope, and to deal with them on a national basis, without at the same time destroying state and local political institutions. On the contrary, cooperative efforts involving different levels of government may have the effect of revitalizing all of them. As Charles E. Gilbert and David G. Smith point out in their essay on federalism, and as Clyde D. McKee, Jr., shows in his analysis of local government, a problem-oriented approach can be quite consistent with the concept of vigorous state and local governmental units.

Some Concrete Proposals

In his essay on the Presidency, Louis W. Koenig draws attention to the adaptive ability of that office. Historically, the Presidency has been able to cope with short-term emergency situations with great effectiveness. But there remain long-term problems of considerable magnitude. Chief among them is whether and under what conditions a majoritarian Presidency can be created. What can be done, Koenig asks, to overcome the limitations that now make it possible for the minority to prevail over the majority?

In evaluating specific changes, Koenig places at the head of his list the proposed Twenty-sixth Amendment, which would provide for the direct election of the President. He feels that the chances for the eventual passage of this proposal are bright. The outlook is also good, he says, for some form of financial aid for Presidential and other electoral campaigning. Some changes in Congressional organization and procedure would undoubtedly strengthen the President's hand, but here, says Koenig, the successes so far have been limited. The prospects for modernization of the Presidency in its administrative role are found to be somewhat better but still "spotty." Finally, Koenig would like to see the general acceptance of a new philosophy toward the public service, so that able men and women from the private sector would as a matter of principle devote some of their working lives to administrative posts in the government. On this front there have been some gains, "but nothing on a dramatic scale."

Much of the literature dealing with reform of Congress, David R. Derge warns, "is explicitly or implicitly built upon distress over what the legislature has, or has not, passed." As a result, what seems to be a discussion of reform or modernization is often in reality a plea for changes in policy. To avoid this pitfall, Derge focuses his own attention on some of the basic issues and techniques in evaluating any modernization proposal.

The detailed analysis of Derge cannot possibly be summarized in a few words, and no attempt to do so will be made here. Yet several related reforms command such widespread support that they deserve highlighting. The reforms in question are designed to increase the ability of Congress to hold its own with the President in the matter of information and communication. In order to overcome the executive's near monopoly in this area, Derge proposes to improve the professional staffs of Congress, to create a Congressional agency operating on behalf of Congress in the way the Bureau of the Budget helps the President, to improve the Congressional auditing effort, to create a scientific advisory and research agency for Congress, and to expand research on U. S. overseas activities. While these proposals would involve considerable expense, they would be well worth the cost, Derge declares.

In analyzing the work of the Supreme Court in the period since World War II, C. Peter Magrath shows the high degree to which the Court has been responsive to changing social and political conditions. Of the various institutions examined in this book, the Supreme Court has probably achieved the greatest success in meeting the new demands placed upon it by social change.

This judicial leadership has been evident in two general areas. In the economic sphere, judicial interpretations "have endowed Congress and the President with constitutional authority to regulate virtually every aspect of the nation's economic life." The Court's second major contribution has been to promote human dignity and "to fashion legal protections guaranteeing individual liberties." In these ways the Court has fully responded to the challenge of modernization. As Magrath asserts, the Court has developed a national, as opposed to the earlier federal, Constitution.

The national security agencies—a term that includes the Department of State, the Department of Defense, the Agency for International Development, and the United States Information Agency—spend together about 70 per cent of the current U. S. government budget. G. W. Thumm observes that many of the arguments regarding modernization that are applicable to the national security agencies are equally apposite for other administrative units. In his analysis Thumm stresses democratization and rationalization as key elements in the modernization of the security agencies. At the present time, he says, the machinery exists for modernization of the Department of State, but machinery alone will not do the job. What is needed even more is strong leadership by the top level of decision-makers, notably, by the Secretary of State himself. In Thumm's view, there is no reason for excessive optimism on this point.

In the section dealing with national political parties, the present writer contends that modernization of the parties depends primarily on their becoming more centralized. Compared to other leading political institutions, the parties have lagged in their ability to alter their structures and operations to meet new demands and conditions. Nonetheless, the movement toward more centralized parties has been consistent, if relatively slow. This movement would be speeded up considerably if any one of several current proposals for Treasury subsidies for Presidential and other electoral campaigns should be enacted into law.

"Federalism is certain to be a leading issue in the 'modernization' of American politics for at least the remainder of this century," declare Charles E. Gilbert and David G. Smith. They foresee federalism and intergovernmental relations at the crux of many disputes that "earlier centered on the separation of powers or the party system."

Gilbert and Smith point out that federalism in this country may evolve in one of two possible directions. In one possible pattern the federalism of the future is one in which the states would be supplemented, displaced, or confined to their current activities, while new programs would be administered under new forms of federal partnership. An alternative prospect is for continued reliance on the states as the basic intermediate level of government. Under this pattern the states would retain a considerable measure of political autonomy and administrative responsibility. Though they prefer the second of these alternatives, Gilbert and Smith stress that it will only be viable and effective if substantial and imaginative reforms—or modernization—are undertaken by state and local governments.

In the concluding essay of this volume, Clyde D. McKee, Jr., considers the modernization of local and state governments from a different perspective and offers some challenging observations. He finds the principal obstacle toward reform of local government to be "the doctrine of insulation." This he defines as "the assumption that the goals of democracy in terms of self-government and direct participation are best served if the activities of local political institutions are made separate and distinct from the political activities of the institutions at other levels." The time has come, he contends, to replace the doctrine of insulation with one of cooperation.

Recognizing the difficulties in actual practice of restructuring state and local governments, McKee suggests that whenever possible such problems be attacked through what he calls "paralegal" methods. These he describes as methods or plans that are political in origin, that are outside but not contrary to law, and that endorse procedures more constructive than those provided in existing law.

In Perspective

The modernization of political institutions in an era of rapid social change may be likened to a continuing contest in which there is no referee and where there are no time limits. There is always a question as to whether institutional adaptations will be made with sufficient speed and skill so as to meet successfully the ever recurring challenges. It is a delicate business, for if institutions do not adequately change, government stagnates. But if institutions react too readily and too violently, government may throw society into virtual pandemonium and chaos. The stakes in this confrontation are obviously of the highest.

On balance, the prospects for continued modernization of American government appear to be favorable. As the essayists in this volume have shown, the responses to new demands have varied with the particular institution. Yet there has been considerable adaptive and adjustive motion, and it seems overwhelmingly likely that this will continue at an accelerated pace in the years immediately ahead. Indeed, if we could tell the forest from the trees, we might well conclude that we are at this time in the midst of a large-scale movement that is in fact quite substantially reshaping our political institutions.